Mary and Alan
  Thank you for being such
wonderful and supportive
friends to me through my
many life transitions since
South Bend days. You make
my life richer. Love,
  Suzanne
  9/5/14

Lessons of Love

in Afghanistan

A Lifetime Commitment to the Afghan People

Suzanne Griffin

Suzanne M. Griffin
3/21/14

B&H Bennett &
Hastings Publishing

Seattle

In memory of my beloved husband Michael,
who patiently guided me through my first encounters
with Afghan and Iranian cultures.

Love
turns thorns

into

flowers.

Pashtu Poem, Author Unknown

Contents

Foreword

Anyone could fall in love with Afghanistan. Flying into the country over miles of undulating desert sand dunes, rivers rushing through lush green valleys filled with small farms, some of the world's highest, most majestic mountains, and villages and cities that appear as geometric patterns because there are, mostly primitive, mud walls built around everything of value, one feels that this is a very special place. It is. But, it **is** Afghanistan. This place is home to a fascinating country and culture, and yet it can be a maddening and frustrating place.

Driving around the country, walking through the bazaars filled with families buying fresh food for their daily meals, one meets so many friendly, gracious, people. For the most part this actually means meeting only men and children. One doesn't meet women. That is a cultural issue. And, that highlights one of the most difficult issues for this very tribal nation. Women are not completely accepted as part of society here. While they may be revered as wives, mothers, and grandmothers in their own families, most cannot fully participate in public society. They are at best "second-class" citizens.

There is one thing that will change that—**education**. Dr. Suzanne Griffin has been working to change this aspect of Afghan culture through education programs and policies for many years. For example, she led teacher-training programs that result in girls having *female* teachers and role models <u>beyond the primary level</u>, something important in areas where girls over ten are not allowed to take classes taught by a man. Through work like this, Suzanne is giving Afghan women an opportunity to live a life in which they can make choices and have freedoms most of us take for granted. This work is her current love; this is her passion. She has dedicated over a quarter of her adult life to this sort of work on behalf of the Afghan people. She believes that educated Afghans will change the cultural norms that underpin tragedies such as their country's inordinately high maternal and infant mortality rates. *Things definitely need to change.*

This book tells Suzanne's story—a remarkable story of how she falls in love with a young man in the U.S. Peace Corps, how she survives the adventures of their first married years in Afghanistan, and how that blossoms into a love for the Afghan people that leads her back to the country when it is in need of rebuilding. It is also a story of how she grieves the loss of her husband and returns to work in a land they both loved. It is a story of love and education, and the education that love provides.

In my work building schools for girls, I've come to the conclusion that when you educate a boy, you educate a boy, but when you educate a girl, you educate a family and a village. An educated girl will grow up to be a wife and a mother who teaches her sons to treat women and girls with dignity and respect. She will teach her daughters the value of an education and of learning job skills in order to help support her family, as well as have a measure of independence. Then, maybe after two or three generations the culture will start to change. The country will be stronger. The international reputation will improve.

Suzanne has worked diligently to improve access to education for Afghan girls and women, and that work is bearing fruit. Today, thousands of Afghan girls walk with backpacks to and from schools every day, carrying colorful umbrellas to shield themselves from the bright sun. It is a wonderful, thrilling sight representing the future of this country. Educated girls will make Afghanistan a stronger country and a better democracy.

My love of Afghanistan began on my first trip there in 2005. I had been to many parts of the world in my forty-one years in the U.S. Air Force but had not seen any place quite like this. But, in five trips to the country when I was in the Air Force, I really did not see Afghanistan and its people for what they are. Only on my third and fourth trips did I have any real interaction with the Afghan people, beyond briefly meeting a few senior Afghan Army Air Force officers.

In early December 2007, I flew with 40,000 pounds of humanitarian aid on the Air Force C-17 cargo aircraft that took me to Afghanistan. My wife, Jan, had collected and boxed it for the trip. The cargo bay was completely filled, containing fourteen military pallets of winter clothing, blankets, and school supplies. She asked me to deliver it to needy people in Afghanistan. In a small rural village, I was handing out blankets to children when a little nine-year-old girl broke through a line of boys and, as my interpreter told me, begged me for boots like the military pair I was wearing. I had no boots for her, but I knew she needed some. It was a cold December day. She was wearing traditional sandals, as most Afghans do. Her name is Lamia. Her courage made quite an impression on me. No one else did what she had done. What I saw in her was a young girl who could someday be a leader, if she had the opportunity to get an education. She could make life better for people living in her primitive village and elsewhere. **This was my lesson of love.**

When I returned home, I told Jan about Lamia and showed her some photographs. We went shopping and then mailed four boxes to the APO address of the security group that had taken me to Lamia's village. With a photo in hand, they found her and gave her the winter clothing and boots we had sent. On a subsequent trip, when I visited Airmen at a base near her village, Lamia and her uncle were invited to our base, and we hosted them for a meal in the military dining facility.

Three months later, I retired from the Air Force. I had spent my adult life in the U.S. military and felt very fortunate, even blessed, by that experience. I had loved my Air Force work—the people, the flying. Now, I wanted to help people who might seem beyond hope. I had found my cause in the wanting eyes of a very small Afghan girl. Jan and I would not be doing what we do had I not met Lamia that day.

Jan and I established a non-profit foundation, which we named for Lamia, to build schools for girls in Afghanistan, to help get humanitarian aid to internally displaced persons (IDP or refugee) camps, and to provide training for job skills to help employ Afghan women and men.[1]

We met Dr. Suzanne Griffin on our second trip into Afghanistan. We wanted to begin building schools, and no one could have been a better advisor to us. She knew the country and she knew honest people who could help us find our way. She was helping Afghans build their education system and working on higher education policy. She introduced us to people in the Ministry of Education whom we could trust.

Jan and I have travelled to Afghanistan together seven times now. We go once or twice a year, staying a month at a time. We are just finishing the building of our sixth school for girls, thanks to our builder, Suzanne's good friend, Walid. He is as fabulous as she describes him in this book. He is a most loyal friend. He now calls us "Brother and Sister." Walid

---

[1]The Lamia Afghan Foundation, www.lamia-afghanfoundation.org

knows where schools are most needed and where they will do the most good.

Let me tell you one story about education. Four years ago, Jan and I visited an IDP camp. I had never seen such poverty and horrific living conditions. (Forty thousand people live in IDP camps in Afghanistan's capital city, Kabul.) Kabul, nestled in the mountains at an altitude above 6,000 feet, is higher in elevation than Denver, Colorado. Imagine living in a tent with your family through difficult winters for years. The "village elder" of this camp was a man, probably in his forties. He likely had no education. He welcomed us into his tent home and, as these gracious, hospitable people do, served us tea and some cookies. We asked him what the camp needed, "What can we do for you?" He gave us the best answer I've ever heard in Afghanistan, "First, please educate our children. Second, please clean up our water, so our babies don't get sick." He asked for nothing more. He knew providing an education would be the best thing he could do for his people.

Suzanne Griffin knows the power and the value of education. What she is doing for Afghanistan and its people will live on for generations. She has certainly returned the love she found in this beautiful, fascinating land.

Lieutenant General John A. Bradley, U.S. Air Force (Retired)
Co-Founder, The Lamia Afghan Foundation

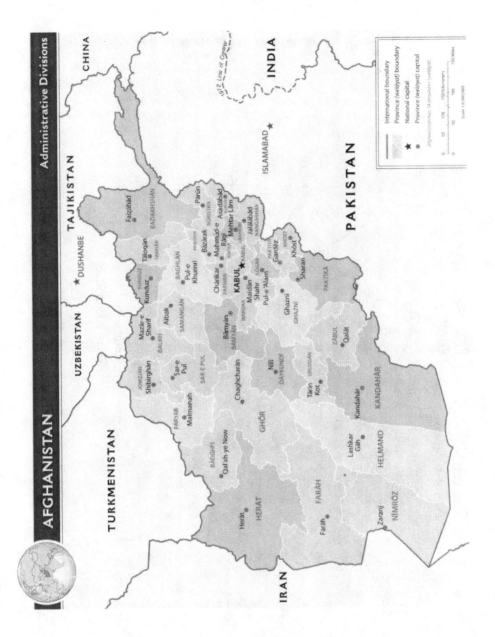

Courtesy of the University of Texas Libraries, The University of Texas at Austin

Focal Points in *Lessons of Love in Afghanistan*

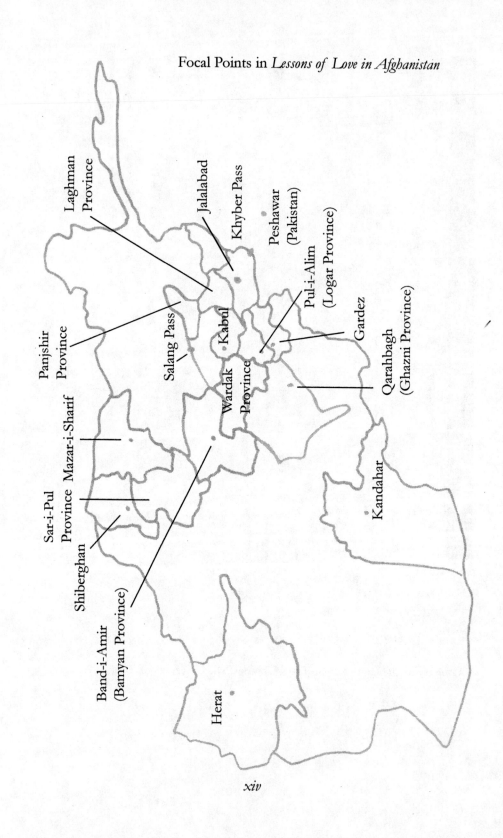

Laghman Province

Jalalabad

Khyber Pass

Peshawar (Pakistan)

Pul-i-Alim (Logar Province)

Panjshir Province

Salang Pass

Kabul

Gardez

Wardak Province

Qarahbagh (Ghazni Province)

Mazar-i-Sharif

Sar-i-Pul Province

Shiberghan

Kandahar

Band-i-Amir (Bamyan Province)

Herat

Chapter 1

A Winter Honeymoon in Mazar

On our first date, Michael took me to see *Dr. Zhivago.* As the love story unfolded against the backdrop of the snow-covered Asian Steppe, he whispered in my ear, "Look at that landscape, Suzanne! Isn't it beautiful? I'm going to take you there someday."

Fourteen months later, Michael kept his promise. We arrived in Afghanistan on January 7, 1968, ten days after our wedding. Our first field mission was to the snowy steppes in the Amu Darya, along the border between Afghanistan and the former Soviet Union. Experienced field workers in Kabul had warned against a trip across the Salang Pass in the winter, but Michael was determined to visit the Peace Corps Volunteers who lived north of the Hindu Kush Mountains before the pass closed for the rest of the winter.

"Ma eech chees nemeetanam mebeenam, Agha!" ("I can't see anything, sir!") Our driver Hashem strained forward towards the windshield and kept his eyes glued there as he shouted over the roar of the truck heater to my husband. We were in a blizzard in the Hindu Kush. I sat squeezed between the two men in the front seat of a battered International Truck as we inched along the slippery Salang Highway toward the 12,000-foot pass. The long gearshift bumped against my left leg. Large snowflakes covered the windshield faster than the wipers could clear the glass. The hood ornament of the truck was barely visible.

Hashem suddenly stopped the truck on the shoulder of the icy road. There was no guard rail. Before I knew it, Michael had climbed out and was holding onto the side of the truck as he made his way toward the hood. My heart was in my throat as I watched him turn to face us. He walked backwards on the slippery ice and mud while he held out his hand to guide Hashem toward the center of the road. My eyes moved downward from his dark hair being whipped by the wind to his brilliant blue eyes, which were offset by white cheeks grown ruddy from the cold. I craned my neck to see how far Michael was from the edge of the road but couldn't see the edge through the heavy snowfall. I couldn't speak as I faced the possibility that I could lose my new husband in a moment. A single misstep would send him hurtling over the side of the steep mountain. Finally, visibility improved for Hashem. Michael returned to his seat next to me. We exchanged looks of relief and I squeezed his hand.

Before we'd started the climb from the Salang Valley, Michael and I had marveled at the ingenuity and hard labor involved in attaching small villages of mud homes to mountainsides. Afghans made their way up icy steep paths with amazing agility, carrying water and firewood from the valley below. Even in these harsh winter conditions, they managed to smile and wave to us as we passed. Snow and dense fog hid from us spectacular views that these inhabitants enjoyed nine months of the year. In clear weather, breathtaking mountain terrain and the sight of Afghan farmers working their land in the lush Salang Valley ultimately made this one of our favorite trips in Afghanistan.

For now, all that we could think about as we approached a long tunnel in the mountain pass was whether the other end of this tunnel would be open or whether we would be trapped for hours in a massive cave full of carbon monoxide. We literally breathed easier when we emerged into fresh cold air and started down the north side of the pass toward Pul-i-Kumri. The blizzard had subsided, but we still had difficult driving ahead on a slick, narrow highway before reaching our destination for the night. We traveled through rolling hills for about an hour, but they gave way to harsher terrain. We were climbing into mountains again. In the deep gorge that paralleled the right side of the road, we watched Afghan men carefully making their way across rickety footbridges over the rushing river.

We arrived in the busy bazaars of Pul-i-Kumri more than ten hours after starting our trip. *"Amadeym!"* ("We have arrived!") Michael declared in a relieved voice as we encountered the chaotic mass of men on the main street. For Michael and Hashem, the crowd was a welcome sight after the harsh isolation and danger of the mountains. Although I was also glad to be out of the mountain pass, this crowd of men—some of whom stared at me through our car windows—was unsettling. I could see no other women on the street and was anxious to get out of the public eye. As we drove past the high school where Peace Corps Volunteers Carolyn and John taught, I looked forward to the privacy of their compound, the warmth of a wood-fired *bokhari*, a meal with newly married Americans like ourselves, and the comfort of lying against my husband's warm body as I fell asleep in a clean bed.

Refreshed by a good night's sleep and motivated by Carolyn and John's animated conversation and enthusiasm for their work at the high school, we left behind the grey, slushy streets of Pul-i-Kumri for agricultural plains that led us toward a smaller group of mountains. Michael's excitement was palpable as paved road gave way to a well-worn track through dormant orchards and across snow-covered farmlands. We shared the narrow road with occasional camel trains making their way north and turbaned men on foot flogging their donkeys so that they could get to the markets in Mazar before dark. I was thrilled to see camels. Since I first saw them in picture books as a child, camels had always been symbols of exotic and mysterious places for me. Hashem indulged me with a few stops for photos until it became clear that these pauses were hampering our efforts to get to Mazar before nightfall.

After several hours of negotiating ruts and breaks in the road, we stopped for *kabobs, naan,* and *chai* at a truck stop in Samangan, the district just south of Mazar in Balkh Province. This quarter mile included a large teahouse, outdoor latrines, and bazaar stands selling almonds, pistachios, hard candy, and dried fruit to sustain travelers on their journey. While Michael and Hashem went inside the teahouse to order our food, I watched men in the shed that served as the tire shop use a huge crowbar to take an enormous truck tire off the wheel rim and repair it. Their shop was part of an automotive repair bazaar that included tires and parts for the wide variety of vehicles that passed through this town on their way north. Samangan has been a stopping place for travelers for hundreds—perhaps thousands—of years.

We drove for long stretches in silence so that Hashem could concentrate on unexpected turns in the road. Hashem was an expert driver, seemingly calm as he avoided washouts in the road and the unmarked gorges carved by runoffs of melted snow. When the air warmed every spring, water rushed down the mountain and across the valley. Once again, we started climbing into hills. My attention turned to the abrupt change in the color of rocky walls on either side of the road from monotonous gray to red sandstone. Further along the road, I saw layers of different colored stone—gray, green, and red—where the wind had swept the dry snow off the hillsides. Everywhere there was evidence of ancient glaciers receding. Suddenly, two spires of red sandstone that nearly met at their tips appeared directly ahead of us. This was Tashkarghan. The icy river rushed along on the driver's side of the truck. I could not believe that there was enough space for both a road and the river between the spires. As we passed between them, the truck door on the passenger side was only inches from the sheer wall of red rock. No one said a word until we rounded the bend and the road widened again.

As we entered the agricultural plains outside of Mazar, Michael spoke with Hashem in Dari. I guessed that Michael was checking on our progress. My guess was confirmed when he reassured me that we would make it to Mazar before dark.

"Mazar is a big city, so I am sure that we will find a reasonable hotel there," Michael told me. As I would soon learn, his information from the Peace Corps Country Office was sketchy about the condition of the hotels in Mazar.

Except for a blue archway with the message *"Xosh Amadeeyn!"* ("Welcome!") over the southern road into Mazar, the entrance to this city was anything but impressive. Both sides of the road were lined with dilapidated bazaar stands selling tires and vehicle parts. Patrons of the shops were men wearing tall turbans and heavy, full-length felt coats called *chapans,* the hems of which were caked with mud from slushy streets. There were no women in sight on the outskirts of the city. Only when we reached the city center did I see occasional women wearing blue *chadris* that covered their faces. I wondered how much they could really see through the blue mesh over their eyes as they mingled among male shoppers in the bazaars. I suddenly felt bad for resenting the fact that once we left Kabul, I had to cover my head with a scarf whenever I was in public or in the presence of men other than my husband. At least I could see clearly.

Lessons of Love in Afghanistan

My eyes were quickly diverted from people, however, as we approached the Mazar Mosque. We were nearly a half mile away when I caught sight of the bright blue main dome and its tall minarets. Even under dark snow clouds, the huge dome dazzled in the daylight. As we neared the city center, I saw that attached to the mosque was a massive turquoise building, the *madrassa,* and surrounding gardens which, combined, filled an entire square block.

"Is it as fabulous as the Meshed Mosque in Iran?" I asked Michael.

"The architecture isn't as graceful," he responded, "but the tile work and scale is as impressive."

"Can we go inside it?"

"We'll have to find out," Michael said. "In some countries, non-Muslims aren't allowed beyond outer courtyard. I'm not sure if women are allowed ..."

"Do you mean that I can't enter a holy place because I'm a woman?!"

"I'm sorry, but that might be the case. In some Muslim communities only men are allowed to pray in the mosque."

As I considered my husband's response, I realized that I had left behind the sense of equality, freedom, and independence that American women take for granted in their own country.

Hashem turned our mud-caked truck down a side street and stopped in front of an aging, foam green, three-story building. The large stenciled blue letters above the entry read "Mazar Hotel."

"This is the place that the Peace Corps Office recommended," Michael said as he got out of the truck to inquire about a room. My heart sank. This wasn't the kind of hotel I had hoped for.

Michael sensed my disappointment several minutes later as I followed him and the hotel manager up the stairs and down a dark hallway to our room. The door opened onto a room with unadorned ochre-colored walls, one naked light bulb dangling from the ceiling, two narrow army cots with graying white sheets and olive-green army blankets, a rickety, wooden straight-backed chair, and a bureau with drawers that were askew in their slots. I wondered how well the wood burning stove in the corner of the room would heat the cold space.

"Aren't there any rooms with double beds?" I asked in a plaintive voice.

A Winter Honeymoon in Mazar

"Probably not. Hotels in this part of the world are set up for men who share a room," Michael explained. "Few travel with their wives." When he saw the distressed look on my face, he whispered, "We can push the beds together."

"Where's the bathroom?" I asked.

"Down the hall," Michael responded. "No private baths here."

With some anxiety, I followed him and the manager down the hall to the *tashnab* (toilet room). The term WC, or "Water Closet," was a literal description of this facility. The door of a closet-sized space opened to a porcelain cover over a smelly hole with foot treads on either side. I had experienced this kind of toilet while traveling as a student in Italy. In that country, it was known as a Turkish toilet.

A large, turbaned Tajik man emerged from the next room, which I learned was the *hamam*, or bathing room. His 6' 4" frame must have barely fit into the claw foot bathtub.

"Here's the bathroom," Michael said. "You need to tell the *baccha* about a half hour before you bathe so he can build a fire at the base of the hot water tank." He tilted his head toward me and whispered, "We'll have to bathe separately."

"Great!" I thought. "We've been married less than two weeks and now we'll be sleeping and bathing separately!"

As Michael negotiated the room price with the manager, my stomach rumbled with hunger and I noted that daylight was rapidly fading, even though it was only four in the afternoon.

"Is there a dining room?" I asked.

"Yes," Michael answered. Shaking his head apologetically, he added "but only men eat there." Seeing that I was near tears, Michael smiled and, with a twinkle in his eye, added "We'll have them bring us dinner in our room. What would you like?"

"I don't know what to ask for. You decide." I suddenly felt as if I was yielding all control of my life to my husband.

Michael discussed options with the manager in Dari. Then he turned to me. "The cook makes good *Kabuli Pilau*. We'll also get some sort of vegetable, *naan* (bread), yogurt, and tea."

"Fine!" I responded. What I really wanted was for the hotel manager to disappear so that I could remove the hot wool scarf from my head.

When we were finally alone, I leaned against Michael. I was cold, hungry, exhausted, and confused. "I don't know if I can do this, Michael," I confessed. "It's all so different and I can't speak the language."

"You'll be fine, Suzanne," he said as he wrapped his arms around me and kissed me softly. The comfort of his warm embrace reassured me that he would help me get through these difficult times in a strange culture.

We were interrupted by a knock on the door. The *baccha* (literally "boy," but also "houseboy") entered carrying wood for the stove and set about building a fire. We would see him several more times before we retired to bed. He returned a half hour later with our dinner—*Kabuli Pilau* mounded on a platter and shining with grease, pieces of mutton swimming in an oily sauce, cooked spinach, round disks of bread, a bowl of curdled yogurt, and dark black tea. We had hardly consumed our meal when he came back to remove the dirty dishes.

With our hunger satisfied and the room now toasty warm, we were looking forward to hot baths and long awaited sleep. The *baccha* visited us again to inquire about a fire for the water heater. A half hour later, he returned to tell us that the water was hot enough for bathing. It was nearly nine at night before we saw the last of him. Private moments with my husband seemed to be another privilege that I would have to figure out how to safeguard in this country.

The next morning I made my way down the hall to the WC. Emerging from the bathroom was the same large man whom I'd seen the night before. I changed my mind about a quick morning bath and retreated to our room where breakfast had arrived. Michael had already started to eat his fried egg that was swimming in oil. He urged me to do the same before the oil congealed and made the egg inedible. The soft, warm bread that came with tea made the greasy egg go down more easily.

Michael drained his tea cup and rose to set off for his morning appointments. "Sorry to leave you, dear, but I have a meeting with the Peace Corps Volunteers in a few minutes."

"How long will you be gone?"

"I'll be back at lunchtime," he said. "You'll meet the Volunteers tonight. We're invited to one of their houses for dinner."

"What should I …?"

A Winter Honeymoon in Mazar

"You'd be best off staying in the room this morning. I think you have a good book there and you can study your Dari lessons."

As Michael departed, the *baccha* came back to remove our dishes. He asked me something, but I didn't understand and could only respond with *"Tashakor"* ("Thank you")—one of the few Dari words that I had learned. Michael was right. I needed to learn the language.

Grateful to be alone, I closed the door, wrapped myself in my coat, and sat down on my cot to think. I shed some tears as I thought of what I'd lost in the last month.

"I gave up a fellowship to study for my doctorate in Shakespeare to come halfway around the world with this man because I love him. I've left my parents, sisters, relatives, friends, and comforts of life in the U.S. for almost two years. No wonder my mother cried so much when we left! I didn't know much more about Afghanistan than she did when I said 'yes.' Now I'm here. I can't speak the language or understand the culture. I don't even know what my role as the Peace Corps Field Officer's wife is supposed to be. What have I done?!" I asked myself.

The answer was clear when I returned to Afghanistan as a widow thirty-four years later: I had entered into a lifetime love affair with a man, a culture, and a country.

Chapter 2

Do You Know What You Are Doing?

I had not been prepared for "love at first sight" when I met Michael at a party in October 1966. During that first semester of my senior year in college, my focus was on life after graduation. I was pursuing a fellowship to support my studies for a doctorate in English Literature and anticipating engagement to Colin, my boyfriend of two years, who was in military training in Missouri. I was also in transition in many ways— from the freedom and adventures of a semester in Europe to a regulated student life at St. Mary's College for women in South Bend, Indiana, and from living in my family home to sharing a room in the college dorm.

When my family moved to California, I had to wait for an available dorm room, so I was temporarily living with the family of my best friend Betty. She and I had been invited to a Saturday night house party where the male guests were graduate students. Since it was the first invitation of this kind for both of us, we were a bit nervous as we arrived at the modest house where Ann, a newly married classmate of Betty's, lived. This was the first party that Ann and her husband were hosting for their single friends.

Ann greeted us with a relieved smile as she opened the door. As she took our coats, she whispered "I'm so glad you both came! My husband promised his graduate student buddies that he'd introduce them to some nice women. So far, the only two who have shown up are the women having a conversation over there." She nodded her head toward the living room.

Ann briefly introduced us to four men who were standing between the entry hall and the living room. Then she circled around behind them to the open plan kitchen as she muttered something about getting appetizers out of the oven. The men stepped forward to introduce themselves. One of them drew my attention. Michael was a handsome, slender, medium-height man with intense blue eyes that twinkled when he smiled. His short, wavy, dark brown hair contrasted nicely with the unmistakably Irish complexion of white skin and ruddy cheeks. He was the only guy in the group wearing a sport coat. The light blue and brown hound's tooth pattern complemented his eyes. Michael captivated me immediately as he introduced himself. While the other guys were talking to Betty, he started a conversation with me.

"What did you do this summer, Suzanne?"

As I started to answer the question, I realized that Michael's eyes were very much like those of Paul Newman, my favorite male movie star.

"I came home from a semester in Vienna, Austria and helped my family move into their new home in California," I replied.

As I detailed my travels, Michael listened carefully, asking follow up questions and smiling often. Finally, I realized that I needed to stop talking about me and find out about him.

"What about you?" I asked.

"I was training Peace Corps Volunteers in Texas," Michael said. "I came home in June from an assignment in Iran."

My eyes widened as I said "Wow!" and frantically searched my information bank from the World History course for appropriate questions to ask about places that I could barely find on a map. Maybe this charming, dark-haired Irishman was out of my league. His dress and manner were definitely a cut above what I had experienced among the undergraduate Notre Dame men whom I had dated for three years.

Michael took advantage of the pause to ask, "Can I get you a beer, Suzanne?"

Even though I didn't particularly like the taste of beer, I smiled warmly and said "Yes, thank you."

Michael came back with two glasses of beer and led me to some easy chairs in the quiet corner of the living room where we could have a conversation away from the music and chatter of other guests. I found it amazingly easy and pleasurable to talk with him, even though we had just met. I didn't mind that he seemed to be studying me when I talked because I was also studying him. There was an undeniable chemistry between us.

As we talked, I was also feeling deeply conflicted. When the academic year started, I had announced to my friends that I was not interested in dating during my senior year because I was committed to Colin. I also had a practical reason for not dating—I had to complete twenty-two semester credits of English Literature courses in one year. Since I'd studied in Austria, I had to make up the junior year second semester English credits in addition to my senior year course load in order to graduate with my cohort. However, Michael's charm broke down my resolve. By the time I left the party, I had agreed to a date with him the following weekend.

When I got back to Betty's house, I sought her counsel.

"I don't know why I agreed to go out with him, Betty! He just made me feel so comfortable and good about myself."

"Listen Suzanne, I know you love Colin, but he didn't try to stop you from going to Vienna and he hasn't formally proposed marriage. You're not even engaged."

"I know, but, I'm not the kind of person to break my commitments."

"Yes, you're very loyal to your friends, but I don't want to see you get hurt or limit your life. You told me that you have reservations about Colin's mother's influence over his decisions. He followed her advice instead of yours in applying to only the top law schools. If he'd followed your advice and applied to second-level schools as well, he might have been accepted. Instead, he's been drafted and may wind up in Viet Nam."

"I do have reservations, Betty, but still …."

"Listen, Suzanne, Michael just asked you for a date. Keep yourself open …"

I followed Betty's advice and resolved to keep the date with Michael, but I agonized for the entire week. I didn't tell Colin. Why should he worry about me going out with someone while he was adjusting to the demands of military training?

I didn't realize that our first date on October 30th to see *Dr. Zhivago* was on Michael's birthday. I was both surprised and intrigued by his whispered comment about the Asian Steppe: "I'm going to take you there someday." Was he proposing on our first date or just flattering me?! Whatever he meant, I felt pleased and comfortable. Something deep inside told me that I might accept his invitation. That reaction was unsettling, because I thought my life plan was already set. I was glad that the

Do You Know What You are Doing?

movie theatre's darkness prevented Michael from seeing the conflicting emotions that played on my face.

During the movie, Michael slipped me a handful of candy corn as a snack. Another surprise, but I simply took the candy and thanked him. After we were married, he told me that he brought candy corn because he didn't have the money to buy the theatre snacks.

Michael kissed me lightly as we said goodbye on the doorstep of Betty's house. I was both thrilled and confused. This was not supposed to happen! I knew then that this would not be our only date.

When I mentioned that I would turn twenty-one in the first week of November, Michael insisted on taking me out for my first legal drink. He took me to Pearl's, a neighborhood bar which he and his friends frequented, and enjoyed announcing my twenty-first birthday to the bartender. That evening, I found out Michael had been home with a bad cold all week. He'd caught it walking home from our first date. After dropping me at Betty's house the previous Saturday night, his VW Beetle had broken down.

"Oh Michael, I'm sorry," I responded.

"Thanks, Suzanne. Our evening was worth it," he said as he squeezed my hand.

I flushed with pleasure as I added, "Well, you won't have to walk down any more rural roads on freezing nights because I'm moving from Betty's house to a dorm on campus next week. The college finally has a space for me."

Our friendship intensified over the next couple of weeks through long telephone conversations that moved quickly from reporting activities of our respective weeks to earnest discussions about things we cared about. Since Michael had also majored in English Literature as an undergraduate, we compared interpretations of Shakespeare's plays and W.H. Auden's poetry. We also shared our views on the civil rights movement and humanitarian aid efforts. Eventually, we described our families and shared our personal aspirations.

One Saturday evening, I was babysitting for a professor and his wife who were friends of my parents. Michael called and asked if he could come over. He chuckled when I said that I needed to get permission from Don and Georgia, the couple who had asked me to watch their children. When I called the couple, Don laughed.

"Of course it's okay Suzanne, you're not a teenager anymore! Listen, this party is pretty boring, so we'll come home early and you two can go out for a little while before your dorm curfew."

When Don and Georgia came home, they smiled when they saw Michael sitting on the couch reading me Auden's poetry. After that night, I'm fairly sure that Don alerted my dad that there was another man in his daughter's life.

For months, I had planned to go with Colin to my college Senior Ball in mid-December. He had been approved for four days of leave to travel to Indiana for the weekend. When I was home during the summer, my mother had made me a lovely aqua satin dress for the occasion. The week before he was supposed to depart for Indiana, Colin's entire unit was confined to base for a disciplinary reason. When I got Colin's call with the bad news, it was on the shared dormitory telephone in the hallway. As I returned to my room crying, the story of my situation started circulating among dorm residents. The residence hall rector was a classmate of Michael's.

"Why don't you ask Michael?" she asked when she saw me in the elevator. "We all know you've been going out with him, and he's so-o-o handsome!"

After a day of thinking about whether it was fair or even polite to ask Michael as a second choice, I decided to risk calling and telling him the story. With hesitation, I asked if he would mind taking me since Colin could not get to Indiana. His enthusiastic response surprised and thrilled me.

"I'd love to take you to your Senior Ball, Suzanne!" he said. He did not tell me that he would have to buy a suit to go with me because all of his clothes were in a trunk that had been lost in shipment from Iran to his home in Detroit.

After I hung up, I danced into my dorm room and told my roommate. Kathy, who was a fan of Colin's, made a noncommittal statement. She had just become engaged to her longtime boyfriend and felt that I should sit out the event rather than be "unfaithful to Colin" by going with someone else.

Do You Know What You are Doing?

The dormitory lounge area was full of young men waiting for their dates to descend from the dormitory floors above. Most of the guys considered khakis and sport shirts a stretch when they dressed for an occasion. They were visibly uncomfortable in their dark suits for this event. Michael, however, looked quite comfortable and very handsome in his new suit.

"Wow!" I thought when I saw him upon entering the lounge. I smiled warmly and said, "Hi, Michael. You look great!"

"You look beautiful!" he countered. "This dress is … it suits you very well."

I felt like a princess with my prince charming as we entered the magnificent, mahogany-paneled lounge of Lemans Hall where the formal reception was held. A roaring fire in the enormous fireplace cast a glow on the whole room and the arched entry way was adorned with evergreen swags and red velvet bows. Michael charmed the college president and nuns in the college administration as I took him through the receiving line. It was a magical evening. Michael held me tightly as we danced to music from a live orchestra, and it became clear that our relationship had moved beyond friendship. While we were sitting on a couch at the edge of the dance floor toward the evening's end, Michael told me that he was falling in love with me and wanted me to think about that over my Christmas break. I told him that I had strong feelings for him but was very confused. I explained that Colin was going to visit me and my family in California over the break and might formally propose marriage at that time. Michael said nothing but looked quite disappointed.

When I got home to San Mateo, a long letter from Michael was waiting for me in which he laid out his feelings and asked me to consider them before I made my decision about Colin. I was stunned. Michael had eloquently written about why he loved me after knowing me for only three months. Colin had not expressed such specific feelings about me during the two years of our relationship.

I was an emotional wreck the next day when Colin arrived. My parents and sisters knew about Michael's letter. They also observed that the dynamic between Colin and me was not comfortable. Colin went through the motions of meeting my grandparents and relatives from my parents' families, but he did not propose marriage.

Lessons of Love in Afghanistan

When I returned to South Bend, Michael was relieved to know that I was still formally unattached. We went out two more times that winter. Michael introduced me to jazz, which he loved, at the Notre Dame Jazz Festival. We barely made it back to the dormitory before my midnight curfew and were confronted by the dorm mother—a large elderly lady who lectured us from the college steps.

"Young man, you have thirty seconds to say goodnight and leave the premises! Suzanne, get up here and sign in or you'll be grounded for next weekend."

"I can't believe this, Suzanne, you are twenty-one years old!" Michael said before he kissed me good night in front of the dorm mother. As he returned to his car, I raced to the front desk and signed in. How ridiculous my living situation must look to a man who has already seen a lot of the world, I thought.

Michael understood that I needed to sort out my "feelings and plans." In February, he said that he couldn't continue seeing me until I made a decision about my relationship with Colin. I knew he was right.

As I considered what to do next, I recognized that Michael presented me with life possibilities that I had never considered. My experiences studying and traveling in Western Europe seemed pedestrian in comparison with his adventures as a Peace Corps Volunteer in Iran and his subsequent travels to Beirut, Baghdad, Istanbul, and Rhodes. For him, graduate school was a way station to a socially significant job. For me, graduate school was a critical step toward an academic career. He was the first man I'd dated who applauded my determination to "have it all"—a career, travel, marriage, and children.

I missed seeing Michael in the spring, but I knew that it would be difficult for both of us if I tried to see him before I had resolved my own feelings. One afternoon in late April, we had a chance meeting when he stopped and picked me up after seeing me walking back to campus from downtown South Bend. We both strained to contain our feelings as we exchanged very general information about our studies.

At the end of my senior year, Michael visited me at the campus after I finished my final exams. We sat together in the lovely garden by Madeleva Lake, and he asked me if I'd made up my mind. I couldn't look at him as I told him that I was going to attend Colin's graduation from

Officer's Candidate School in Georgia immediately after graduation. When I finally faced him, I had tears in my eyes.

"I'm sorry, Michael, but this graduation is important to Colin. I have to see him before I can decide."

Michael was disappointed, but did his best to mask his feelings.

"Suzanne, if this visit helps you make a decision, don't apologize. I know that it's been hard for you to sort this out when you haven't seen him in six months. If you change your mind, look me up."

My mother came alone to my graduation from St. Mary's because the airfare was too expensive for both of my parents to come. Mom was very emotional that weekend. She was upset that Dad, who had just completed his Ph.D. and was so proud that I had just received a fellowship to study for my own doctoral degree, could not be there to see me graduate. Mom had completed her BA degree at St. Mary's just two years earlier, having interrupted her education to join the WAVES during World War II. I was their eldest daughter, and my parents had high hopes for me. They were clearly concerned about my relationship with Colin. I sensed that they were afraid I might marry him despite their misgivings about the match.

The next week, I attended Colin's graduation from Officer's Candidate School and then visited their family home in Delaware.

My dynamic with Colin during that time was marked by emotional highs and lows. We enjoyed hopping the waves at Rehoboth Beach together on one day. The next day, he accused me of being indecisive because I didn't care what color VW Beetle he bought. The visit ended badly when I accidentally crashed his mother's car into a tree the night before I left.

"I don't think that having me learn to drive stick shift at night on roads that I don't know is a good idea, Colin," I said.

"Not a problem, Suzanne. Hardly anyone around here is out driving at night. Besides, you leave tomorrow, so this is your last chance," Colin said.

I was tense and sweaty while we practiced for an hour in his mother's VW Beetle. As we headed back to his family home, Colin told me to turn left as we approached an intersection.

"I can't. The car's going too fast, I can't shift and make the turn!" I pleaded.

Then Colin yelled into my ear, "Yes, you can. Now turn!"

Since people in my family didn't yell at each other, I was shocked. I reacted by trying to make the turn, but overshot and hit the tree.

Shaking from fear and crying over the damage I'd done to his mother's car, I expected Colin to comfort me and apologize for yelling. He didn't. Instead, he expressed his anxiety about the reaction his mother would have to her wrecked car. In that moment, it became clear to me that I would never be the most important woman in his life.

Our last days together were excruciating for me. Colin didn't want his family to see that our relationship was in trouble, but he and I had a few private heated conversations.

We had both changed during our many months apart. More importantly, I discovered that we had very different visions of our future lives together. I realized that I couldn't live within the constraints and expectations that Colin's family—especially his mother—and relatives had for his life. Though he never admitted them, Colin must have also had misgivings about our anticipated marriage. He never formally proposed.

I started graduate school at Michigan State University in early September feeling depressed. However, I was also relieved that I was finally reaching resolution about my feelings while I moved forward with my academic plans. By October, I knew that I had to see Michael again, but I was not sure if he still wanted to see me. I had the chance to find out when I was invited to join in a carpool that was driving to South Bend, Indiana for the Michigan State/Notre Dame football game.

When I arrived at St. Mary's campus, I connected with my dear friend Mary to visit our former boss at the college admissions office.

After visiting with the Admissions Dean, Mary took me to the inner office. There sat the old desks we had worked at, side-by-side for four years. Mary turned to face me and said, "I know you want to call Michael. There's the phone, let me know how it comes out."

My heart raced as I picked up the receiver. My hand shook as I dialed his number. Maybe Michael wouldn't be at the house. Maybe he wouldn't be glad to hear from me.

"Hello, is this Michael Griffin?"

Do You Know What You are Doing?

"Yes. Is that you, Suzanne?!" Michael answered with a voice full of enthusiasm.

"Yes. I'm here in South Bend for the Michigan State game. From the background noise, it sounds like you have a lot of people at your place right now."

"Yes, we're getting ready to go to the stadium for the game. We're having a post-game party for out of town folks who're visiting us. Can you join us?"

"Yes, I'd like to see you." That was a gigantic understatement.

"Terrific! My brother Terry's here from Detroit. I'd like you to meet him."

Aside from meeting Michael's brother, I paid no attention to anyone else at the party that night. Neither did Michael. All evening, we sat in a large, navy blue easy chair, with our eyes locked on each other as we talked. I told him about what had happened with Colin. Michael told me that he'd applied for a position with the Peace Corps in Afghanistan. He was expecting an answer after he completed his Master's degree exams in less than two weeks.

"I'll be coming up to East Lansing to see you right after my exams in mid-November," Michael said. "If I get the job, I want you to think about going with me."

Shivers ran up my spine.

"What about my graduate program?" I asked.

"Don't worry, Suzanne, we'll make sure that you get that doctorate."

I was both stunned and elated at the directness of his proposal. I promised to think about it, but my heart already knew what my decision would be.

Months later, Michael told me that his brother Terry grilled him about our relationship after watching us at the party. Michael admitted to him, "She's the one."

The car was quiet on the early morning trip back to East Lansing, both because MSU had lost and because we were all tired from late night partying. I was uncharacteristically silent, lost in daydreams of what it would be like to marry Michael and go to Afghanistan.

We got back to MSU late in the morning. As soon as I got to my dorm, I made a beeline to my friend Kathleen's room and burst through the door with my news.

"Kathleen, Michael has applied for a job in Afghanistan. If he gets it, I'm going with him!"

Kathleen's screech was so loud that she woke up the late sleepers in neighboring rooms. "Omigod, Suzanne, this is like a storybook romance!"

Michael arrived in East Lansing, flush with success. He had passed his Master's exams in American Studies and had been offered the Peace Corps job in Afghanistan.

A free-spirited graduate student friend who hosted social gatherings for us English department teaching assistants offered to have Michael stay at his house. He had converted an attic space into a sitting room that doubled as a guest bedroom and served us a delicious dinner there that he had cooked himself. After sharing dinner with us along with a glass of Chivas Regal scotch that Michael had brought as a gift, our host diplomatically withdrew from our space.

Michael and I alternately sat on the large floor pillows or lay together on a mattress as we discussed our options all night. We were certain of one thing: We wanted to be together. In the morning, Michael called the Peace Corps Office in Washington, D.C. to inform them that we wanted to come to Afghanistan as a couple.

"No marriage certificate, no plane ticket for Suzanne," they said.

Michael looked at me and a huge smile spread across his face. "She'll be coming as my wife."

Ecstatic with love and excited at the life ahead of me, I raced back to my dorm room to pack for a trip to meet Michael's maternal grandmother in Ann Arbor and his parents in Detroit. Michael's mother and father celebrated our short engagement over dinner with us that evening.

My mother answered when we called my parents' home the next day with our news.

"Hi Mom!"

"Suzanne, nice to hear from you. Are your exams over? We're looking forward to you coming soon for Christmas."

Do You Know What You are Doing?

"Yes, exams are over and I can hardly wait to get home. I also have some big news."

"Oh, what is it?"

"Mom, I'm getting married to Michael! We're getting married right after Christmas."

"What?! Isn't this a bit sudden? Six months ago you thought you'd be marrying Colin! Suzanne, we haven't even met Michael!" She was starting to cry. "Why are you getting married so soon? What's the hurry?

"Michael's got a job with the Peace Corps in Afghanistan. It starts in January."

"I'll have to talk to your father about all this," she said as she continued crying. "He's taking you to Afghanistan?! I don't even know where that is!"

"Afghanistan is near Iran, Mom. It's in Central Asia."

"Where are you planning to get married?" Mom asked tearfully.

Not thinking of the impact, I said, "All our college friends are in the Midwest, so we thought we'd get married in South Bend or Detroit, where his parents live."

Mom was now sobbing. "You're getting married to a man we haven't met and we won't even be able to come to the wedding," she cried. "You know we can't afford to fly the family there on short notice during the Christmas season!"

"I'm sorry, Mom, we didn't think of that. We can get married in San Mateo. I hope Michael's parents can fly out. Mom, I know this is a bit of a shock. Can I call again tomorrow?"

"Yes, honey. Do you know what you are doing?"

"Yes, Mom, I do." As I said this, I turned and smiled lovingly at Michael.

Meanwhile, my father, who approached big life decisions by researching the options, contacted his fellow professors at Notre Dame to check out Michael's character. He was pleased with the feedback he got and enthusiastically shook Michael's hand when they met at the arrival lounge in San Francisco Airport two days before Christmas.

It didn't take long for Michael to win my mother over. I could tell that she thought him handsome and was charmed by his easy manner as he hung out in her kitchen while she bustled around preparing holiday meals for the family. By the time we finished our traditional Christmas

Eve fondue dinner and opened some of our gifts, Michael was establishing his place in the family. However, I could tell that my parents were not comfortable with the situation.

My youngest sister Beth made the family sentiment quite clear: "You are spoiling our Christmas, because everyone is so worried about you."

The thirty guests who were able to get to San Mateo for our modest wedding on December 27th included our parents, maternal grandmothers, the family of a paternal uncle who lived nearby, some local friends and neighbors, and two of my high school classmates. My three sisters were bridesmaids, but none of Michael's seven siblings could come. Ron, his Peace Corps roommate, flew from Philadelphia to be best man, but his plane was delayed. He finally made it to the reception, but my cousin Frank had to stand in for Ron at the ceremony.

Immediately after the wedding dinner at Moffett Field Officer's Club, Michael and I drove to Carmel River, California for two precious days alone together. Since Michael's dad, Garn, was an avid golfer, my parents drove Garn and Betty (now I had both a mother and mother-in-law named Betty) to Pebble Beach and Carmel the day after our wedding. We managed to avoid bumping into them in this small idyllic resort on the ocean.

As we relaxed on the sunny beach, Michael exclaimed, "They're freezing back there in Detroit right now and we're lying here on the beach! Now I know I don't have to endure those hard winters anymore. I'm never going back there to live." From that point on, Michael was an enthusiastic transplant to warmer climates.

After a teary farewell to my family at San Francisco Airport, we flew with Garn and Betty to Detroit for a second reception attended by Michael's relatives. Michael's parents proudly informed the flight crew that we were newlyweds. The crew, in turn, broadcast the news over the plane's intercom. So instead of having some private time together on the long flight, we graciously accepted the good wishes of passengers passing by our seats while we sipped complimentary champagne and ate a tiny wedding cake.

In Detroit, I learned that marrying into an Irish clan means you are never alone. Nearly 200 relatives from the Griffin and Buekers families filled the house and celebrated our marriage under the approving

Do You Know What You are Doing?

gaze of the 4'10" matriarch of the Griffin family known as "GG," who interviewed me early in the evening's festivities.

"Suzanne, dear, I understand that you are the oldest of four daughters, is that right?"

"Yes, GG. I don't have any brothers."

"Well, that's okay, dear. We have a lot of boys in this family. Michael is not the oldest in his family, but he's Betty and Garn's first son, you know. We're all really proud of him and his Peace Corps service."

"Yes, you should be," I said.

"We are. We thought he'd be the priest in the family, but that doesn't seem to be Michael's calling. We're very happy that he found a nice girl like you to marry."

"Thank you, GG," I said as I digested the news that Michael had been marked as a potential Catholic priest. Given what I knew about Michael, the family's observation that it "was not his calling" was an understatement.

"How do you feel about going to Afghanistan, dear?"

"It sounds like an adventure. I've been reading the Peace Corps manual for the country since Michael asked me to marry him. It will be very different from the places I've travelled so far. I've only been to parts of Europe, the UK, Mexico, and Canada."

"Well, I'm sure you'll be fine, dear. You're a bright young woman, and Michael will take good care of you."

"Thank you, GG. I'm sure he will," I replied as she extended her small hand and gave me a surprisingly firm handshake.

When we left the United States, we had not seen most of our formal wedding pictures. We never would. My dad had sent them "regular mail" to Afghanistan. The package may have wound up in the hands of someone who found a better use for the photos than delivering them to the intended recipients. Afghans who are aware of Western cultures are fascinated with photos of Western weddings. We saw many such photos for sale by street vendors in Kabul, so we surmised that our wedding photos probably found their way onto the shelves of cabinets in Afghan homes.

During the flight across the Atlantic, I realized that I had not developed a clear notion of our life ahead. With the turmoil surrounding our wedding, I had read the thick Peace Corps manuals on Afghan culture at a superficial level. Michael had tried to make the information more concrete in his daily letters during our three-week engagement: We would have electricity. We'd need a pressure cooker, blankets, and medical supplies. I would need to find some "meaningful activities" to occupy me as a Peace Corps staff member's wife. Would this experience, I wondered, have the storybook label that my friend Kathleen had given it, or would it become a nightmare?

We were blurry-eyed from lack of sleep by the time we had a twelve-hour stopover in Athens. The Acropolis, a building that I had imagined since my early teens, was directly in front of me, but we were too tired to get out of the car and walk around the site. Our Greek breakfast with my Uncle Bill's family introduced me to foods that would become familiar over the next two years: fresh yogurt, flat bread, goat cheese, fruit, and tea.

Our next layover was in Beirut, where we crashed for the night on the floor of an apartment rented by a female missionary whom we'd met on the flight from Athens. In the morning, we flew to Tehran, our last stop before Afghanistan. In the Tehran airport, I saw women in full-length *chadors* for the first time. Dark, printed, tablecloth-sized fabric draped over the women's heads and bodies, leaving only their eyes exposed. They looked exotic and foreign. I never dreamed that forty-four years later I would be wearing the same kind of *chador* every day on the streets of Herat. Michael and I sat on cold, hard benches in the departure terminal of Tehran airport for five hours because our flight to Kabul was delayed. A visit by Yugoslavia's President Tito had temporarily closed Kabul Airport.

The sky was clear blue as our Arianna Airlines plane passed over the dazzling white peaks of the Hindu Kush. These barren mountains were different from those I knew in the western United States, which were covered by lush evergreen forests that thinned as the altitude increased. I could see that there were few trees on these mountains even at low altitudes, as our plane descended toward the plateau of 5,900 feet where Kabul is situated.

Kabul Airport looked and felt like the utilitarian regional airports common in the western United States in the late 1960s. The blue cement

Do You Know What You are Doing?

building had no distinguishing architectural features. Turbaned men in loose-fitting pajamas known as *shalwar kameezes* far outnumbered the women in the terminal. Many of the women wore *chadris:* light blue, pleated, floor-length garments with embroidered grating covering the wearer's eyes. A few women wore headscarves and heavy winter coats over skirted business suits like those worn by older women in the United States in the 1950s. Stern-looking customs agents in Western-style uniforms stamped our passports. One of them was holding our documents upside-down as he inspected them. Few Afghans in low-level government or military positions were able to read English in the 1960s, so it didn't surprise us that the official couldn't read our documents. We eventually learned that about 60% of Afghan men and 85% of Afghan women were illiterate in their native language (i.e. Dari, Pashtu, Tajik, Turkoman, Uzbek or Hazara).

Helen and Joe Michaud, a friendly, middle-aged couple with the United States Agency International Development (USAID) team, met us at the airport. Their layers of bulky clothing topped by felt coats, scarves, and hats made them look like cheerful Christmas carolers. Michael and I learned the practical reasons for their wardrobe choices during our ride in their drafty International Truck across the frozen Kabul plain. We were chilled to the bone. I also realized that the short, wool kilt, knee socks and white turtleneck sweater that I was wearing were completely wrong for the culture and the climate.

The winter landscape on the Kabul plain was harsh and breathtaking. The thin air of the high altitude and the winter sun made the January sky look brilliant blue and the white slopes of the Hindu Kush sparkle. We drove from the airport towards the opposite end of the city, where Michael and I would be living in a small house near Kabul University. As we approached the city center, the clarity of the air was diminished by the khaki-colored haze of traffic stirring up dust on the road. Traffic was light for a city of 750,000, where motorized vehicles of all kinds made their way through the city: battered buses, gaudily decorated English lorries, motor scooters, old models of American cars and Japanese pickup trucks. Interspersed among the mechanical transport vehicles were donkeys loaded with burlap sacks, bicycles pedaled by men with baskets of produce, wooden wheeled carts—some pulled by oxen and others by Mongol-featured men—and plodding camel trains carrying large, colorful

Lessons of Love in Afghanistan

wool bags. The variety of vehicles produced a cacophony: accelerating motors, large and small, screeching brakes, deep horn honks interspersed with high-pitched toots, clanging camel bells, braying donkeys, tinkling bicycle bells, and squeaking wheels. In the background, music in Hindi, Arabic, and Dari blared from bazaar stalls while metalworkers hammered steadily and people shouted their transactions in several languages.

The smells and sights competed with the sounds. Foul exhaust fumes and the stench of open sewers full of rotting produce and human and animal waste were offset by the scents of spices, fruits, and vegetables that wafted from the bazaar stalls. The aroma of baking bread from outdoor ovens mixed with the tangy pungency of charcoaled meat from kabob braziers and clashed with the raw odor of freshly slaughtered animals as we travelled along Butcher Street. I felt sick as I watched flies swarming onto sides of beef that hung on large hooks in unrefrigerated stalls.

"This is where you'll be shopping for food," Michael informed me. I thought about this challenge as we passed stalls of brass, copper, tin, glass, and cloth. Finally, there were the "general store" stalls that stocked a bit of everything from bars of soap to gallon tins of shortening.

The customers at these stalls were as diverse as the wares sold there. Women in blue *chadris* threaded their way through the crowds, bargained for goods at the stalls, and attempted to see well enough through the embroidered gratings of their *chadris* to navigate the narrow, muddy streets. Tall Pashtun men with felt hats or white turbans who carried old rifles and wore huge bandoliers of bullets across their chests were the first tribesmen to catch my eye. The ethnic differences between them and other, shorter Tajik, Uzbek and Hazara men were clear in their facial features, languages, and variations of headgear—turbans, colorful skullcaps, and karakul hats. Some men carried small bamboo cages that contained songbirds or scrawny roosters. At one intersection, men were preparing spaces for fighting birds to begin their matches.

As we proceeded south from the main bazaar, the stalls thinned out and primitive storefronts became more common. We traveled along the Kabul River, which was a buzz of activity despite the fact that it was freezing cold and chunks of ice lined the riverbanks. Everything was being washed in this river: personal laundry and dishes, beautiful red carpets, donkeys, and heavy trucks. I wondered why trucks were driving

Do You Know What You are Doing?

over some carpets after they were washed. I later learned that old carpets were more valuable than new ones. The truck-tire treatment made the new carpets look worn and old.

The road widened as we left the city center and approached a circular intersection known as Jade Maiwan. To the left was a mosque at the head of Darulaman Boulevard, which led toward the mountains. Straight ahead were large government buildings and schools that lined the road adjacent to the campus of Kabul University. On the Karte Char (Fourth District) side of Kabul University, we entered a residential neighborhood of tree-lined streets. Not far from Rabia Balkhi Girls' High School, we turned onto a street that led to our first home. When we arrived at the gate to the compound of our little house, I was exhausted and full of questions about what I had just seen, but I was excited about the adventure.

Chapter 3

Gul Hassan

A young Uzbek man, about five and a half feet tall and of slight build, greeted us at our house in Karte Char. Gul Hassan would be our "houseboy," cook, and my primary interpreter of Afghan culture for the next eighteen months.

"*Salaam alekum!*" ("Peace be with you!") Gul Hassan smiled shyly as he greeted us at the compound gate. There was a look of anxiety in his soft brown eyes. The limits of Gul Hassan's English became clear immediately. He shifted into Dari as soon as Michael spoke to him in that language.

As Gul Hassan showed us around the modest, three bedroom, single-level white stucco house that was to be our home, he explained the idiosyncrasies of the three small buildings (our house, his house and a storage area) to Michael, who translated for me.

As we moved through the compound, Gul Hassan referred often to "his friend John," the man who had formerly lived in the house with his wife Nancy. Gul Hassan clearly missed John, a fluent Dari speaker who was popular among both the Afghans and Americans in the Peace Corps family. After suddenly becoming ill and partially blind, John, accompanied by Nancy, had been evacuated to the United States several weeks before our arrival. At the end of our tour, Gul Hassan asked Michael for news of John's health. Gul Hassan's face fell when Michael responded that, unfortunately, we had no news. Michael reassured the young man that he would let him know when any news of John arrived.

Finally, Gul Hassan pointed to the small white cottage near the compound gate where he lived from Sunday through Thursday. "I ride my bicycle to visit my family on Thursday afternoons," he said. He added that he needed to leave right after lunch, as he had to be in the outskirts of

Kabul before darkness came, which is at 4:00 p.m. in January. We knew, of course, that *Joma* (Friday), the Muslim Sabbath, would be his day off.

Gul Hassan acknowledged me, but related directly to Michael. As I had not yet learned Dari, Michael was the only person who could talk to him. Gul Hassan was also more comfortable doing business with the male head of household. Every morning after breakfast, he asked Michael for his orders for the day, told Michael what items our household needed from the bazaar, and estimated the amount of money he needed for purchases. Each evening after dinner, Gul Hassan went over his list of purchases with Michael and gave him change from the day's shopping. They also discussed long-term needs of the house and future meal plans. Even when I learned enough Dari to talk with Gul Hassan myself, he only talked to me if Michael wasn't available.

Gul Hassan planned and cooked all of our meals during the first month. Every meal featured platters of food swimming in hot oil. His delicious dishes lost their appeal after fifteen minutes, when the grease congealed in the chill of our unheated dining room. During dinner on one frigid January evening, I waited until Gul Hassan was out of earshot to ask Michael what to do about this problem.

"Michael, Gul Hassan is buying a ten-pound can of *Shapazan* (a brand of shortening) every week! All of that oil is unhealthy."

Michael responded with another cultural lesson for me. "Gul Hassan is using a lot of oil because the amount of oil that the cook uses is a mark of the station and affluence of the family, Suzanne. He wants to make sure that the amount of oil in our meals reflects our status. Iranians have the same practice, but I finally convinced our cook there that we didn't need our food to have a lot of oil in it to impress other people. I'll talk to him."

The next morning, Michael explained to Gul Hassan that he appreciated the respect that Gul Hassan was showing in using plenty of oil to cook our food, but that too much oil was not good for our health. John might have had a similar talk with Gul Hassan, because he didn't show offense at Michael's request. In the days following their talk, the *Shapazan* consumption of our household declined by half.

In the spring, our shipment of freight arrived from the United States. It included canned and packaged food that my parents had bought for us. (My father reported that some shoppers became alarmed when they saw my parents stockpiling so many packages of certain items. A few asked if my parents had news of an impending disaster.) Packaged and canned foods from home made it possible to vary our weekly menus. Gul Hassan and I struck a deal. We would alternate our menus between Afghan, American, and European cuisine. I would show him how to cook American and European dishes if he would teach me the secrets of Afghan cooking. I bought each of us a notebook with a colorful plastic cover. When he taught me an Afghan dish, he gave directions in Dari, which I translated and copied down in English. When I cooked an American or European dish, I translated the English recipe into Dari and he recorded it in his notebook. We made a good team.

Our collaboration in the kitchen was essential when we entertained large groups. We shopped, cooked, and prepared food for days ahead of time. Our first big effort was an outdoor barbecue. Michael and Gul Hassan dug a pit in the backyard and had a long spit made in the iron bazaar. We roasted a whole lamb. Gul Hassan smiled broadly in response to compliments from our guests, and he carried home slices of roasted lamb to his family.

Preparations for Thanksgiving and Christmas started with the capture of our turkeys. Michael and Gul Hassan paid a farmer to allow them to catch a pair of turkeys. They ran across the farmer's land after the squawking, flapping birds. One of them tried to hold the turkey still while the other tied the bird's feet. The turkeys were then thrown into our jeep and brought back to our compound. Michael and I named each pair that we got that year: The Thanksgiving couple was Martha and George, and our Christmas couple was Bonnie and Clyde. The turkeys roamed freely about the front yard for several weeks, eating as much corn as we could feed them. When the turkeys were fat, Gul Hassan, assisted by his friend Majid, slaughtered them according to the Muslim ritual. I made a point of being away from the house at these times.

Martha fed eighteen hungry Volunteers who arrived for the Thanksgiving feast with their own silverware wrapped in cloth napkins since we did not have enough cutlery for all of our guests. Clyde was the main dish at a Christmas buffet for thirty-five. Near the end of each party, Gul Hassan appeared in the living room doorway and smiled triumphantly as he watched our guests enjoy the meal that the three of us had created together. Toward the end of the evening, his shoulders sagged with fatigue as he washed scores of dishes in a small tin kitchen sink. When he finished the final clean up from the party the next morning, he set off on his bicycle with a large, plucked turkey tied to the back: George went home to Gul Hassan's family at Thanksgiving, and Bonnie was his family's Christmas gift.

Preserving the good name of our household was a constant source of anxiety for Gul Hassan. I made his job difficult when I refused to have my activities limited by the cultural restrictions on Afghan women. Although I wore a headscarf in the countryside and in the bazaar, I did not cover my head when I was going across Kabul in a taxi or when I was moving about in our neighborhood. I was not alone. In the late 1960s, Western women in Kabul rarely wore headscarves, although many of us respected cultural custom by covering our arms and our legs.

Since western style pants were considered immodest because of their tight fit, I had some culottes made in the bazaar. These allowed me some freedom of movement. One day, I decided to wear my culottes while riding my bike through our neighborhood in Karte Char. Gul Hassan was humiliated. He came running out into the street and begged me to return to the compound. When Michael got home that evening, Gul Hassan relayed the message that I should never do that again because I would be considered "a bad woman."

Another cause of concern for Gul Hassan was occupancy of the guest room for Peace Corps Volunteers who sometimes stayed at our house. Although that room was at the opposite end of the house from our bedroom, Gul Hassan was uncomfortable when the guest was a single male because Afghan men never allow men outside the family in the same living space where their mothers, sisters, wives, and daughters live. For Gul Hassan, the situation was bad enough when Michael was in Kabul, but the arrangement was scandalous when Michael occasionally had to leave me behind while traveling. When a male guest was using our guest room, Gul Hassan remained in the kitchen, which was across from the guest room, until very late at night and returned to his station early in the morning to ensure that nothing was amiss. I, in turn, only visited with male Volunteers in the "neutral zones" of our living and dining rooms, both of which had windows to the hallway through which Gul Hassan could—and often did—observe our interaction.

My arrest by the local police was the greatest test of Gul Hassan's ability to protect *Mem Sayb* (i.e., the lady of the house) and our family name. My friend Suraya came every Wednesday afternoon to give me a Dari lesson. Michael came home for lunch and a short nap most days. Suraya took pains to arrive after Michael had left the house. Whenever she came, Gul Hassan also left the house, since Afghan custom did not allow her to be in a house with a man who was not related to her. One day, however, Michael overslept at naptime. Suraya was nonplussed when he greeted her at the door on his way out of the house. As soon as his jeep left the driveway, there was a loud knock at the gate. Four local policemen, armed with rifles, announced that they were arresting Suraya. Our omnipresent gate guard—whom we later learned doubled as an informant for the local police—had reported that Suraya had been in the house with a Western man who was obviously not related to her.

With great agitation, Gul Hassan tried to explain the mistake to the police. In spite of his and my protests, they were determined to arrest Suraya.

"Okay! If you are going to take her, you'll have to take me!" I stated firmly in Dari.

Neither the police nor Gul Hassan expected this reaction. The police conferred with each other. Then they gruffly motioned to both Suraya and me that we should get in front of them and aimed us toward the police station. Suraya and I walked several blocks through Karte Char on a hot August day with the rifles of four policemen pointed at our backs. Gul Hassan trailed us on foot, keeping me in sight. When we arrived at the station, I asked in Dari to make a phone call to my husband. I was allowed this "favor." When Michael came on the line, I told him what had happened, including what the arresting officers had said when we arrived at the station. While I was speaking, the station chief, an intelligent-looking middle-aged man, entered the room. He spoke English, so he understood what I had just relayed to Michael.

"How do you know what the police told me?" he demanded in English.

Gul Hassan

"Suraya is my Dari teacher," I answered. "I've been studying the language for six months. Of course I understood. I am not stupid. You should also notice that I have been speaking Dari to everyone here except you. My husband is coming to get me and Suraya, now!"

"Who is your husband?" the police chief demanded.

"He is a Peace Corps Field Officer," I replied.

The police chief didn't understand. I searched my head for the Dari translation, but the best I could come up with was "Assistant Director of the Peace Corps."

The police chief suddenly turned pale. He had recently had an unpleasant encounter with our Peace Corps Director, who was an imposing man with a legendary temper. Michael's title having been lost in translation, the chief assumed that this same man was coming for me.

"Let her go!" he ordered the arresting policemen.

"I'll not go unless Suraya comes, too!" I retorted. "I'm not leaving her here. She's my teacher and my friend."

The chief agreed reluctantly to my demand. When Michael walked into the station, the chief was visibly confused and relieved that Michael was not the director whom he had dreaded seeing, but he did not interfere with our release. Suraya, Michael, and I went home with Gul Hassan, who was still agitated about the incident.

Suraya and I tried meeting in the neighborhood park a couple of times, but my Dari lessons eventually ended because she was never again able to come to our house.

In 2004, I learned that Suraya was living in the United States. We had a joyful reunion in the Washington, D.C. area. She was pleased that I had continued developing my Dari skills.

Gul Hassan often went to see Western movies at the cinema. When we sent our list of freight shipment requests to my parents, we asked Gul Hassan if there was anything that he wanted from the United States. He requested a pair of Levis with a matching Levi jacket. Since Gul Hassan didn't know his size, Michael measured him and sent the measurements to my father. When the Levi set arrived, Gul Hassan smiled in delight. Then he disappeared into his cottage. A few minutes later, he emerged proudly modeling his Levis and headed for a photographer's shop in the bazaar. I still have the black and white photo of him staring at the camera with a look of bravado. He has drawn himself up to his full height and his thumbs are thrust in the pockets of his Levis. A black cowboy hat adds to his "bad guy" look, but his substitution of brown leather oxfords for cowboy boots gives him away as a "city slicker."

Toward the end of our Peace Corps tour, Gul Hassan began worrying about his next employer. He urged us to invite to dinner our most highly placed Afghan friends: an Afghan general who was a cousin of Zahir Shah and his wife, who was the official English translator for the Crown Prince and an instructor in the Agriculture Department at Kabul University. The couple had lived in the United States while the general studied for his graduate degree and had developed a taste for Italian food during their time there. Gul Hassan and I labored for two days to prepare a complete Italian meal for them. The meal began with homemade minestrone soup and ended with spumoni ice cream that was made in our hand-cranked ice cream freezer. Gul Hassan was delighted by their profuse compliments. A week later, he was off on his bicycle for an interview at the general's house. He returned with their son on the back of his bicycle and beamed as he announced that he had been hired as their cook.

My album includes a photo of a farewell dinner with Gul Hassan's family in June, 1969. We are sitting around a carpet on the earthen floor eating from common platters of food with our hands. The ten people in the picture include Gul Hassan's parents (who look decades older than their fifty years), his two younger brothers, his lovely young wife, and their children: a two-year old daughter and an infant son. Although Gul Hassan's family seemed poor by our standards, Afghans in their neighborhood considered them fortunate. They had food, clothing, and a home of their own. Gul Hassan was proud of being the main provider for his extended family. When we left Afghanistan Gul Hassan took our German Shepherd, Djinn (which means "mischievous spirit") whom he'd helped us raise, to guard his family compound. We hoped that Djinn would be a reminder of our shared experiences.

I returned to Afghanistan in June of 2002. During the long journey there, I thought about the recent admonishments of colleagues and supervisors who were concerned that I'd chosen to spend my summer sabbatical in Afghanistan. They'd asked me the same question that my

Gul Hassan

mother had asked thirty-four years before: "Are you sure that you know what you are doing, Suzanne?" They added "It's a very dangerous place for a woman to be going alone."

On this trip to Afghanistan, I knew exactly what I was doing. I was coming back to where I'd started my life with Michael. Since he had suddenly died of a heart attack three years previously, I knew that the experiences of this summer would be bittersweet. We had planned to return here in our retirement. "Perhaps," Michael had said optimistically, "the U.S. government will establish a formal program for Retired Peace Corps Volunteers."

If Michael were alive, he would have wept with me as we watched news videos of bombs dropping on some of the water and irrigation project sites where our Peace Corps colleagues had toiled for years. He would have agonized with me at the thought that our dear Afghan friends could be among the civilians who were "collateral damage" in bombing raids. Coming to Afghanistan after the 2001 U.S. bombings that ousted the Taliban would be just the kind of thing that Michael would want to do. I was returning on behalf of both of us to let the Afghan people know that we had not abandoned them, and to do what I could to help them rebuild after three decades of war.

As the plane began its descent, the view of Kabul from the air showed me that the city had changed dramatically in thirty-four years. The city limits were further out and there were many more homes and buildings. Instead of the clear blue winter sky that used to amaze me, I looked down through thick brown smog over a barren landscape between buildings damaged by rockets and gunfire. Gone were the tree-lined streets that I remembered. I looked in vain for the lush green gardens that had surrounded public buildings and been the focal point of private homes. What I saw was an ugly, sprawling, traffic-clogged metropolis inhabited by over two million people.

The rich agricultural land that once made the Shamali Plains outside of Kabul City a retreat from the summer heat was not green with summer crops as it should have been in mid-June. Instead, the land lay desolate and brown, destroyed by a quarter century of fighting and drought. The trees had been cut down and the soil poisoned by the Taliban. I later learned that undetonated land mines were everywhere among the fields, another deterrent to their use.

Lessons of Love in Afghanistan

As we taxied toward the terminal, I saw huge scrap heaps of bullet-riddled airplanes lying along the edges of the runways. On many, the smoke streaks were so fresh that it seemed as if the fighting had ended only days before. While Afghan airport workers, shepherds, and farmers from adjacent land wandered freely across the runways, the area closest to the terminal was guarded by heavily armed International Security Assistance Forces (ISAF) personnel. Several tanks were stationed near the terminal building.

From the outside, the terminal looked the same as I remembered it—a three-story white granite block with light blue trim and signage. Inside, however, the building showed the effects of thirty-four years of hard use and neglect. Without electricity to light it, the terminal was dark on a sunny day. The windows had a yellow film from the incessant smoking of passengers waiting inside. The floors were dirty, the seats were broken, and a few mice scampered past incoming passengers who formed lines at the doorway to the two-windowed wooden booths where Afghan men in military uniforms reviewed passports.

Once through the passport line, passengers jostled with each other and with would-be porters to retrieve their bags from the single luggage belt. When the belt broke down, the luggage handlers passed the bags from old, rickety carts through the hole to two men who placed them onto the belt by hand.

"Ena bag az ma!" ("That's my bag!") I hollered as one of the self-appointed porters grabbed one of my bags. I was amazed that I remembered Dari so quickly.

Since no car was waiting for me, I took a taxi to the international non-government organization (INGO) office in the northeast section of Kabul. The INGO guards and motor pool supervisor were surprised and concerned when the taxi deposited me and my luggage at the office nearly two hours after the flight arrived. They had sent a driver, but when I hadn't emerged with other passengers from my flight he assumed I had missed the flight. I had been inside trying to file a claim for a lost bag. This was before cellular phones were available in Kabul, and there were no phones in the Kabul Airport, so I had taken transportation into my own hands. I soon learned that American INGOs consider taxis risky for foreigners because of the possibility of kidnapping.

Gul Hassan

Sigurd, the INGO Country Director and a veteran humanitarian aid worker, greeted me warmly and handed me over to Sam, the Human Resources Director, for orientation and transport to the INGO guesthouse. Sam had arrived in Kabul from his home in Sri Lanka just one week before me, but I never guessed it based on the completeness of his briefing. Sam and I immediately hit it off.

Soon, it was lunch time, so a white Land Cruiser transported me to the INGO guesthouse in *Shar-i-Nau* (New City) district of Kabul. I recognized the guesthouse as the former residence of the U.S. Embassy Deputy Chief of Mission in Afghanistan while I was there with the Peace Corps. This man was later posted in Iran and became one of the fifty-two American Hostages held in Tehran from November 4, 1979 to January 20, 1981.

I met the house cook, Baba ("old man") Mohammad, and his wife, Nassim. After I got settled, Baba Mohammad showed me a certificate that said he was trained in the American Women's Association Food Handler's course in Afghanistan in the late 1960s. He had worked for Americans and other foreigners ever since. I soon learned that Baba made great apple pies.

Baba and Nassim greeted me in Dari and were delighted that I could respond in their language. I had not lived in a group setting since my college days. However, Baba and Nassim made my adjustment easier by assigning me to the former DCOM's master bedroom suite, which had just been vacated by a visitor from the INGO headquarters. It was the only room in the house with a private bath.

Before I drifted off to sleep the first night in the INGO guesthouse, I recalled again my first moments in our house in Karte Char so long ago. I resolved to try to find the shy man who cooked and cleaned for us and who guarded me when Michael was not around. The next day, I asked the venerable house cook if he knew of Gul Hassan and could tell me his whereabouts. A week later, he told me that he had inquired among the cooks for the expatriate community and that the only information he could get was that Gul Hassan had gone to Mazar-i-Sharif many years ago.

When I visited Mazar later that summer, I was unable to find Gul Hassan or any trace of his family.

Chapter 4

Finding My Niche

"Welcome, Suzanne!" Sigurd's wide smile was magnified by his twinkling blue eyes. To my surprise, he gave me a warm embrace instead of a handshake. He was as enthusiastic in person as he'd sounded on the phone when we spoke about the contributions that I could make to his organization's mission in Afghanistan.

"The staff members are very excited that you're here," he said. "I copied the *Seattle Times* article on you from their website and posted it on the bulletin board. We're pleased to have a volunteer with qualifications like yours. There's a lot for you to do in Afghanistan. As I told you on the phone, I want you to develop our agency's English Language Training plan for the country. To do that, you'll have to travel to the other cities, except Kandahar, of course. How do you feel about traveling outside of Kabul?"

Traveling around Afghanistan is just what I'd hoped to be able to do. A shiver ran down my spine and I felt like dancing around in a circle, but my professional persona took over.

"I love the idea!" I said, flinging out my hands as I always do when I'm excited about something. "I traveled around much of Afghanistan with my husband when I was here in the Peace Corps, especially the northern and eastern provinces, which was Michael's assigned territory. All I need is my backpack and a notebook. When do I start?!"

"You should visit Herat, Mazar, and Jalalabad, at least. First you need to meet with the Provincial Education Directors in each regional city, and then go see the high schools. That's where they teach English now. Interview the students and teachers. Let us know what you think of what they're doing and what our agency needs to do to support the English programs and make them better. Oh! Don't forget to include the private English schools. I understand that they're pretty big."

I couldn't believe my luck! I was getting an assignment to do exactly what I love to do—visit classrooms, observe and evaluate how things are going and design programs to help teachers improve so that students learn better.

"Okay. I'll make a travel plan and a work plan for your approval," I replied.

"There are two people that you should involve in developing your plans," Sigurd added. "Walid, who is head of the Umbrella Grant Program, will be your Pashtu interpreter. He can link you to the NGOs that are running private English programs. He can also take you to meet the Ministry Officials who are Pashtuns. Aziza, who will be your Dari interpreter, is head of our Educational Unit. She'll be your link to the Ministry of Education both in Kabul and at the provincial level. I think you met them briefly yesterday."

"Yes, I did. They both seem eager to help me."

"They are. Both are very bright and capable people. You'll like working with them. Okay, get that work plan to me by the end of the day, if you can. I'll see you tomorrow and we'll talk about it. Then you can start traveling."

"Thank you, Sigurd. I'm looking forward to working together."

"Me, too, Suzanne. Bye."

I was walking on air when I left my first meeting with the Country Director. This volunteer position was everything I'd hoped for. I was going to make a significant contribution to Afghanistan and I was going to be able to travel! I was thrilled to be back in Afghanistan and this time they wanted my skills! I would be valued in Afghanistan for what I could do, rather than for what my husband did. Knowing that gave me a very different feeling about my role than I'd had during in my first visit to this country with my husband.

When we arrived in Kabul in 1968, I was seen primarily as Michael's partner and supporter. No one seemed to particularly care about my training as a teacher. Peace Corps wanted Michael for his proven leadership, his cross-cultural experience in Central Asia, and his excellent command of Farsi, which he had learned during his Peace Corps service in Iran.

Beyond my orientation as a Peace Corps staff wife, I was left on my own to figure out my role in the country. During the first six months, I dutifully carried out the expectations of a staff wife. When travelling with Michael, I observed female Volunteers at work in places which men could not visit—such as girls' schools, classes for girls in schools that serve both boys and girls, and training programs for female nurses. I also listened empathetically to the Volunteers (especially the females), and communicated their needs to my husband and other relevant staff members in the Peace Corps Office. I also provided hospitality to Volunteers who came to Kabul from the provinces.

The combination of culture shock and having no defined professional role in Afghanistan hit me hard one cold spring morning in the city of Kunduz, the provincial capital of a province with the same name in northern Afghanistan. (The province of Kunduz became a Taliban stronghold in the 1990s and still has a strong Taliban presence twenty years later.) I remained in the hotel room while Michael went out to meet with Volunteers and government officials. I had worked all four years of my undergraduate studies in the college admissions office and I'd taught English as a Second Language (ESL) while I was in graduate school. Part of my self-image was tied to being valued for my academic training and my professional skills. Being defined simply as Michael's wife was not enough for me, and Michael was so focused on his new job that he did not immediately pick up on my sense of loss. He was shocked when he returned from his busy day in Kunduz and found me sitting on the spartan cot in the hotel room with eyes still red from crying.

As he often did, Michael came through the door with a smile of satisfaction, which was usually followed by a report of whom he'd seen and what he'd accomplished that day. As he came forward to embrace me and greet me with a kiss, he looked at my red eyes with concern.

"What's wrong, Suzanne? You've been crying!"

"I need my own job here," I told him. "I was a good teacher and a promising graduate student two months ago. Now I'm just 'Michael's wife.'"

He tightened his hug. "I'm sorry, Suzanne. I didn't realize you were so unhappy. I'm sure that we can find you a teaching job here. We'll work on it when we get back to Kabul, okay?"

54

"Okay," I said. As I nestled my head on his shoulder, I wondered why I had waited so long to tell Michael what was bothering me. It had taken me awhile to understand how willing my new husband was to help me work out solutions.

In summer of 1968, I became the ESL teacher for the American International School of Kabul (AISK). Merton, the principal, hired me after learning that the woman from India who had been expected to start teaching ESL to the non-American high school students during that summer would not be able to come to Kabul until September. The school needed someone to work with these students immediately so that they could improve their English enough to move to the next grade level with their cohorts when classes resumed in the fall. Although I'd be the youngest teacher on his staff, Merton felt that my enthusiasm for teaching combined with my training had prepared me well for this assignment.

The progress that my ESL students at AISK made during the summer led to another teaching job, this one at Ahlman Academy for the 1968-1969 school year. My class at this private, church-supported school consisted of sixteen non-English speaking children from eight different countries. Luckily, I had two small classrooms adjoining each other, so I could split up the class for parts of each instructional day. The principal had forgotten to order books for the ESL class, so I was faced with the challenge of teaching all the children enough English for them to be able to do school work at each of their grade levels without any teaching materials to help me. Most of the children were in grades three through six, but there was also an eighth grade girl from Czechoslovakia. She had been attending the Russian school in Kabul, but her parents withdrew her from that school when Russia invaded Czechoslovakia in 1968. The youngest student was a six year old Turkish girl whom I tutored for an hour each day before the other students arrived.

I loved the students and the challenge of creating lessons that appealed to this diverse group. I borrowed educational movies from the Columbia University team and made worksheets at three different levels of English so that all the students in the class could use the movie to improve their English. I wrote audio tape scripts so that half of the students could listen to tapes in the adjacent classroom while I worked with the other half. Michael read the scripts into the tape recorder at night while I developed worksheets for the movies. Periodically, he fell asleep

Lessons of Love in Afghanistan

while recording the tapes. When the students got to those parts of the tape, they broke into laughter.

Since I had to balance my teaching responsibilities with the travel demands of being half of the husband-wife Peace Corps field team, I split the teaching schedule at Ahlman Academy with Margaret, a Polish woman about my age who would become my lifelong friend. Margaret and I regarded the children in our class as an international family. At the end of the school year, Margaret and I celebrated the students' achievement of learning enough English to progress to the next grade level with their English speaking classmates by inviting them all to a picnic in the garden of my home.

When I returned to Afghanistan alone in 2002 as an experienced educator, program manager, and administrator, I was thrilled to have my credentials acknowledged by the Country Director and recognized by the Afghans with whom I worked. Sigurd was the perfect supervisor for me. He made it clear that he wanted me to use my expertise and that his role was to provide me support and advice on strategy, culture, and politics. He also seemed to know what kinds of assignments I loved.

One day he called me into his office to say, "Suzanne, I know that your area is Education, but I need you to branch out a bit today and go with Peter to our project sites in Logar (a province adjoining Kabul Province). He's going to photograph them and I want you to interview our staff members who are implementing them."

"Okay, I haven't been to Logar since I got here. What kinds of projects are they?"

"Agricultural projects, mostly—especially one that involves drying and preserving fruit. There's also a water reclamation project underway. We're trying to reroute some river water to aqueducts that can water the farmland so that people can start growing crops again. Another is a Female Education Project. It's the project that Nina has designed with our Afghan staff in Pakistan. We weave health education with women's literacy and offer classes in homes in the villages."

My ears perked up at the mention of the women's literacy class. My original intention in coming to Afghanistan was to see if I could apply my dissertation findings to improving women's literacy classes in the country.

Finding my Niche

"Combining women's literacy and health education sounds promising," I commented. Leaning forward and looking more intensely at Sigurd, I added, "Women's literacy is a major interest of mine."

Sigurd smiled and nodded his head affirmatively. "I know it is, and that's another reason I want you to make this trip. Our donors are very interested in this project. They want photos of it, but Afghans don't like foreign men taking photos of their women. So it's your job to help Peter get the photos and keep him out of trouble."

I chuckled as he said this. Sigurd and I both knew that Peter was a terrific photographer, but he was so focused on getting good photos that he sometimes needed a handler to slow him down a bit and deal with cultural issues in this conservative country.

As I rose from my seat, I said, "I'll do my best, Sigurd," as we shared another chuckle.

"I'm sure you will, Suzanne," Sigurd said as he walked me to the door of the office.

Peter, a tall, sandy-haired photographer from New York City, had been photographing humanitarian aid projects in Afghanistan since the 1990s. The Taliban actually chased him across the Afghan border into Pakistan on one of his early assignments. He and I set off in an agency pickup truck heading for the field office in Pul-i-Alam district in Logar Province where Hassan, the Field Office Coordinator, would assist us. We were to spend the morning visiting our agency projects there and then proceed to Gardez for lunch and a visit to more agency education projects.

Peter sat in the front seat with the driver. He looked tired and said he was feeling a bit ill, but he was focused on our mission. As we traveled, we discussed our strategy for the day.

"Our priority is photos of the Female Education Project," Peter said.

"We may have trouble getting those photos, Peter. Logar is a pretty conservative province," I said.

"I've photographed women all over Asia," Peter shot back. "I don't see why I can't do it here. I am sure that Hassan will help us."

I didn't share Peter's optimism. I knew how strongly Pashtun men felt about having women from their families photographed by anyone—particularly a foreign man. Our colleague Walid had rejected Peter's request to visit his home and photograph his family. Walid and his brothers did not want a single, foreign man visiting their family home because they were worried about damage to their family's reputation if Peter was seen there. If a friendly colleague said no, what chance did we stand with strangers?

When we got to the Logar Field Office, we were greeted warmly by Hassan and his program officers—all of whom were men. Hassan was a large Pashtun man with an easy smile. In his turban, he was taller than Peter—about six feet, five inches. After we finished the formalities of greeting, we all settled into chairs that nearly touched each other in a small office where three people might have been comfortable. Six of us made it uncomfortably cozy—especially for me, as the only female. As an old man squeezed his way between our chairs to serve us tea, Hassan asked which programs we wanted to visit and what our schedule was for the day. Peter responded with a list of programs that we needed to photograph and emphasized that the Female Education Project was his priority.

"We can take you to the fruit preservation projects and the water reclamation site, but not the Female Education Project," Hassan said.

Peter was visibly upset. "The agency needs photos for the website because that's the project that donors are most interested in supporting. In fact, that's the main reason we have made this trip. Sigurd has also prioritized this project; that's why he sent Suzanne with me. Of course, we'll also document your good work in agriculture and water reclamation."

Hassan placed both of his large hands on his desk, sat up a bit taller in his chair and responded in a firm, authoritarian voice. "The people here are very conservative. We've had to work hard with community leaders to allow us to start the Female Education Project. The women meet in private homes in the villages and the locations are kept secret. They will never agree to let the women be photographed."

The three Afghan men on the Logar program staff agreed with Hassan. For half an hour, the debate went on in the tiny, crowded, and oppressively hot office. Finally, it was agreed that we would go to one of the project sites. I would go into the room ahead of Peter and Hassan to observe the class and talk to the female instructor and women in the class. Peter and Hassan would remain in another room where they were out of view, but where they could observe my progress. If the women agreed to be photographed, Peter would be allowed into the room.

We traveled to the village in one car to keep a low profile. Since Afghan men don't usually sit next to women (especially women who are not part of their family) in any situation, I was surprised when Hassan got in the back seat with me instead of contesting with Peter for the front seat. Peter sat in stony silence as we as we traveled to the village. Since I was sitting behind him, I couldn't tell if his silence was due to his frustration over the lack of support from the Afghan staff or because he was still not feeling well. Most likely, it was a combination of both.

After a few minutes of driving, Hassan pointed to the scattered rubble of a large building on a plot of land along the road.

"That is where the girls' high school used to be," he said as he turned toward me.

"A girls' high school was a big step for this province," I remarked. "There weren't any girls' high schools here when I was in the Peace Corps. I am sure that having it destroyed was a big loss to the community."

I had hit a nerve.

With a few tears trickling down his cheek, Hassan said in a soft voice. "Yes, it was a big loss. It took twenty-five years to convince the community to build this school, and now it's gone."

Our pickup truck bumped across an open field and navigated a rutted, narrow road into the center of the village. Finally, we stopped next to a *juey*—an open sewer—which I had to jump over after opening the truck door. As Peter, Hassan, and I set off on foot down a narrow alley, a barking dog approached and tried to bite Peter's leg. This only added to his bad humor. Finally, we were in front of a small room with a thin white curtain blocking the door frame. The female instructor met us outside the room and indicated that Peter and Hassan should go into a room on our left. Then she ushered me into the classroom where twenty Afghan women of various ages sat on a woven plastic mat. Half of them were holding young children and some of them were nursing their babies.

As I entered, the women looked at me with interest and surprise. They recognized that I was a foreigner, so they did not expect me to greet them in Dari.

"*Salaam alekum,*" I said with a smile and immediately removed my shoes and sat down on the floor opposite the class.

"*Walekum A Salaam,*" ("Peace be with you and welcome") the women responded in unison.

In Pashtu, the female facilitator explained who I was and why I was there. As she did so, I quietly moved to a place off to the side of the room near the only window. As I prepared to talk to the women, I thought, "I was made for this. This is why I am back here in Afghanistan!"

The facilitator had to translate my statements for most of the women, as few of them knew Dari. However, communication flowed pretty well. Initially, I asked the women to each tell me how many children they had. After we went around the room, I said in Dari,

"It looks like Mariam is the winner. She has eight children and half of them are boys!"

The women all laughed, as they realized that I understood their cultural value for lots of children and the social and economic importance of male children in keeping the family line going.

I asked the women how they liked their class, what they had learned and how the classes had helped them and their families. Their responses varied, but were all positive:

"I know why I need to keep flies out of my house. They cause disease."

"I am learning to read my language. Someday I will be able to read the labels on the drugs that I get from the pharmacy."

"I now know why I need to have my children immunized."

"We all know why we should breast feed our babies."

When they finished, I explained to the women the interest that agency donors had in this project and the importance of having additional funds to keep the classes going. I added that a few photos of the project for the agency website would help us continue to get donations to support it.

Since no male relatives of these women were present to give us permission to photograph them, I would have to leave that task to Hassan. If necessary, he could talk to the women's husbands later that day. Instead, I addressed the question directly to the women in Dari.

"We would like to take some photographs of you in this class, with your permission."

Finding my Niche

As I spoke, I saw expressions of concern on many of their faces. I bowed slightly to acknowledge their feelings.

"If you don't want to be photographed, you can pull your veil over your face like this." As I demonstrated by pulling my veil across my face, they giggled.

"You can also turn your backs to the camera like this." As I turned my back, I heard more giggling.

"Or you can leave this room, if you want to." I pointed toward the door. Then I stopped and waited while the women talked among themselves. Some agreed to have their photos taken, but many of them drew their veils across their faces so that only their eyes were visible. A few turned their backs or moved toward the door.

I took out my own camera slowly. After I had taken several photographs, I mentioned that there were two men in the next room, one of whom wanted to take some photographs with a better camera than I had. Then Hassan stepped through a door and spoke to the women in Pashtu. I could see Peter behind him. After the female facilitator and the women remaining in the classroom nodded in agreement, Peter stepped into the room and started taking photos. While he was doing so, I was focused on the little boys who were standing at the cracked window behind me and looking in. I took a couple of photos of them.

As we walked away from the classroom and back down the alley, Hassan and Peter seemed relieved to have gotten the photos without any incident. I was elated about my experience with the women. From that point, I knew that I would come back to Afghanistan after I finished my summer sabbatical there.

Next we traveled to a farm to photograph the drying and preserving of apricots. Hassan was very enthusiastic about this project. While Peter took photographs, the project supervisor showed me the drying trays and explained that eight varieties of apricots grown in Afghanistan were being raised in Logar.

As we drove from that project to the water reclamation site, Peter again sat in the front seat next to the driver. I was directly behind him in the back seat, uncomfortably aware of Hassan's large body crushed against me because he'd scooted from the opposite side of the car to the middle seat to accommodate the German-speaking Afghan project engineer whom we had just picked up. The engineer's male assistant was already occupying the luggage space behind the back seat, so there were now five men and me in the car.

"Peter," I whispered. "It's not appropriate for me to be in the back seat with two Pashtun men. Can't you change seats with me?"

"No, I can't," Peter replied. "There isn't enough room back there for two big men plus a third medium-sized one. Relax and just look at the smile on Hassan's face." Then Peter grinned and added, "This is probably one of the best days of his life. How many times do you think he's ever had a chance to sit next to an American woman who speaks Dari?"

When we arrived at the water reclamation site, I saw at least fifty men digging, pushing wheelbarrows, and carrying metal pipes.

"Peter, I can't get out of the truck," I said in a desperate voice. "There isn't another woman around."

"Do you want to stay in the truck?" Peter asked.

It was over a hundred degrees in the cab. I decided I would risk it.

"Okay, I'll get out. I can't bear the heat in here. What's my job?"

Peter tried not to smile, but I knew that he was getting a kick out of watching me try to cope with this situation. He nodded in the direction of the men working and replied. "Just distract them while I take pictures."

As I got out of the truck, all the men stopped working and stared.

"I don't think this is what you had in mind, Peter. What now?"

"Do you have a camera here?" Peter asked, trying not to laugh aloud.

"Yes, but it's just a little Olympus."

"Grab it and start taking pictures."

I did as he asked and it worked. The Afghan engineer who escorted Peter and me around had studied engineering at a university in Germany. He did not speak English, but was delighted to know that Peter and I spoke German because we both had German-speaking grandparents and had studied the language in college. Since not many German speakers visited Logar Province, the engineer seized the opportunity and animatedly explained the project in that language while I was taking pictures. Wherever I pointed my camera, the men began working industriously. Meanwhile, Peter approached from a different angle and got some good shots. He seemed energized by every shot.

I gave Peter another moment of levity as I jumped across a couple of ditches to get from the aqueduct back to firm land. I could feel the

Finding my Niche

men watching in dismay and holding their breath as I jumped. Peter later described the looks on their faces. "No one wanted to be the one to drag you out of the ditch full of water," he laughed. "They were really nervous when your sandal slipped on the bank."

"It worked!" Peter said as I got back in the car. "I should take you on more shoots."

Now it was my turn to laugh. "I enjoyed this trip, but I'm not sure that Sigurd will let me do this full time," I replied. "I have a big job to do in the Education sector."

When we returned to the Logar field office, there was an urgent radio call from John, the Security Officer in Kabul. "Don't go to Gardez!" He shouted. "There's fighting there. You need to come back to Kabul."

"We need to go Gardez!" Peter said. "We have several more sites to photograph. The field staff in Gardez just called and they have our lunch ready. We're already late."

"Sorry, Peter, you'll have to skip lunch," John said. "You need to get back to Kabul."

Peter and I both knew that lunch was the most important meal of the day in Afghanistan. If you had been invited to be a guest for lunch, it was a major insult to not show up. Peter tried one more time to get clearance to go. "How bad is the fighting?"

"It's a serious conflict," John answered in a rising tone. "I'm ordering you to come back now!"

Reluctantly, we said goodbye to Hassan and his colleagues, who could not understand why we couldn't stay and have lunch with them before our departure. Peter and I were both disappointed. We'd hoped to cap our success in getting good photos in Logar with some photos of the projects in Gardez. Peter offered me the front passenger seat and climbed into the back seat of the truck for the return trip, saying that he was exhausted and needed to rest.

We had traveled for less than fifteen minutes when a fleet of six Blackhawk helicopters heading for Gardez flew low over our truck.

We weren't particularly alarmed, as we'd grown accustomed to helicopters flying over Kabul and the sound of rockets being fired at night by insurgents who refused to concede to the Afghan and NATO forces that protected Kabul. We also had daily reports of continued battles in the provinces that bordered Kabul Province. Those of us working in

Afghanistan that summer knew that the term "post-conflict" was not an accurate description of the context in which we were working.

"I guess it's a serious battle," I remarked in a voice that people at home would consider ridiculously calm for the situation.

"Yes, John wasn't exaggerating," Peter observed in an equally tranquil voice.

In the first half of 2008, INGOs working in provinces that border Kabul Province—especially those working in Logar Province—began to experience increasing threats, harassment, and violent aggression from Taliban insurgents. By summer, military convoys traveling through Logar were actively attacked, injuring dozens of soldiers and causing some fatalities. In August 2008, three female agency employees—one American and two Canadians—were shot and killed by Taliban extremists while they were traveling near Pul-i-Alam in their marked agency vehicle on their way back to Kabul from a site visit in Gardez. Their murder shocked the Humanitarian Aid community in the country and caused all of us to reassess where we worked and how we traveled. We could no longer assume that everyone welcomed our help in the rebuilding of Afghanistan.

In fall 2009, I visited Logar with an Afghan family. Because of the security situation for foreigners there, no one could know that I was an American. I wore my Afghan village clothes—a long skirt over loose-fitting black pants, topped by a long sleeved loose tunic and a *chador* (veil) hung from my head to the edge of my skirt, thereby covering my entire body—and was wedged in the back seat of their car between two female family members wearing *chadris*. Only the immediate family knew that I was a foreigner. Relatives, neighbors, and domestic help at their house were told that I was a visitor from Iran, where many Afghans still live. Since I spoke Dari to everyone (except in private to the two English speaking young people in the family), no one outside my host family guessed my identity.

The abundant crops on the property reflected the excellent weather of the growing season that year. There had been a lot of snow in the winter, which filled local streams and rivers as it melted. The spring rainfall had extended into early summer. After that, we had four continuous months of sunshine and heat. As a result, limbs of apple trees were so heavy with fruit that they touched the ground, the corn crop was the biggest in years, and the family invited neighbors to help them harvest and eat tomatoes and green vegetables in their garden.

On this lovely Indian summer day, the boys in the family flew kites and picked apples to take back to Kabul, the women and older girls made *bolanee*—an Afghan dish made from bread that has the consistency of flour tortillas—in the outdoor oven, and the young girls carried water and played tag. The men's activities depended on their position in the extended family. Some herded the animals and cut wood for the stoves, others surveyed the agricultural yield and inspected the progress of re-construction and renovation of buildings that had been destroyed by rockets in the fighting of previous decades, and a few took naps and conversed with each other between lunch and dinner.

I felt totally at home walking among fields of crops ready for harvest and through orchards of trees laden with fruit. I told my hosts that this day in Logar reminded me of childhood days on my paternal grandparents' farm in Oregon. On this occasion I also understood what peace means for most Afghans, many of whom are farmers. They want conflicts to end so that they can reclaim their family property, harvest their crops as they have done for hundreds of years, and live without interference from outsiders.

Chapter 5

New Afghan Friends

Two women shared the agency Education Office with me—Aziza was head of the Education Team and Nina was an energetic American who had developed the successful Female Education Project in Logar. Aziza received her high school education in Pakistan where her family had been in exile during the Taliban years. Since a Bachelor's degree program was not accessible to her in Pakistan, she took all the post-secondary certificate programs in English and Education that were available (many of them offered by the agency) in order to prepare for being an English teacher. She quickly became an excellent teacher and then advanced to being a teacher trainer, earning the respect of her peers and the notice of her trainers and supervisors.

Aziza's intensity and intelligence is evident as soon as you start working with her. You can imagine her mind working at warp speed behind those warm brown eyes that glow through her glasses and see right through you. When you are talking to her, you can almost see her making connections and generating new ideas. She is simply one of the most intelligent women whom I have ever known.

Aziza and I worked well as a team right from the beginning. She gave me cultural, political, and historical context for projects that I was planning. I shared with her my educational and management experience. We quickly developed the kind of relationship that allowed us to share our views on matters rarely discussed between expatriate and Afghan colleagues but which are critically important to our being able to function effectively in each other's cultures. Aziza had a way of making her points with me in a quiet and respectful voice but in a very firm manner.

One very hot July day I rebelled against the Afghan dress code, which requires opaque stockings or lightweight pants under long skirts no matter what the weather. I decided to come to work with bare legs under my long navy flowered skirt and wore open sandals.

As I walked into the office, Aziza looked at me with slight disapproval.

"Suzanne, you know that we have a meeting at Ministry of Education today."

"Yes, I know," I answered.

"You cannot go to the Ministry of Education dressed like that."

"Why not? I have on a long skirt."

"Your legs are bare. You at least need to wear stockings under your skirt to go into that place," she said firmly.

"But it's so hot, Aziza. I just can't bear wearing stockings in this heat," I protested. "You are used to wearing so many clothes in this heat, but I am not."

"Do you have any stockings in your computer bag?" she asked.

"Of course not," I responded, realizing that she would not be moved.

"Then we will have to stop at your guesthouse on the way to the Ministry of Education to get some," Aziza said with finality.

"Okay, Aziza. I give up," I conceded. "I'll do it if you think it's important."

"It is," she said with authority.

When we got to the Ministry of Education and started up the open stairway towards the third floor, I understood immediately why Aziza had been so firm with me about wearing stockings. When I saw all the men on the first floor looking up the open stairway at us, I wished that I also had pants under my skirt like Aziza did.

I appreciated Aziza's connections with the Ministry of Education. The department heads knew and respected her. We never waited long for appointments. Even the Deputy Minister for Curriculum made time for us and listened carefully to our suggestions about curriculum development and teacher training. By the end of summer, the Minister of Education and his team had accepted our recommendation that English be introduced in the Afghan schools in the fourth grade instead of the seventh grade in order to take advantage of the psycholinguistic window (ages four to twelve) during which time children have the greatest opportunity to become fluent in other languages.

Ultimately, Aziza participated in the implementation of this rec-ommendation. She was recruited by Ministry of Education to be part of an English language curriculum development team from Columbia University on a UNICEF-funded project to provide textbooks and train-ing for Afghans who would be teaching children in grades four through six. I was very pleased to know that Aziza had joined this development team because I had consciously mentored her to follow up on my work with the Ministry of Education.

My model for working with Aziza and all of my subsequent Afghan colleagues was the Peace Corps Counterpart model. In each position that I have held, I have mentored an Afghan colleague (often a woman) to follow up my work or take over my role.

Early in the summer, Aziza discussed with me her interest in getting a Bachelor's degree in a university or college in America. After three weeks of working with her, I told her about the four-year Lilly Foundation Scholarship for an Afghan Woman being offered by St. Mary's. Aziza ex-pressed interest, so I wrote to the college to tell them that I had found the perfect candidate for the scholarship's inaugural year. Aziza scored very high on the Test of English as a Foreign Language (TOEFL) and got SAT scores above the average scores achieved by native English speak-ing applicants. Her application was going well until Aziza announced that she was getting married. She had been engaged for some time and Afghan cultural custom would not allow her to travel anywhere during the engagement period unless accompanied by her brother or her fi-ancé. Moreover, her family would not allow Aziza to delay her marriage until after completing her degree. Getting her husband a visa would de-lay Aziza's enrollment. Both Aziza and I were frustrated by the delay. However, Aziza was caught between the expectations of her conserva-tive family and her drive to get a college education. She got her visa but had to reapply because her husband's visa process took two years. I did what I could to support them.

I visited Aziza during her second and third years on the campus. She was thriving on the intellectual stimulation of her studies. She noted that her college experience was quite different from that of her classmates because she lived in married student housing off campus. However, she and her husband had found community among the married international students at the University of Notre Dame.

Aziza graduated with honors in Psychology in 2008. She and her husband have returned to Afghanistan to "give back to their country" and we have been able to work with each other on Education projects once again. A mutual Afghan friend and former colleague noted on Aziza's return to Afghanistan that her increased capacity to contribute to Education in Afghanistan was one of my legacies to the country that would outlive me. From the progress she has already made in her work on Afghan Education, his prediction appears to be correct.

"Hello, Susan!" Walid's voice boomed with his daily greeting as his tall Pashtun body filled the small doorframe of my office on my first day of work at the office. He had to duck his head to come through the doorway. As he strode quickly toward my desk, he extended his large brown hand and gripped my small white one in a firm handshake.

"How is your health?" he asked, literally translating into English the Dari phrase *"Hale-tan xubas?"*

Ignoring the fact that he called me "Susan" instead of Suzanne,[1] I answered by directly translating the Dari response *'Xubastam, tashakor'* into English.

"Hi Walid. My health is fine, thank you."

As I responded to his greeting, Walid's smiling face with a trim beard and head of thick, wavy hair tilted slightly towards me. He looked directly at me, an unusual but not necessarily threatening action between an Afghan man and an expatriate woman. Walid's manner simply meant that he had experience interacting with the outgoing American women in our agency and responded in kind to their friendly, informal manner. For me, it was both a relief and a compliment that Walid was able to relate to me with the same comfort that he showed in interacting with other American women in our office, even though I was two decades older than they were. His understanding of American informality would make it much easier for us to work together.

Walid's warm greeting is well known among his colleagues and acquaintances. When he greets close male friends and relatives, his

---

[1] *(Most Pashtuns call me Susan, as that is the name given to Pashtun women and the name Suzanne is not familiar to them.)*

Lessons of Love in Afghanistan

handshake is followed by a hug or a slap on the back and a hearty laugh. His extrovert personality, good looks, political acumen, charismatic leadership of his peers, and the respect for him among the Afghan government agencies impressed the Country Director. He appointed Walid as the Project Officer for the Umbrella Grant Program a few months before I arrived in Afghanistan. Walid was responsible for oversight of eighty Afghan non-governmental organizations (NGOs) who were implementing agency projects throughout the country. In addition, he had agreed to take on the role of being my Pashtun interpreter and facilitator of my meetings with Pashtun Ministry Officials and Afghan NGOs.

"I am just a simple person from a village in Wardak," Walid would often tell people. Only half of this statement is true. He is from a village in Wardak, but he is not a simple man. He is a complex person with a high degree of intelligence—more education than 95% of Afghan males—and political skills that are recognizable to veteran politicians from any culture. He speaks English fluently, holds a Bachelor's degree in Agricultural Science, a Master's in Business and has recently been elected to a national political position.

I was immediately impressed by Walid's passion for helping his fellow Afghans out of poverty and his willingness to work twelve-hour days for the agency toward that end. Like other devout Muslims, however, he interrupts his work five times daily to respond to the calls to prayer.

Although Walid is thoroughly Afghan, contact with American and European co-workers has acquainted him with the trappings of Western cultures. He alternates between wearing traditional Afghan dress and sporty Western clothes. He likes traditional Afghan music and Hindi love songs, and he has developed a taste for American rock-n-roll. When I met him, Walid had bought his first car and was teaching himself to drive. When I asked about driving schools where he might get some coaching, he laughed and responded, "We don't have such things in Afghanistan."

One day Walid and I were scheduled to meet with the director of one of the largest Afghan NGOs.

"Are we still meeting this morning with Asad?" I asked.

"Yes. The car is waiting. Shall we go?"

Walid held the door for me, guided me down the narrow stairs and stood aside as I gathered my long skirt in order to get into the back seat of the waiting Land Cruiser without tripping. I could tell that he was

New Afghan Friends

relieved that I didn't expect to sit in the front seat. I knew that, tradition-
ally, women in Afghanistan sit in the back seat of the car and men sit in
the front except when there are multiple male passengers and only one
female in the car. In that case, the woman sits in the front passenger seat
and the male passengers sit in back. When foreign women sit in the front
seat with the male driver when there no other passengers or sit in the
back seat with Afghan men, Afghans are uncomfortable. They know that
this violation of the expected seating arrangement could cause a scandal
because conservative onlookers would suspect that there is an illicit relationship between the women and men in the car.

Since Walid was continuously in conversation with someone—the
driver, a person calling on the radio (our means of communication before cell phones arrived in Afghanistan) or me—I saw Walid's face in
profile for most of the trip across Kabul. Like most Afghan men, he
looked older than his thirty-three years. The lines in his face showed that
his life had not been easy. My expatriate colleagues and I had often noted
that the effects of warfare, poverty, and suffering of twenty-three years
made most Afghan adults look at least a decade older than their actual
ages. I later learned that Walid had lived in Pakistan as a refugee since
he was nine years old. At first he lived alone with his older brother, but
his entire family ultimately migrated to Peshawar. They had returned to
Afghanistan in April 2002, just two months before I arrived in Kabul.

As we drove to our meeting, I described to Walid the school visits
that I had made in Herat. I also voiced my hope that poor Afghan children would soon be able to stay in school through high school, rather
than being forced to drop out of middle school to help support their
families.

"They can do it," Walid said. "My family was very poor, but all five
of us went to school. My mother had three hens, and she sold the eggs
from those hens to make sure that my brothers, my sister, and I had
notebooks and pens to take to school."

"She sounds like a wonderful mother," I remarked.

"She is. Because of her, all the sons have completed university degrees."

"That's a real accomplishment. She must be very proud of all of
you."

"Yes, she is happy that we finished the university." Then he paused, turned around in the front seat, and looked at me in a way that said he was about to say something important. "Susan, I would like you to come to my house to meet my family and hear our family story."

I was surprised and pleased at this invitation to visit Walid's home, as we'd just started working together. However, I suddenly recalled how many times Michael and I were invited to the homes of Afghans we had just met.

"Thank you, Walid. I'd like that. I'm going to Mazar next week, but I'd like to come to your home when I'm back in Kabul." At the time, I assumed that Walid must have invited many foreigners to his home. I was wrong.

Two weeks later, Walid escorted Joanna, who was Walid's supervisor in the Karte Se Field Office, and me on a walk from our office to his house for a Friday lunch. "You two are the first foreign staff members that I have ever invited to my family's home," Walid said.

Upon our arrival, it was clear that this would be one of the big "guest meals" that Afghanistan is famous for. Over the space of a half hour, Joanna and I met a succession of family members in the garden of the house, which was dominated by the huge *Shah Tut* (King Mulberry) tree. The large garden was a point of pride for the family. Walid drew our attention to the elaborate irrigation system that supplied water to the healthy tomato plants and other vegetables that fed his household. Walid's three brothers and their families were there, as were his mother, his sister, and his cousin's family. Prior to entering the guestroom on the second floor, Joanna and I met Walid's lovely twenty-seven-year-old wife. She did not linger with us, as she was supervising the work in the kitchen.

Joanna and I settled onto the large floor cushions lining the perimeter of the sunlit guest room that faced onto the vegetable garden. Two of the older children placed bolsters behind our backs. At least ten children, five of them Walid's, were in and out of the room during the afternoon. The older boys helped serve the meal and stayed in the room to eat with us. At other times, they left the room to play in the yard. The older girls made brief appearances before lunch. Walid's two youngest children came and sat on his lap until it was time for Walid to help his brothers lay the tablecloth on the floor and serve the meal.

New Afghan Friends

As a preliminary to lunch, mulberries from the tree in the garden were served with tea. During this time, Amini, the oldest of the four brothers, told the family story in English.

"Susan, you said that you would like to hear our family story, so I am going to tell it to you and Joanna."

"Thank you, Amini, I'm anxious to hear it," I said.

"Our family is from a village in Wardak Province," Amini began. "My father and I organized the village against the Soviets. I was a resistance fighter. When Walid was nine, the Soviets retaliated against our family. They bombed our family compound two times—in winter 1981 and in spring 1982. Our compound was hit by a total of twenty-two bombs (some of them napalm) in the two attacks. Amazingly, the humans in the compound survived, but forty head of livestock did not."

For nearly an hour, Amini described the details of the Soviet efforts to kill him, which prompted him to assume a false identity and make a nighttime escape by taxi to Ghazni. He described his discovery by opposition forces in Ghazni and a second escape to Pakistan, followed by his three years of fighting with the *Mujahadeen* on both sides of the Afghanistan-Pakistan border. Amini stayed in Pakistan, enrolled in medical school and asked that his younger brother, Walid, be sent to live with him so that Walid could go to school.

(In a private conversation five years later, Walid told me about how his family survived the bombings and about leaving his family to go to Pakistan. I will relate that here, to fill out the story his brother told me upon our first meeting.)

"We lived in caves for up to six weeks at a time during the bombings," he told me. "We survived by eating leaves and berries. We were often thirsty. It was a very hard time, and it's painful for me to talk about it."

"The schools in our province were closed after I finished third grade, because of the fighting and the bombings," he explained. "The night I had to leave was the worst night of my life. I was nine years old. My mother came and picked me up from my bed, where I was asleep. She carried me into the living room and told me to say goodbye to my father, brothers, my sister, cousins, aunts and uncles. Two male travelers who knew my brother were in the room. She told me that I was going to

Lessons of Love in Afghanistan

Pakistan with these travelers to live with my brother. We were very poor. My father, who was a farmer, had only ten Afghanis and gave me five of them for the journey. It was terrible to say goodbye to my family, but it was almost unbearable to say goodbye to my mother. I asked her to give me something to remember her. She had nothing, so she could only give me a coin worth twenty-five cents. As I walked toward the mountains, I heard my mother crying behind me. I can still hardly talk about it ..."

After a pause, Walid continued. "We were on foot the entire way. I had cheap Pakistani shoes. They rubbed against my feet and hurt them. So I took my shoes off after a short time and strapped them to my backpack. I walked for five days to the Pakistan border in bare feet. When I got there, my feet were cracked, bleeding, infected, and swollen. At Torkham, an old Afghan man saw me and started to weep. He chided the two men who accompanied me. 'How can you let this boy suffer like this?' he cried. 'It would take only two rupees to give him medicine that would help him!' Then he took some of his own money to the pharmacy and bought some ointment to put on my feet. When I finally got to Lahore and Amini met me, he also cried. I stayed there in Amini's room at the university for five years. We celebrated *Eid* alone together for all of that time. The day that I got on the bus to leave Lahore and rejoin the rest of the family in Peshawar, Amini stood in the road and cried as he waved goodbye."

"Everyone in our family travelled to Pakistan on foot," Amini said. "The roads to Pakistan were closed to Afghans, so we came over the mountains. The young men in our family led the women, children, and old people over the mountains."

"How fortunate that your entire family made it safely to Pakistan," I said.

"Yes, we all made it," Amini's voice changed as he went on. "But we lost my uncle soon after that. He was assassinated at the gate of his compound. I was the intended victim. He left nine children." Amini's eyes clouded. The grief in the room was palpable as everyone lowered their eyes.

"I'm sorry," I whispered.

New Afghan Friends

Amini continued. "Our time in Pakistan was very difficult. At first, I was supporting thirty people on my salary as an employee of an NGO in Pakistan. After my uncle died, I was responsible for forty people. Luckily, Walid also found work with an NGO when he was twenty-five, so he helped me support everyone."

I felt uncomfortable that none of the brothers who were sitting on *toshaks* (large, flat floor pillows) around the room added to the family story. However, I assumed that it had been pre-arranged that Amini, who was the oldest male family member present, would speak for all of them. I also realized that only two of the brothers—Walid and the youngest brother—spoke English.

Amini's account ended with the statement, "In April 2002 our family marked the end of twenty years of being refugees!"

"Did you have a party to celebrate?" I asked.

"No. We couldn't, because we were still building this house," Amini answered. "The work is complete now, so we'll celebrate soon ... maybe this fall, when the weather is cooler."

"That will be a great occasion," I remarked. The room of listeners murmured in agreement.

When Amini finished his story, I asked if I could take pictures of the family for the agency website. Since I had asked Walid in advance for permission to do this, everyone readily agreed. Walid's mother and sister remained in the room for the pictures with the male family members. All of the wives, including Walid's, stayed out of the room.

Our delicious Afghan meal included *Kabuli Pilau* (a dish of rice, beef, carrots, raisins and spices), two kinds of kebabs (chicken and lamb), *bouranee* (an eggplant, tomato and yogurt dish), a salad of fresh tomatoes and cucumbers, yogurt and fresh fruit of the season (melons, grapes and apples from Wardak Province). I was surprised that the men and older boys took on all the serving and cleanup responsibilities for our lunch. They were very attentive to Joanna and me. Walid even cut slices of apple for me when he saw me struggling with the dull fruit knife. Since this was considered a "business entertainment," the family women, girls, and young children ate in another room.

During the meal, our conversation turned to the national politics of our respective countries and their likely implications. Much of the discussion was between Amini and me. It felt awkward to be having a dialog with someone who sat at the head of the room, about ten feet away from me, with several people sitting in between us, even though I knew that it's normal in Afghanistan for the honored guests and the Afghans with the most status to do much of the speaking. Amini's brothers listened and offered occasional comments. When the comments were in Pashtu, Walid translated them for me.

The meal in Walid's home was a turning point for me. I had missed the experience of spending time with an Afghan family during my first month back in Afghanistan. I now felt that my return to the country and to Afghan culture was complete. When Walid came to my office the next day, I thanked him for the wonderful afternoon with his family.

"This was my best weekend so far in Afghanistan," I said.

He responded with an emotional statement. "Your coming to our house and your interest in our family story was a wonderful act of love for us. You do not need an invitation next time. Our house is your house."

On my first visit to the family home, I had not met Walid's father, who was traveling outside of Kabul at the time. I finally met *Haji* nine months later. Walid wanted me to see the family's ancestral village in Wardak Province. Because of security concerns, we took two cars. Walid's younger brother rode with me in the agency car and Walid, his father and a cousin rode in another. As we prepared for the journey, Walid mentioned that his family had been discussing my safety as an American in Afghanistan at the same time that my country had begun bombing missions in Iraq. His family was worried about my agency's ability to protect me from Afghans who sympathized with Sadaam Hussein's regime. Before we set out, Walid's father, a tall, imposing man with piercing eyes, came to my car and spoke to me in Pashtu. As I had not yet learned that language, Walid translated:

"He said 'You can have the salt from our table. You are our guest and we will protect you.' He means that whatever we have is yours."

Walid and his father have kept their word. I have been to Walid's home many times in the years since that first visit. I have shared in holiday celebrations such as *Eid* and *Nawrooz* and was the only foreigner among several hundred guests—including more than seventy women— to participate in family celebrations: the naming party for Walid's younger son, the engagement party and wedding for his oldest daughter, and for

New Afghan Friends

weddings of other family relatives. I have also been included in intimate family dinners where I have had a chance to see how much Walid enjoys being a family man. When he comes home, his younger children run to greet him, while the older ones greet him respectfully at the door. His youngest son and daughter often curl up in his lap. Walid and his wife are generous hosts. They remain my family away from home. Walid's younger son calls me *"Niya,"* which means "Grandmother" in Pashtu.

The warm reception of Walid's family helped me deal with the loss of former friends from our Peace Corps days in Afghanistan. I had hoped to reconnect with two families with whom Michael and I shared many meals more than three decades ago. The families we knew then were very different from Walid's family and very different from each other. The late 1960s were peaceful and relatively prosperous years in Afghanistan, so the conversation topics were quite different from the survival issues that I discussed with Walid and his brothers.

One family that Michael and I saw often was headed by a learned man named Mayel Herawi, a native of Herat, who supervised the Kabul Museum. At Mayel's house in Kabul, Michael and I had examined his Persian miniature collection, compared the work of Persian and Afghan poets, talked about his daughter's plans to study in the United States, and enjoyed intimate meals with Mayel, his wife Nassim, his three daughters and a son.

Another family that we visited was that of Hassan Sharifi, an Uzbek from Mazar-i-Sharif who had graduated from the University of Texas and was President of the Afghan Gas and Petroleum Company. Dinners at Sharifi's house in Mazar were big events. They often included other foreign visitors and were usually attached to a special occasion or activity—hunting songbirds, trying out his new badminton set, or saying farewell to Peace Corps Volunteers who were completing their tour.

I had hoped to find these dear friends when I returned to Afghanistan in 2002. However, I underestimated the difficulty of finding any Afghan who was prominent in Nadir Shah's time. Many had left the country, gone into hiding, or died. Despite many inquiries in Herat and at the Kabul Museum, I could not find Mayel Herawi's family. When I visited Mazar, I learned that Hassan Sharifi had died the previous year. I can no longer anticipate the enthusiastic welcome of this energetic man, the promise of his generous hospitality, and the surprise adventures that he arranged for his foreign visitors.

I'll always miss our former friends in Afghanistan, but I soon came to understand that the openness and ease of interaction that foreigners had with Afghans in the 1960s would not be possible in these times. Since the Russian occupation of the country, many Afghans—especially conservatives—had developed a negative attitude for foreigners. I slowly realized that my new Afghan friends were taking personal risks when they were seen with me in public places and that their families took risks having me to their homes. The depth of their love and friendship is demonstrated in their willingness to continue seeing me despite these risks. I reciprocate by lowering my profile (e.g., wearing conservative clothes and riding in a car similar to those owned by average Afghans) and asking my friends to choose the time, places and circumstances of our meetings.

New Afghan Friends

Chapter 6

Recovering from Loss

In the weeks before I returned to Afghanistan in 2002, I revisited memories of evenings with Michael in our first home together. We arrived in January—the coldest month of the year in Kabul. On winter evenings, we lay on the carpet in front of the *bokhari* in our living room, listening to music, reading, and playing with our German Shepherd puppy, Djinn. When warm weather arrived, we had picnics in the back yard. Our picnic dinners included fresh greens that I had planted in a corner of the yard. Since I used pure water to keep them fresh, we could enjoy eating them without worrying about getting sick. In early fall, we ate apples freshly picked from the tree in our yard.

I wondered how our former home had weathered the thirty-four years. Sigurd must have intuited my affection for that house. Before I left for Afghanistan, he called me in Seattle to warn me that my old neighborhood in Karte Char had been on the Kabul battle line for over twenty-five years.

"Others who were here in the Peace Corps have had a difficult time coping with the devastation they have found in their old neighborhoods," he said. "I know that you'll be impatient to see your old neighborhood, but I'm asking you to wait a couple of weeks after you arrive. You need to get used to the destruction in other parts of Kabul before you go to Karte Char. There's not much left there except rubble."

Choking back the tears, I said, "Okay, Sigurd. Thanks for preparing me. I look forward to seeing you soon."

Several weeks later, I was in Kabul and thinking about my house. My colleague Shakeela and I had finished an afternoon meeting in the agency's Karte Se Office. I asked her if we could try to find my house in Karte Char before heading back to the main office in Shar-i-Nau. Shakeela's family home was also in Karte Char, so she agreed. She directed the driver toward Rabia Balkhi Girls High School, which was near my former home.

Despite Sigurd's warnings, I felt shaken by the extent of the devastation. Blocks of rocket-damaged dwellings surrounded me as the car rolled slowly down Darulaman Road past side streets that were once lined with trees. Families inhabited the shells of some large buildings, despite the fact that the structures were missing outside walls and some of the timbers intended to support the upper floors. Women were hanging clothes on lines stretched between exposed wooden studs. I caught glimpses of young children playing dangerously close to the edges of the floors on which they lived. Older children were playing in the garbage-strewn yards outside their temporary homes. A slight tremor in this earthquake-prone region would collapse these buildings, crushing hundreds of families.

I took in the scenes in stunned silence. These ruins were particularly stark. There was no sign of roofs, doors, or any ornamentation that would give the buildings character.

Shakeela explained, "The owners took away every portable item for rebuilding. They even took the roofs that were intact."

My eyes searched among the ruins for features that would help me identify my former home, but I could not find any.

"Was this a nice part of Kabul when you lived here?" Shakeela asked. As she turned toward me, her *chador* slipped backwards to reveal long blonde hair that framed the light olive skin of her face.

I broke my silence to respond in a cracking voice. "Yes, the newest houses were in Karte Char. Both Western workers and middle-class Afghans lived here. We all had gardens with trees and flowers."

Shakeela noted the change in my voice and her green eyes widened with concern. Then she called my attention to the only landmark in the area with a compound wall still intact: Rabia Balkhi Girls High School, her alma mater. International Security Assistance Force (ISAF) soldiers were overseeing the reconstruction effort there. Green army tents, ISAF stenciled in large red and black letters on their sides, filled part of the school courtyard as classes continued to be held in the undamaged wing of the building.

We drove for a while longer, turning up and down unidentifiable roads searching for any sign of the little house where Michael and I started our married life. I was both anxious to see it and afraid of what I might see. I finally gave up and asked the driver to take Shakeela home.

As we neared Shakeela's home, I asked if her family had left before the shelling and rocket attacks began in this area. Her response put my own loss into perspective.

"We were in the basement," she said in the short, direct statement that characterizes the spoken English of many Afghans. "When the shelling stopped, we walked out. My little nephews were barefoot. There was no time to find their shoes. We all walked on Darulaman Road toward the middle of Kabul. There were no buses or taxis. On the way, my brother-in-law, the father of my two nephews, was killed by a rocket shell that warring Afghan factions were firing at each other."

"I'm so sorry," I whispered, realizing as I spoke that "sorry" was an inadequate response. Not wanting her to dwell on that terrible day in her past, I tried to refocus Shakeela on the present. "How do you feel about being back?"

"I don't like it. We had better schooling in Peshawar, and we had running water and electricity all day. Here, we have many difficulties. But where else can we go? We are Afghans. My family has to stay here. We're rebuilding our house."

As the agency driver stopped our car in front of her compound gate, Shakeela turned to me. "This is my family's house. Please come in for tea."

"Thank you for the invitation," I said, "but it's late and I have to be at my guesthouse by 5:30 p.m."

Following polite Afghan custom, Shakeela repeated her invitation two more times. When I had refused her third offer, she understood that I really could not stay. We agreed that I would come for tea on another day.

The next day, my colleague Peter proposed doing a series of illustrated interviews for the website on "returnees," families who had returned to Afghanistan after spending years in refugee camps. He wondered aloud where we might find families to interview.

"Peter, we don't have to go looking for them. There are returnees here in our office." Then I told him about Shakeela's family.

Recovering from Loss

"If her family will agree to be photographed, we can do it this week," he said.

The next day, Shakeela greeted us at her gate with her four-year-old nephew, who gazed at us through one brown eye and one blue one. He was clearly fascinated by Peter's height of 6' 2" and by his blonde hair. There were no men with blonde hair in his Pashtun family.

Shakeela introduced us to her parents, who looked decades older than their mid-fifties. Her father was stooped, and her mother was blind in one eye. An abundance of flowers and vegetables grew in a well-tended garden plot divided into quadrants by neat concrete walkways. Its permanence and order seemed out of synch with the house. The sight of the fresh white stucco and red tile roof of the new section of the house directly adjacent to the old section—a rocket-damaged, earthen structure with crumbled walls and a collapsed roof—was somewhat jarring.

Shakeela's parents led us into the newly rebuilt wing of their home. As we settled onto the new *toshaks* arranged around the red floral-designed carpet, the children tucked bolsters between our backs and the walls. I sat next to the window and the flies immediately tried to light on the limited exposed flesh on my body. Shakeela's father apologized for not yet having glass in the new window openings, while his wife and grandchildren batted away flies with fly swatters.

It was a hot afternoon. Peter and I were sweaty from carrying camera equipment into the compound. My face became flushed because the *chador* prevented heat from escaping from the back of my neck. Shakeela's parents noted our discomfort and responded by producing paper fans that they waved rapidly in front of our faces until we took over the task ourselves. The electrical outage in their district of Kabul that afternoon made the new ceiling fans inoperable. The family did not have the funds to purchase generators, which expatriate guesthouses had as a backup system for frequent interruptions of electrical power throughout Kabul.

Shakeela reminded us that they did not have safe drinking water in the compound, as their well had not yet been dug. To ensure that our thirst was immediately quenched, one of the grandchildren brought cans of pop on metal trays. Another grandchild was carrying water for tea from a neighbor's well. Early in our visit, the drilling equipment for their well arrived. Shakeela's father excused himself several times to ensure that the setup of the equipment did minimal damage to the garden.

Lessons of Love in Afghanistan

During most of our visit, family members were posing for photos taken by Peter while they related their stories to me. Shakeela translated her parents' description of their decades as refugees in Pakistan, as well as their current difficulties. Her father noted that three related families had lived together in one house in Peshawar.

"For a while, Shakeela, two of my sons, and I operated a small tailoring business out of that house," he said in Pashtu. "But we couldn't make enough money to support the family. My sons and I were always trying to find work. The Pakistani police made it impossible. They made us pay them bribes for protection. Sometimes they beat us for loitering."

Eventually, Shakeela, the only member of the family fluent in English (thanks to her education in Pakistan), was hired to work in our agency's Female Education Project. "I supported twenty people on my salary," Shakeela said. "No one else in the family was able to find work. It was very difficult for us in Pakistan."

"It seems that things are better for you here," I remarked. "You are building your new house and getting settled again."

"No, we still have many troubles," Shakeela responded. "The biggest problem is my brother. Come into the other guestroom. You need to talk with him."

Shakeela's handsome thirty-three-year-old brother was sitting on a large *toshak* in the guestroom with his back leaned against the wall. The fair-skinned, dark-eyed young man raised his hand in greeting as we entered. "*Salaam alekum,*" he said.

"He has a degenerative spine condition," Shakeela said, "from being tortured by the *Mujahadeen* while he was a soldier. He was working at the Ministry of Defense when they took over. They kept him in the basement of that building for eight months. He sits like this all day and all night. He gets up only to be assisted on his trips to the bathroom. We help him while he leans on a walking stick for support. His neck is immobilized to lessen pain. The doctors have given him painkillers, but he still wakes us up in the night when he screams because his pain is too much."

Her brother added to her explanation. "You see my situation," he said in Dari. "Here are the papers that the doctors wrote. They say that the surgery that can correct my condition is not available here or in Pakistan. What can I do?"

Toward the end of our stay, we briefly met other family members who lived in the house: Shakeela's widowed sister and her six children, her unemployed brother and his two sons. Shakeela's mother told us that her son's wife was expected to return from her parents' home later that day. "His wife contracted malaria while we were in Pakistan," she said. "Her family has been taking care of her because she has been bedridden for nearly a year. We could not take care of her because we are already taking care of her six children."

Shakeela wanted us to meet her aunt, uncle, and their son's family of six who lived in the compound next door. They were "squatting" in temporary shelter on the second floor of a damaged, abandoned house. We crossed the poorly kempt compound, made our way up the packed dirt stairs, and entered a large, dim room with a dirt floor. Two young sons and Shakeela's cousin were sitting on the only covering on the floor—a flattened UNICEF tent. The wife, aunt, and uncle came and went from the room as Shakeela explained their situation to us in English. When they spoke to us in Dari (which Shakeela translated for Peter), they stood on the exposed dirt floor, since there was not enough room for them to join us on the tent. The thin cloth curtains in the window openings offered scant protection against heat, dust, and flies.

I could smell that one of the two young children in the net-covered beds was sick. Flies covered the top of the mosquito netting across the cradle, directly over the face of the sleeping toddler. They were attracted by the smell of the little girl's saliva. Her face was flushed with fever.

"Have you taken your daughter to a doctor?" I asked the girl's father in Dari.

"Yes, they gave my wife some medicine to make her well," he responded. Then he changed the subject. "I cannot find a job here," he said. "I am ashamed that I cannot support my wife, my four children, and my parents. I was trained as an electrician in Pakistan."

"What kind of job do you want?" I asked again in his language.

He responded, "I want to be a teacher or an electrician, but I will take any job."

"What about your wife? Did your wife finish high school?"

"No, she only finished fifth grade. She cannot work. She has to take care of our four children."

Shakeela's aunt and uncle had rejoined us. In Dari, the uncle volunteered information about his employment status. "I was a farmer for fifty years. I am looking for work in Kabul, but I don't know what I can do here."

Shakeela's aunt shook her head. "I don't know how to work outside our house," she said. "But I am a good cook. I cook for the family."

I responded in Dari. "A good cook is important to a family. What is your specialty?"

"Ashak," she answered.

"That's one of my family's favorite dishes," I told her. She nodded approvingly.

I left the compound understanding why Shakeela, a lovely woman who is nearly thirty, says that she cannot consider marriage. She is the only adult in her extended family with a job. She worries about how they will survive without her income. As Peter and I thanked her and her family for their hospitality, Shakeela hugged me emotionally and said, "Suzanne, you see that we have many difficulties. I hope you can help us."

"I will do my best," I said. "Sharing your family's story is a first step."

When we returned to the car after the two-hour visit, I sighed. "Whew! That was tough!"

"Yes," Peter said grimly. "It was."

"Let's make a list of what we can do to help them and assign ourselves some of the tasks," I suggested.

Together, we brainstormed strategies for helping Shakeela's family connect with persons and agencies to get assistance. We wondered aloud how many other families in this neighborhood had similar needs. After completing our list we lapsed into silence for the half-hour car ride back to the middle of Kabul. I was trying to process the multiple levels of suffering that we had just confronted. My depression at realizing the depth and extent of suffering that Afghans had experienced for the last twenty-three years left me barely able to speak for hours. At a personal level, I understood why Afghan government officials and volunteer agencies describe the task of rebuilding this country as a huge, long-term effort.

Two years later, I made another attempt to find my former home in Karte Char. By now, rubble had been cleared from the neighborhood streets and from many of the lots on which houses had been completely destroyed. There was so much new construction going on in the neighborhood that Darulaman Road, the main road to Karte Se district, was lined with newly established construction materials suppliers. My friend Marnie accompanied me on this search as she had already found her former home in Karte Char. Her family had lived on the same street as Michael and I did; however, we hadn't met at that time because Marnie was still in high school. (Marnie and I met many years later in Seattle while working on a program to help women on welfare.) Marnie's family home was damaged, but the structure was still intact. We narrowed the possible locations of my previous home to two gates. From the Land Cruiser I could see a large apple tree rising above the walls in the yard behind one of the gates.

"This is it!" I said.

"How do you know?"

"It's the apple tree! I have pictures of that tree when it was much younger, but the shape is still the same. Also, this house is on a precise diagonal from Rabia Balkhi High School, which I remember from photos that I took from the roof of our house."

"Okay. Let's go find out," Marnie suggested.

We knocked at the gate and a young man answered. Behind him, I could see a new one-story home being built on the same foundation where our home had been.

"*Salaam alekum, Agha.*" I said. Then I continued in Dari. "Excuse me for bothering you, but I lived in this neighborhood long ago and I've been trying to locate my former home. I think this may be where it was. Do you own this property now?"

Since multiple claims to property are currently a big issue in Kabul, the young man was justifiably wary.

"Yes, I do," he answered.

"What was the name of the landowner from whom you bought it?" I asked.

The young man called an older man to the gate.

"The owner was Ghafoor Khan," the older man said. "However, he is dead now."

"Were there three structures on this property?" I asked. "Was there a one-story house with seven rooms where your new house is now?"

"Yes," both men answered.

"Was there a small house for household help in front of the main house and a storage area at the end of the house over there?"

"Yes, yes," they both said as they nodded their heads vigorously.

With tears in my eyes, I said, "Then this was my house. I lived here with my husband over thirty years ago. Ghafoor Khan was our landlord."

Marnie added in Dari "We both lived on this street." Pointing to the eastern end of the street, she stated, "I lived down there. We both came back to help Afghans like you rebuild your country."

"You are most welcome," the men said. "Would you like to come in for tea?"

"Thank you very much, but we see that you are busy building your house," Marnie and I responded.

"Thank you for letting me see where my house was," I added. "I am glad that there is a new house there now, and I hope that you will be very happy here."

"You are most welcome. God go with you," the men replied in Dari.

As we drove away, I concluded that it was better that I had not seen my old house in rubble. I didn't take a picture of the new house being built on the site. I prefer to live with the memory of our old house as pictured in my album of aging photographs. That house holds the sweet memories of a couple who were very much in love and who were enjoying the adventure of starting their life together in their first home, which happened to be in Kabul, Afghanistan.

Chapter 7

Memories of Herat

My senses remembered Herat for decades after Michael and I first visited this lovely city near Afghanistan's western border in late spring, 1968. The smell of pine needles and flowers, the graceful arched entrance of the main mosque decorated with dazzling lapis and turquoise tiles, the domed shrines that honor poets and important people in Afghan history, the bird songs, and the poetry recited by Sufi mystics sitting in lush green gardens made this a magical place for me after months of travel across the barren brown plains and mountains of Afghanistan.

When we first visited Herat, Michael took me on my first ride in a *gadi*—a passenger carriage drawn by horses whose bell-covered red halters create rhythmic jingling sounds as they canter along the thoroughfare. Having fallen under the spell of the sensuous, romantic atmosphere of an early summer evening in Herat, I persuaded him to forego the taxi ride from the hotel to a local restaurant and take a *gadi* ride through the city. In the midst of the ride the driver handed Michael a dark, palm-sized resinous substance and asked if he wanted buy it. Michael turned it down. I asked him later what it was.

"Raw opium," he responded.

"Really?!"

I was shocked. I wasn't yet aware of the easy availability of opium in this country or the prominence of opium production in the Afghan economy

"Yes," he answered. "The driver says that most foreigners our age who visit Herat come for the opium and *hashish*. He was surprised that I turned down the offer."

Michael was in his element on our first trip to Herat. The residents of the city appreciated his beautiful Iranian Farsi (which many Herat residents spoke in addition to Dari) and his enthusiasm about the Iranian influences in the mosques, shrines, and gardens. *Mullahs* at the graceful Herat Mosque were so impressed with him that they granted permission for me to enter the mosque courtyard with him if I wore a *chador*, which they provided.

When our family lived in Isfahan, Iran, for six months in 1978, I fully appreciated what Michael had been telling me about the Iranian influences on the Herat mosque. In the center of Isfahan, visitors are surrounded by huge, sparkling turquoise domes and enormous archways decorated with intricate floral-design tiles. The mosques of Isfahan mesmerized our young daughters, Rachael and Sarah, who loved to stand under the arched entry of the Shah Abbas Mosque and clap their hands—as the guards encouraged them to do—so that they could listen to the echoes reverberating off the great building's walls. The vast, marble-tiled squares and well-tended gardens adjacent to the Isfahan mosques made them places of peace and refuge from the city's noise. For our daughters, they were firsthand experiences of the exotic, magical illustrations in their best fairy tale books.

Across the street from the Herat Mosque were several shops selling the famous Herat glass. An abundance of brilliant turquoise vases, glasses, and pitchers lined shop windows and stood piled in bins inside the stores. Michael and I were lucky enough to visit one shop where the glass blowers were at work. I stood transfixed as the hot turquoise liquid was blown and swirled until it took the shape of a vase. We purchased a small turquoise glass carafe and ten small liqueur glasses on that visit, which I have managed to preserve all these years by carefully packing each piece every time we moved.

Michael and I passed through Herat again in the summer of 1968, at the beginning of an overland trip to Iran. That was the last time I saw the city until three decades later.

I've now made a half dozen trips to Herat, to oversee the establishment of a computer-learning center and lead workshops for English Department instructors at Herat University.

As we cruised along the boulevard from the airport to Herat's city center in July 2002, the familiar scent of pine trees wafted in through the open car windows. In the midst of the oncoming vehicles, I was delighted to spot a *gadi*. I watched the *gadi* driver trying to keep his horse out of the path of other vehicles and remembered when *gadis* owned the streets and motor vehicles pulled over to let them pass.

When we entered the city center, I spotted the minarets of the Herat Mosque, which I still consider the loveliest mosque in Afghanistan. Its graceful lines are complemented by the lovely plaza and spacious gardens that surround it, and by the wide boulevards that separate the plaza from the shops and crowds of the city's commercial center.

Across the street from the mosque, I spotted the glass shop where Michael and I purchased our tiny turquoise glasses. When I visited the shop two days later, I was amazed that the owner was the same glass blower whom I had admired decades before with Michael. Incredibly, he recognized me after I talked to him about being in his shop a long time ago. He showed me a 1968 news clipping of him in his shop to verify that he had been working there at that time.

I discovered another connection to our Peace Corps past in Herat when I visited the Provincial Minister of Education at the start of my 2002 visit.

"Dr. Griffin, do you know Mr. Jerry, who was my English teacher in 1968?" he asked.

"I knew him then, sir," I said. "Unfortunately, I don't know where he is now."

Smiling through tears, the Minister described how happy he had been as a student in Mr. Jerry's class. Then he said, "Thank you, Dr. Griffin, for not forgetting us and for coming back to help us."

It was my turn to get choked up. "Sir, it is my privilege to be here. I am grateful to have the opportunity to come back here and help you rebuild the country."

I explained to the Minister the objective of my visit and he readily gave permission for me to visit the girls' and boys' high schools in the city.

"You came just in time," he said. "The students are taking their final English exams for the school year tomorrow. You will see that our schools don't have enough room for all the students who came back to school this spring."

At the end of the first day of my memorable return to Herat in 2002, I saw the impact of Taliban rule when I visited the site of the gardens that included remains of the Musalla Complex, built in 1417. The beautiful gardens were gone and the monuments that remain—four minarets, Gawar Shad's Mausoleum, Mir Ali Sher Nawai's Mausoleum, and the Tomb of the Poet Jami—stood in a stark landscape of hilly red earth.

I asked Mustafa, a slender, boyish, eighteen-year-old Tajik who was my staff interpreter, what had happened to the park and gardens that were there before.

"This used to be The Women's Park, Suzanne," Mustafa said.

"What happened to the gardens?" I asked.

"The Taliban used this place to bury the bodies of the thousands of people whom they massacred outside the city."

I was horrified. "So we are literally standing on mass graves?"

"Yes, Suzanne. That's why you don't see many people here. We don't like to come here."

As if to underline Mustafa's explanation, the sun was setting behind the minarets as we spoke. It was blood red.

The morning after my arrival in Herat, Mustafa and I visited the boys' high school. Although it was only 9:00 a.m., the air was already hot. Because additional classrooms for the school were still under construction, about half the boys took their exams outside. Their desks were arranged under tarps strung between trees, to shield the boys from direct sun.

Mustafa hoped to accompany me to the girls' high school, but the principal appointed an elderly man who would be my guide until a female instructor could take over as interpreter. I arrived at the girls' high school just as the students were finishing exams and departing as quickly as possible from the large tents made of UNICEF tarps. I did not blame them. Although the tents gave protection from the sun's rays, air could not flow through the rainproof fabric. It must have felt like taking an exam inside of a sauna.

I was able to observe a few classes. I was pleased to see female instructors, but the content and their methods used did not encourage student involvement. An English lesson was stilted and more appropriate for a primary school class than for thirteen-year-old girls. The students knew more English than their teachers.

The principal invited me to have tea with her and the female instructors who had gathered in her office to hand in grades. Her office was set up like those of most supervisors in Afghan public agencies. The principal's desk was at the far end of the room facing the door. Next to her desk were two chairs for important visitors. The remaining chairs lined the walls on both sides of the room. Those chairs were for less important visitors who needed to wait awhile or for all-staff meetings called by the principal. In this setting, I sat with the principal and asked questions in Dari about the school and about how they pursued their profession during the Taliban period. The women teachers sitting around the room acted as an audience but periodically chimed in to reinforce the principal's main points.

"We are happy that so many girls came back to school!" The principal said this with the broad smile of someone who has accomplished a major goal. She gestured toward the window onto the courtyard where hundreds of girls in black uniforms and white headscarves were milling around. "We expected 2,000, but nearly 3,000 have come back. As you can see, we don't have enough classrooms. We also have to run in two shifts. This shift ends at 11:30 a.m. and the next one begins at 1:30 p.m."

"It will be very hot at 1:30," I remarked, already feeling the heat rising from my neck under my dark veil.

"Yes, it will be, but what can we do?" she asked with resignation as she settled behind her desk.

I leaned forward and asked in a low tone, "Were you able to teach girls during the period of the Taliban?"

"Not officially," the principal added in a tone that carried to the center of the room. She nodded toward the teachers to indicate that she wanted to include them in this conversation. "The schools were closed and we were told to stay home," she said angrily. The other women nodded.

"It must have been a very hard time for you." I looked at her and the other women with a mixture of sympathy and admiration for their resolve to return to teaching.

"It was. We were bored and our lives were very hard. We couldn't go out or we were beaten." As she paused, some of the listeners looked

Memories of Herat

down and nodded their heads. "We had problems running our houses. Electricity was unreliable and we did not always have running water." Then she added in a defiant tone, "Some of us secretly taught girls in our homes."

My eyes widened. "I read a book about those secret classes. I'm so glad to meet you! What you did was courageous and wonderful for the girls of Herat!"

The principal and teachers beamed. Some teachers added comments from their own experience to affirm what the principal had said. They thanked me warmly as I got up to leave. My heart was full as I shook hands with the principal and with each of these remarkable women. The fact they had suffered was etched on their faces, but the satisfaction that they had survived and were now openly teaching thousands of girls was evident in their smiles and in their warm, firm handshakes. It was hard for me to leave these women. I wished that we had had more time together so that I could hear their stories. I also wished that we could adjourn to a less formal setting where they might feel free to speak more spontaneously. These women were some of Afghanistan's many unsung heroines.

The growth of private courses offered by NGOs in Herat was a response to the dissatisfaction of high school students with the public education system's limitations—especially in the areas of English and computer skills. After the fall of the Taliban, private learning centers and schools rapidly expanded in major cities and provincial capitals throughout Afghanistan. Their continued popularity is an indication of the determination of middle class Afghan families to educate their youth—particularly their boys—in subjects not offered in the public schools.

I visited the multi-age classes offered by two private educational centers in Herat. Most of the center managers and instructors were ambitious young men who had learned English while they were refugees. The demand for English and computer classes was so high in 2002 that the centers operated six days a week from 5:00 a.m. until 10:00 p.m. Separate classes were offered for male and female students. English classes cost 500 Afghanis (approximately $10.00 U.S.) per month. Computer classes cost 1,500 Afghanis ($30.00 U.S.), the equivalent of the monthly government wage earned by teachers and doctors at that time.

Lessons of Love in Afghanistan

I asked students in these classes what improvements they wanted to see regarding their education, and they were unified in their response: "We need better teachers and more books. We need new books, not these old ones." I heard this request repeated in every city that I visited that summer.

Nine months later, I was able to respond to students' need for books. Thanks to the assistance of Seattle Area Rotary Clubs, columnist Lance Dickey of the *Seattle Times*, and over a hundred donors and volunteers, INGO staff distributed a container load of 10,000 books to Kabul University and Afghan high schools.

Mustafa, my interpreter on that 2002 trip, and his peers in the agency office had graduated from high school only two months before my visit. They spent hours surfing websites looking for post-secondary education opportunities outside of Afghanistan. They didn't realize the hurdles they faced: few young men got acceptances and fewer received student visas. Today, Herat's high school students do not have to look overseas for their university education. Herat has a brand new campus offering more courses than any Afghan university outside of Kabul.

In 2009, I visited Herat University's new campus to evaluate the English and Computer Skills classes offered in a computer-learning center established through the support of the higher education project that I was managing. As we drove from the airport to the campus, I noted that both the physical appearance of the city and the mood of the population had changed. While new commercial buildings were springing up in the city center and on the Herat University campus, women on the street were disappearing behind *abbayas*, full-length black coats with matching veils worn by Arab women in the United Arab Emirates, and full-length Iranian *chadors* made of dark grey or black printed material. The occasional women in blue *chadris* on the street were identified by my Afghan colleagues as women who came from "outside" of Herat City.

There was evident dissonance between the physical revitalization of the city and cultural repression that resulted from the spread of the religious conservatism of Iran, across the border from Herat.

My plane arrived late on that hot summer day; I was barely in time for my appointment with the Dean of the Herat Education Faculty.

Remembering the summer apparel worn in Herat seven years previously, I arrived in a light blue Pakistani *shalwar kamize* with a matching blue veil. The minute I embarked from the plane, I knew I had made the wrong choice of dress for this trip. As Najib accompanied me across the campus to the Dean's office, I endured the disapproving stares and murmured remarks of female university instructors clothed in dark colors and black veils. The dean was personable and cooperative during our meeting. Though I suddenly felt like I was in my pajamas, I could not offend him by declining the standard request provincial officials make when they have foreign visitors—a photograph taken with him before I left the office. As I stood next to him, I could only wonder about the comments his family and the colleagues would make regarding my clothing.

"Najib, please take me to the guesthouse before I have another visit!" I pleaded.

"You're okay, Dr. Suzanne."

"Thank you for being polite, Najib, but I'm not okay. I need to wear dark clothes here, now. The women don't wear bright colors on the street anymore."

As I rushed into the guesthouse to make a quick change into a black, full-length skirt and black embroidered shirt, I glanced at the other expatriate women in the guesthouse. They all wore black pants or black skirts and muted-colored shirts.

My interaction with men and women on the campus confirmed my assumption that the more conservative dress on city streets reflected an overall move toward conservatism in Herat. Virtually every woman on the campus wore a *chador*, and they sat apart from the men in the classroom. Only when the doors of the departmental offices or classrooms were closed did women feel comfortable removing their *chadors* to reveal the headscarves, tunics, and slacks that are the standard attire of university women in Kabul.

On subsequent visits to Herat, I also wore an Iranian *chador*. Soraya, a young English instructor and mother of two little boys, gave me some pointers on proper wearing of the *chador*. "Suzanne, you put the *chador* on like this and hold it under your chin with your right hand."

"How can I do that, Soraya, when I am carrying a computer, a purse and my books?"

"You hold them inside the *chador* like this. See what I'm doing?"

"This will take a while," I replied with resignation as I walked carefully down the stairs. The hand holding the *chador* under my chin left me without a free hand to hold the handrail.

The inconvenience and discomfort of wearing conservative coverings on the campus, however, allowed me the opportunity to move about and observe without being noticed. I even passed through crowds of men at the entrance to the Theology Building without heads turning. By blending in while living and working in the city for several months, I knew Herat's citizens better.

While I observed tensions between the conservative and liberal citizens on the streets and on the campus, I remarked on the calm manner in which they expressed their differences. Even occasional student demonstrations ended without violence. A peace and calm prevailed in this city, just as it had when Michael and I first experienced it more than forty years ago.

Heratees are once again finding their own identity. The gardens of the city are again green and fragrant with flowers, the Herat Mosque still dazzles visitors daily, and the old Citadel is being restored. When I stood on the roof of the hotel (where I lived for six weeks at a time) and watched the sun reflected off five ancient, red minarets as it set on the western edge of the city skyline, I felt that Herat still held the magical spell it had cast when I first saw it. I think Michael would agree.

Chapter 8

A Holiday on the Caspian

Michael wanted to take me to Iran, where he had served as a Peace Corps Volunteer (PCV), so that he could introduce me to his favorite people and places there. I was looking forward to experiencing the country about which he had told me so many stories. We planned a visit to cities near the sites where he had worked as an English teacher—Mashhad, near his PCV site in Kuchan, and Babolsar, on the Caspian Sea near his site in Shahi. Michael also wanted me to see the cities of Tehran, Isfahan, and Shiraz.

Since much of Michael's salary went toward paying off our student loans, we had little money set aside for the summer "R and R" trip in 1968. Rather than pay for two of us to fly internationally from Kabul to Tehran, we took a domestic flight to Herat and hitched a ride on an oil tanker to Mashhad. The tanker drivers were used to young foreign men traveling this way, but they were surprised to see that Michael had a female companion and even more amazed that he was bringing his wife on such a rigorous trip. Four of us—the driver, an Afghan male passenger, Michael, and I—were crammed into the tanker cab and rode together for several hours until we got to the first town on the Iranian side of the border at nightfall. It wasn't comfortable, but we got to our destination without mishap.

There were no hotels in the border town where we arrived after dark. The teahouses were reserved for male travelers. I kept my eyes down and my head veiled as we passed through the shadowy room full of men. Kerosene stoves added to the room's smoky look and smell, and its walls were smudged with black soot. I didn't pause to look at the furnishings, but if it was like other teahouses I have seen, the patrons were likely sitting on *charpoys* (wooden beds with bases of woven rope) and *toshaks* stained with spilled tea.

The teahouse owner and Michael solved the dilemma of accommodating me by having the guards and workers carry a double bed out into a flower garden behind the teahouse. It felt quite romantic to fall asleep beside my husband in a moonlit garden in Iran. Reality set in the next morning, when I woke to the scratchy feel of a chicken walking across my chest and saw that "our garden" included a chicken yard. Then, I turned toward the sound of running water and realized that the wall serving as community bathroom was only about thirty feet behind our bed. Even with the awareness that this garden wasn't idyllic, I wasn't angry about the placement of our bed. What I thought about, instead, was the effort the teahouse owner had made to make us comfortable in an awkward situation.

(My subsequent experiences with Afghan and Iranian hospitality helped me realize that the teahouse owner's choice of the flower garden behind the teahouse for our "bedroom" was his interpretation of the Afghan and Iranian custom of surrounding guests with the prettiest things they have to offer, no matter how humble the setting or how barren and ugly the external environment. Even the occupants of makeshift dwellings in IDP camps outside of Kabul have invited me to share tea and offered me the most colorful pillow in their tent to sit on or place behind my back.)

I had hoped that my eight months of studying Dari would allow me to communicate with Michael's Iranian friends and the people we would encounter on this trip. However, I quickly learned that there are significant differences between Farsi and Dari and that Iranians don't have a high opinion of the Dari language. The taxi driver who drove us from the border to Mashhad dashed my hopes of having my new language skills appreciated in Iran in his conversation—in Farsi—with Michael.

"Where did your wife learn our language?" the driver asked.

"She learned her Dari in Afghanistan," Michael responded.

"Well she sounds like a village woman from the center of Iran," he said. Then he added, "If she's really an educated woman, she needs to learn to talk like one."

I understood the conversation and decided to let Michael do most of the talking to Iranians for the rest of the trip.

At last we were in Mashhad and standing in front of the Imam Reza Shrine and Mosque, which is stunning in its size and beauty. The afternoon sun glanced off the golden dome and minarets as we circled around the mosque exterior. I was disappointed that a prayer service was in progress, so we could not enter the holy shrine that draws Muslim pilgrims from all over the world. The tomb of Iran's most famous poet, Ferdowsi, is also in Mashhad. As Michael had often talked about the beauty of Ferdowsi's poetry, he was enthusiastic about having me visit the tomb.

The old woman who had been Michael's cook was the most memorable person for me from our visit to Kuchan. She spent much of our visit smoking her opium pipe—a common practice among older people in Iran. The old people say that it helps them deal with their aches and pains. In this woman's case, the opium was effective. She was kind and genial throughout our visit.

Michael's former teaching colleague said that the most economical way for us to get from Mashhad to Babolsar was via a shared minivan. He helped us locate a van that was going to Rasht and would pass through Babolsar. It had two seats left. The rest of the seats were occupied by a family from Rasht. The driver was also a Rashti. We started out early in the morning. By mid-day, we understood why Iranians tell so many jokes about Rashtis. We had had two flat tires and another mechanical problem. With each mishap, family members and the driver spent more time arguing about how to fix the problem than getting the problem fixed. We grew concerned that we would not make it to Babolsar by nightfall, so we decided to find another way to get there. Over the protests of our fellow passengers, who were still dealing with the second flat tire, we grabbed our bags and hailed a long distance Mercedes Taxi to get us to our destination.

Babolsar was everything that Michael described to me and more.

"Wow!" I said after the bellman closed the door. "This is amazing, Michael! I can't believe we got this beautiful room for the price. It costs less that an economy hotel room in the U.S." As I moved toward the far end of the large room, I opened the door to an enormous bathroom with four walls covered in brilliant turquoise mosaic tile. "Oooh Michael! Look at this! We can shower like royalty in this bathroom!"

I sensed that Michael was looking at something even more amazing. It was the Caspian Sea sparkling in the sunlight. Michael was chuckling as he threw open the doors to the balcony and stretched out his arm toward

A Holiday on the Caspian

our unobstructed view of the Caspian. I ran across the large room to join him there. He drew me close to his side as we took in the view of this marvelous body of water. He knew how much I'd been looking forward to seeing the Caspian. Then he pointed to the colorful cabanas on the beach below us.

"Do you see those cabanas down there?" he asked with a smile.

"Yes. They look comfortable. Do you think we can rent one tomorrow?"

"When I stayed here as a Peace Corps Volunteer, I slept overnight in a cabana because that's all I could afford. I never thought I'd be staying up here looking down at the cabana dwellers! We can rent one during the day if you want to, but I'm pretty happy up here."

"So this is kind of a dream come true for you, right?"

"Yes, Suzanne, it is," he said as he turned me toward him, smiled broadly, and bent down to give me a long kiss. With the first eight months in Afghanistan behind us and a rigorous road trip to Babolsar finally over, we were due for a second honeymoon.

We did a little exploring of the city of Babolsar, but we spent most of our daytime hours on the beach. After being in a landlocked country for eight months, we wanted to be in or near the water as long as we could. Having spent most of my life on the West Coast, I had missed visits to the beaches on the Pacific Ocean, so I was thrilled both to spend time near the sea and to be able to swim in a bathing suit—an impossibility in Afghanistan. Our favorite dinner was the one Michael often talked about when he described Babolsar to me before our visit: sturgeon steak with the juice of an orange squeezed over it, cooked and served at a wooden bar in a shack on the beach. Upon request, the sturgeon was accompanied by a cold mug of beer, a rare treat in a Muslim country.

We reluctantly left the Caspian behind to travel over the mountains in another Mercedes Taxi to Tehran. Kabul in 1968 was like a provincial town compared to Tehran. I didn't expect the paved streets and sidewalks, orderly traffic, western-looking shops and variety of restaurants offering European, Middle Eastern, and Asian cuisine. During the day, we visited historic sites and saw the Crown Jewels in the national museum. At night, we sampled fare at restaurants that were within our budget.

As Michael predicted, I loved Paprika, his favorite restaurant in Tehran. We ate in a beautiful garden full of flowers with water flowing through an Italian-style fountain behind our table and caged birds chirping from the trees. To be in such a magical setting with the man I loved felt like being in a fairy tale.

Michael managed to get away from me during one of our shopping trips to buy me a lovely gold and emerald ring. We had gotten married so quickly that I never got an engagement ring. At my birthday dinner in Kabul several months later, Michael surprised me as he opened the ring box and slipped the dainty ring on my finger. He said, "It's about time you finally got this. I think it will go well with your wedding band."

"Oh, Michael, it's beautiful! I like it much better than a diamond."

Michael and I had been so wrapped in our own world during the first days of our trip to Iran that we had not paid attention to the news or reported our whereabouts either to the Peace Corps Office in Kabul or to our family. We were planning to travel from Tehran to Isfahan and Shiraz, so we stopped in at the Peace Corps Office in Tehran to get some travel advice.

When we got there, we were greeted with, "There you are!" and were then chastised for not checking in sooner.

"Don't you know that there have been major earthquakes in Iran?" the Peace Corps staff person asked.

"No. We came overland from Herat to Mashhad and Babolsar. We didn't hear anything about it when we were up on the Caspian," Michael said.

"Your families have been sending us cables asking for your whereabouts. They knew you were traveling near the quake area and were upset that the Peace Corps Office in Kabul couldn't tell them where you were. We here in Tehran didn't even know you were in the country."

"How bad were the quakes and where were they?" Michael asked.

"Well, the epicenter of the first one on August 31st was in Dasht-i-Bayaz, where five villages were destroyed. That quake measured 7.3 on the Richter scale. On September 1st, an aftershock hit Ferdows and destroyed the villages there.[2] Look at a map. When you came into Iran from Herat, you were traveling just north of the quake area a few days before the two quakes hit."

---

[2] *(Ultimately, 175 villages were destroyed or damaged.)*

A Holiday on the Caspian

"Whew!" Michael commented. "We had considered going south before going to the Caspian, but changed our minds. We were lucky!"

"Yes, you were!" the staff person responded emphatically.

We all discussed the loss of life and the government's ability to get aid to them. Finally, we got around to how the quake would affect our trip.

"You can't travel to Isfahan and Shiraz," the staff person said. "Although you'll be going west of the quake area, we're advising PCVs to stay at their sites until everyone is accounted for and not to travel until we have assurance that the quakes aren't the first of a series."

This is not what we wanted to hear, but we also knew that it was a realistic response to the situation.

"What do you suggest?" we asked.

"First, contact your families and the Peace Corps Office in Kabul to let them know you're okay. We can help you contact the Kabul PC office from here. Then, book a flight back to Kabul. We don't know how bad the aftershocks will be or if there'll be more quakes. Come back and visit when the situation settles down."

We left the office shocked but feeling lucky that we hadn't traveled south before we went to the Caspian. We felt guilty that our families had worried so much while we were blissfully unaware of the tragedy. We were also disappointed that our long-anticipated trip had come to an abrupt end. We resolved to get back to Iran someday and visit Isfahan and Shiraz. When we finally got to those cities ten years later, we were a family of four. Michael was again able to pass on his appreciation for Iranian culture as he introduced these beautiful cities to me and our daughters. Sadly, that time in Iran also ended abruptly when the Iranian Revolution began in 1979.

Chapter 9

A New Culture in the Palm Springs of Afghanistan

Although Jalalabad is northeast of Kabul, whenever I travel there by road it feels like I am traveling south. I associate going south with warmer weather and loss of altitude. Both of these conditions characterize the trip from Kabul to Jalalabad.

In the hour descent from the Kabul Plain, which is at 6,000 feet, to the bottom of the Kabul River gorge at 1,000 feet, a driver negotiates formidable switchback curves at Maipur Pass on a two-lane road without consistent guard walls. The road is so narrow that I could open the car windows and touch the craggy stone walls if I dared. Toward the bottom of the gorge, the curves in the road become wider, the stone walls stretch to the sky behind us like monstrous skyscrapers, and the green valley of the Kabul River opens ahead. The temperature changes just as dramatically as the scenery. For six months of the year, we start the trip wearing heavy coats to ward off the cold, as it is often snowing at the top of the pass. As we descend into the sunny river valley, we shed layers of clothes until we are down to our light cotton *shalwar kamizes*.

During the time of Zahir Shah, Jalalabad was the winter retreat for wealthy Kabulis who owned winter homes there or who spent the cold months of the year with relatives. From November to late March, Kabulis took advantage of any business or family matter as a reason to escape the frigid temperatures and muddy streets of Kabul for Jalalabad's soft breezes, sunshine, and palm trees.

Michael and I were happy to join this annual exodus. A trip to visit the Peace Corps sites in Jalalabad was a welcome relief from the endurance tests of our trips to the snowy north. We looked forward to a room at the Spingar Hotel, surrounded by a lush garden of sweet-smelling tropical flowers, tall palm trees with fan-shaped fronds that rustle in the wind, and the music of birds chirping in the flowering shrubs outside our windows. It felt a bit like Palm Springs, California.

In the late 1960s the Jalalabad Road was paved and the trip could be made in about two hours. Even on the paved road, the return trip from Jalalabad to Kabul could be dangerous during winter. When temperatures dropped below freezing as the road rose to higher elevations, the pavement became icy and treacherous. One winter night, Michael and I thought we were making the last road trip of our lives. As we left the Jalalabad Valley and began the steep climb from the river gorge to the Maipur Pass, the road turned to ice. Michael struggled with the steering to hold the Willys Jeep on the road. Then we lost our brakes. I will never forget the frantic look on Michael's face as he explained why we were sliding backward. His blue eyes were wide and he was flushed from the effort of controlling the steering wheel.

"Hold on, Suzanne! I don't know if I can stop this!" he exclaimed through gritted teeth.

I instinctively grabbed my seat and braced for impact as I cried out, "Michael, what's wrong with the Jeep?!" I fell silent as I helplessly watched him struggle to control our vehicle. I don't recall how we regained traction, but we made it to the top of the pass and did not attempt another through the Jalalabad Gorge until spring.

By 2002, the Jalalabad Road had been completely destroyed by tanks and constant truck traffic. The trip took more than five hours over a bone-rattling rutted road that gave riders headaches and required constant repairs to tires, shocks, and other vehicle parts. When the long-awaited repair of the road finally began in 2005, traffic could only flow in one direction each day. During the rainy season, vehicles bogged down in mud. I became so used to delays on my bimonthly trips to my agency's projects there that I often fell asleep before we got to the Maipur Pass, slept through the two hours that traffic was stopped, and awakened only as the car approached the outskirts of Jalalabad.

As difficult as my trips were, I never had to endure the ordeals of some of my colleagues who were stuck on the road for as long as seventeen hours. An American midwife told me of a night spent without food or water and of babies being born in cars caught in the blocked traffic. After hearing similar stories, agencies started flying their international staff members to Jalalabad. The flights took only twenty minutes once the plane actually took off; however, the wait for the plane's departure from either direction could last several hours because the Jalalabad airfield was often used for military flights. We also had the unnerving experience of corkscrew landings as a defense against rockets, which insurgents might fire at us.

When the road was finally finished and it was again possible to travel between Kabul and Jalalabad in less than two hours, international staff members were advised not to travel on the road at all. Insurgents had set up unauthorized checkpoints, improvised explosive devices (IEDs) occasionally exploded on the road, and both robberies and kidnapping attempts increased. Today, travel on that road is not recommended for foreigners. I miss the road trips to Jalalabad, particularly the return trip to Kabul on which we were expected to bring some of the delicious fruit and vegetables from Nangarhar Province. On my last solo trip, the driver and I came back loaded with produce for our coworkers in Kabul. The back of the SUV was packed with at least twenty heads of cauliflower harvested from roadside fields, crates of tangerines, and bags of Sarubi pomegranates—all purchased at a fraction of Kabul prices.

In the time of Zahir Shah, Jalalabad was a colorful city that assaulted the senses as soon as you passed from the dusty main road to a boulevard of eucalyptus and palm trees. Orange and lemon trees scented the breeze, sounds of Pakistani and Hindi music competed with the chatter of shoppers in the bazaar, and the sights included nomadic Kuchi women wearing pomegranate-red *chadors* and heavy jewelry that jingled as they moved among market stalls with their turbaned male relatives to buy food for their families, camped outside the city limits.

There was an air of tolerance among the resident population for the unusual activities and dress of Kabul vacationers and foreign visitors, as well as for illicit activities—such as the open sale of *hashish*—of transient outsiders. The entire city had the relaxed pace of people on holiday, with residents showing only naïve curiosity about foreigners. When a red-haired expatriate Peace Corps Volunteer caused scandal by riding her bicycle through the middle of town, she received only a reprimand from one of the elders. Local residents simply observed in wonder as over fifty

A New Culture in the Palm Springs of Afghanistan

expatriates, including me, rode camels through the desert one weekend thanks to arrangements between Kuchi tribe leaders and the Peace Corps doctors stationed in the city. The money we paid for the ride financed the medicines needed by the tribe on their winter migration route through Pakistan, Afghanistan, and Iran.

These days, Kuchi women are rarely seen in Jalalabad and females are absent from the bazaars. The few women who venture out to shop for food are in *chadris*. It makes me sad to see women who wear the brightly colored cotton *chadors* and *shalwar kamizes* of Pakistan when I visit them behind compound walls forced to wrap themselves in uniform sky blue polyester *chadris* when they go out into the street. The repressive influence of conservative Pashtun culture is everywhere. The streets belong to the men who cluster together on street corners, cast disapproving glances at cars carrying foreigners, and go about their business with somber faces. During long droughts, streets are dusty all year round. Any music played in shops is drowned by the noise of postwar reconstruction and by horns from trucks, cars, and Pakistani taxi carts. Personal security in Jalalabad and the surrounding provinces is uncertain—especially for foreigners. We keep a low profile because we know that IEDS, including car bombs, can go off anywhere without warning. Demonstrations and fights can materialize within minutes, and gunfire or rocket attacks can disrupt the city at any time.

During the four years (2002-2006) that I visited Jalalabad to monitor program activities, my male Afghan colleagues seemed determined to mitigate the toll that living in this situation takes on foreign women. When my female colleagues and I were on the street, our Afghan male colleagues were vigilant about our safety and security. Drivers took us inside the compounds before they allowed us to get out of vehicles. We could not walk on the streets at any time. When we were behind the compound walls of our office and guesthouse, the Afghan men who worked with us went out of their way to provide for our comfort and to make us feel welcome.

I made my first return visit to Jalalabad in August 2002, just a few weeks before the end of my summer sabbatical in Afghanistan. I bounced along in the back seat of a Land Cruiser driven by Safi who held a running conversation in Pashtu with Walid, who was my translator on

Lessons of Love in Afghanistan

this trip. Occasionally, Walid would turn around to summarize what they were saying and to ask about my welfare.

"Susan, how are you? Are you okay?"

"I am okay, Walid," I responded (even though I felt my teeth rattling in my head over some of the roughest parts of the road), "but I am very hot and dusty. How much longer is the trip?"

"Two more hours, Susan, *Enshallah,*" he answered.

Walid's answer was the standard Afghan response, which means "God willing." It indicates the strong belief that only God can control what happens in our lives. This attitude runs counter to Americans' firm belief that we have control over our own lives, and we therefore expect certainty when we ask for information. In that first summer, I had not adjusted to *Enshallah.* I kept asking anyone who used the term to give me a definite answer. They just laughed and pointed out that nothing is certain if God does not will it. After several years in Afghanistan, I began to understand that perspective and ultimately learned that in Afghanistan, very little is certain.

At one point, Safi decided to let Walid, who was teaching himself how to drive, take the wheel for a while so that Safi could give him some pointers. I was a passenger in a car on a bad road with a novice driver, and at first, I was too concerned about my safety to say anything. I just kept hoping that Walid wouldn't make any serious errors. Since Safi didn't seem too concerned, I gradually relaxed. When Safi took the wheel again, I sighed in relief and said, "That was pretty good, Walid. Do you know that I can drive a car like this?"

"Really, Susan?" he asked in surprise.

"Yes, I'm a pretty good driver. We had a Jeep Cherokee with a stick shift transmission. My husband used it for his work outside of the city, but I drove it a lot of the time because my job was a long way from our home."

Now Safi got into the conversation. I don't think he believed that a woman could drive a Jeep.

"How far did you drive it, Susan?" he asked with a doubtful look.

"About seventy miles each way to Olympia, the state capital, where I worked."

"Really, by yourself!?" Safi was incredulous.

A New Culture in the Palm Springs of Afghanistan

"Yes, Safi, by myself." I answered with smug satisfaction as both men looked at me in astonishment.

"So, Susan, you are an experienced driver in addition to being smart," Walid said with a wink.

"Yes, I am." I answered firmly and with a little smile.

"Okay, Susan, do you want to drive us?" Walid asked with chuckle.

"No, but if Safi gets sick or can't drive for some reason, I think that I should be the backup driver."

Both men laughed at my remark.

Our agency's building in Jalalabad was a combination office and guesthouse. The residents of the building were six Pashtun men. Safi and Walid brought the total to eight. Because of the security situation, I could not stay in the Spingar Hotel on my own, so the men had decided to accommodate me at the agency's building. Professor Reza, the agency Education Program Manager for Jalalabad, was thrilled to have another academic visiting and had a room prepared for me on the top floor. I was touched at the care taken to prepare the room for a lady, but dubious about sharing the bathroom with the four men who would be occupying the other sleeping rooms on that floor. Soon after we arrived, I was shown to my room to rest while the men had tea downstairs.

I gratefully changed out of my dusty travel clothes, washed while I had the bathroom to myself, and sought respite from the oppressively hot room—which had no fan because there was no electricity to power one—by sitting on the open deck adjacent to the sleeping rooms. Walid and one of the local program managers joined me there before dinner for a conversation in English. The program manager said that he rarely had a chance to practice his English in Jalalabad. When dinner was announced, I put on my most modest *chador*—it hung to my ankles and was green, the color of Islam—and started downstairs. Walid and Safi intercepted me on the stairway. They looked as if they had bad news.

"Suzanne," they said, "Please listen. We have to tell you something."

"What's the matter?" I asked.

Walid looked at me earnestly and said, "These men have never eaten with a woman who was not their relative. They wanted you to eat alone in the kitchen, but we told them you would never agree to that."

I couldn't believe that they were going to make me eat alone as if I were some sort of pariah. I was their professional equal and I was not going to be treated like the kitchen help. "You are right," I said. "That's insulting! I came here on business for our agency."

"We know," Walid assured me calmly. "So we made a deal with them. You will sit next to Professor Reza because he is in charge of this field office and the oldest man here. You will not be able to talk unless someone talks to you. I know this is not what you are used to, but this is not a comfortable situation for these men."

"Okay. I will be like a good Afghan woman," I said with a tone of reluctant concession. I realized that they had gone out on a limb to have me included in the meal, so I needed to accept the compromise. I also knew that I needed to be careful not to offend the other men if I was going to be able to deal with them in professional situations.

Walid and Safi chuckled and were clearly relieved that I had not gotten angry. Then they conducted me onto the outdoor porch where we all ate seated on the floor.

Since we were eating with our hands, I realized that one issue regarding who would sit next to me was who would be willing to share the food bowls with me, as Afghan men usually don't share food bowls with women—especially with women not related to them. I was extremely grateful when Professor Reza took some food from the bowl between us and then offered it to me. I was still getting used to the Afghan custom of starting their meals in relative silence out of respect for the food. After everyone had their first serving, they gradually relaxed and started talking. However, only Professor Reza talked to me. Walid was sitting across from me and observing the situation. Safi was eating in a separate group with the guards and other drivers. As the fruit was being served, other Dari speakers, including Walid, finally spoke to me.

"How do you like Jalalabad, Susan?" one of them asked.

"I like it," I said. "It reminds me of a winter vacation place in California called Palm Springs."

"Why is that?" another man asked.

"Because it has palm trees and orange trees and the weather is warm here when it is cold in the capital city," I answered. Then I added, "In the summer, Palm Springs gets uncomfortably hot, just like this."

A New Culture in the Palm Springs of Afghanistan

"Yes, Jalalabad is very hot in summer," a third man added. "It's over 50 degrees (122 degrees Fahrenheit) in the summer!"

"I think that it's nearly that hot today," I remarked. It really felt that hot to me.

Darkness fell as tea was served and the men returned to exclusive use of Pashtu, so I excused myself and asked to have my tea upstairs. I later learned that this was the appropriate thing to do, as good women don't sit in the company of men outside of their family after dark. Everyone wished me a good sleep and I went upstairs alone. Eventually Walid came up to see how I was doing and joined me for a cup of tea. I told him that I didn't want to offend anyone, but I could not sleep in my room, as it was too hot. He got two of the other men and they moved a bed out to the open air deck. The wall was high enough to protect me from view of those on the street, so we agreed that I could safely sleep there. I knew, however, that I would have to sleep fully clothed if four other men were to eventually come upstairs to the sleeping rooms. As I fell asleep, I heard the men in lively conversation downstairs.

About 2:00 a.m., I woke because I was drenched in sweat from sleeping in ankle-length cotton pants topped by a long tunic. It was completely silent on the floor and I realized that no one was in the other rooms. I crept across the deck to my room and found that the heat had dissipated. I was grateful to disrobe and sleep under the sheets for the rest of the night.

The next morning, Walid came up to check on me when I was in the midst of my yoga exercises. I was embarrassed to be seen doing yoga postures, but I was modestly dressed in loose trousers and an oversized shirt, so I completed the posture before I stopped. He stood a moment in the doorway and observed.

"*Salaam alekum*, Susan, good morning," he said cheerfully as he crossed the deck to sit in the only chair. "Is this your exercise?"

"*Salaam alekum*, Walid. Good morning. It's called yoga." I finished my yoga session by going into the warrior pose while giving a short explanation of yoga basics. "We try to slowly stretch like this. We inhale and exhale slowly while we are starting and finishing a position."

"No wonder you are so smart," he remarked.

Surprised by this remark, I thanked him and changed the subject.

"Walid, where did everyone sleep last night? I was the only one up here."

"We thought that you would be more comfortable without men up here, so we all slept downstairs."

"But there are only two rooms downstairs for eight men and it was hot last night!"

"Yes it was hot," he admitted, "But that's okay. You are our guest."

"Thank you, Walid. Please tell everyone thank you. That was a very nice thing to do."

"I will, Susan," he said. "I came to tell you that breakfast will be served in ten minutes and you are welcome to join us."

Relieved, I said, "Thank you. I guess I passed the test last night."

"Yes you did. They really like you because you speak Dari and respect our customs."

With each meal over the next three days, the Pashtun men became more relaxed in my presence. The few men who could speak English came to my roof deck before and after dinner each evening to practice their English and ask me all the stored up questions that they had about life in America. On the third day, the weather was so hot that we could not eat our lunch on the outdoor porch as we usually did. Instead, we sat together on the floor in the cool hallway. My face was flushed because even the thin cloth of the *chador* held enough heat on my head and neck to make me feel faint. My hair was soaked with sweat.

Seeing my situation, Professor Reza said, "Susan, please remove your *chador* so that you will become cooler. You are like our sister now and we will not be upset. We don't want you to be so uncomfortable or to faint."

Relieved, I thanked him and removed the *chador*. At the urging of the others, Walid grabbed my camera and took a picture of me sitting bareheaded and eating my lunch with eight Pashtun men as if this were a normal occurrence.

After lunch, we made final arrangements for the first project bidders' conference of potential NGO subcontractors that our agency had ever hosted in Jalalabad. Our office had no large meeting space, so chairs were arranged theatre style in the courtyard in front of our office. All the men wore white *shalwar kamizes*, because the weather was far too hot for suits. I wore dark green *shalwar* pants with a white flowered *kamize* and matching veil over my head and draped across my chest. It felt more like a party than a workshop when the guests arrived. As usual, I was the only woman present. Despite the heat, the male NGO leaders were genuinely glad to see each other and to be meeting as a group. The house staff was so pleased to have such an event that they started serving lemonade and cookies before the presentation instead of following the custom of waiting until the end of meeting.

Walid and I were here to conduct an informational workshop to ensure that every NGO working in the Eastern Region had the same information to bid on our proposed projects. We had given several presentations on other topics together during the summer, but this was a new one for us. We had presented it only once before in Kabul. There, we had both Dari and Pashtu speakers in the workshop, so Walid had to translate in both languages.

In all of the workshops that we did together, Walid formally introduced the participants and the topic in Pashtu. Then he summarized for me in English what he had just said and turned the presentation over to me. On this day, I took notes during Walid's portion of the presentation. When he turned to me to translate what he said in Pashtu, I showed him my notes.

When he saw my notes, he looked at me in surprise. "I don't need to translate. You have it all down."

"But I don't speak Pashtu," I protested.

"No, but you apparently understand it," he said with a broad smile. "You have translated exactly what I said in Pashtu into those notes in English."

"Really! I just tried to get down what you were telling them." I was as surprised as he was.

I gave the presentation about the process of submitting proposals in English, stopping after each sentence for Walid to translate into Pashtu. He also answered the participants' questions, since only two or three of them spoke English.

At the end of our presentation, a nice-looking man who sat in the first row and smiled frequently throughout the presentation first spoke to Walid and then came over to me and addressed me in English.

"You are a guest in our country. I would like to invite you to come to my restaurant tonight. It is air conditioned and you will be comfortable in this heat," he said. I was taken aback at this invitation and was anxious that he not think that I was a loose foreign woman.

"Thank you very much for the invitation," I said, "but I am afraid that I have to refuse. I have been a guest of these men from the agency for three days and they have been very good hosts. It would be impolite for me to not to have dinner with them on my last evening here."

"As you wish," he answered. "Maybe you can accept next time that you come here."

As the young man wandered toward the departing guests, Walid motioned me toward a shaded area of the courtyard. As he faced me, he held out his open hand as if to ask why. He looked at me anxiously. "Susan, why did you say no to that invitation? That man is my friend," Walid said with mild dismay. "He asked both of us to come to his restaurant."

"I'm sorry, Walid. I didn't know that he was your friend, and I didn't know that you were also invited. Besides, I don't want to offend Professor Reza and our other colleagues by not being here for dinner."

Walid nodded agreement with the last remark. "You are probably right," he said. "I will explain to my friend."

As he walked toward his departing friend, I was happy to retreat to the roof after a long, hot day. I was both tired and relieved that this first workshop in Jalalabad had gone well.

The dinner that night was very relaxed. The men of the house expressed their pleasure at having had me as their guest. At the end of the meal, Walid noted that there was no fruit and asked Safi to go to the bazaar and buy a watermelon. After Safi cut it, he brought the first piece to me as the guest. I understood that this was an honor normally given to the most senior male and felt glad that I had made the choice to stay with my colleagues for my last dinner in Jalalabad.

Although I spent most of my time with men on this first trip to Jalalabad, I got insights into the lives of women in this conservative area when I visited the girls' high school in the city center. Students had just finished exams so they had already left the school grounds. However, the female principal and her female instructors agreed to see me, Professor Reza and the Assistant Provincial Minister of Education. The two men were enthusiastic about accompanying me on this visit because, as they explained to me, they were unable to visit the female institution on their own in this conservative community.

Our agency Land Cruiser pulled inside of the compound and the gate was locked before we got out. The principal and her faculty were waiting for us on the building's front porch. All of them wore white or pastel-colored lightweight cotton *chadors* that hung below their hips. The principal was a lovely, dignified woman with grey hair showing around the edges of her *chador.* The women warmly greeted me and my male colleagues. The principal's office had a decidedly feminine feel. The room was painted light blue and there were white, lacy curtains in the windows. Each upholstered chair had a white crocheted doily on the back. They reminded me of the chairs in my paternal grandmother's living room.

Our conversation covered the same topics that I would discuss with administrators and teachers most places in the world: school attendance, student achievement, curriculum, teacher preparation, operations challenges, and the lack of adequate funding. I was impressed with the professionalism of the women, the determination of the principal, and their collective passionate commitment to girls' education. My male colleagues were equally impressed. They asked questions and smiled with pleasure at the quality of the responses. They enjoyed being served "special tea"— tea reserved for special guests that is accompanied by good-quality cookies and candy as well as sugar cubes—and basked in the attention of the women. Before we departed, I took photos of the principal and teachers, who exuded pride at having their work recognized. As we departed, Professor Reza and the assistant minister thanked me for having made this visit with them. It had been their first chance to see this school and appreciate firsthand the dedication and professionalism of the teachers at work there.

On subsequent visits to Jalalabad, I was an employee of an agency that trained health care workers and operated clinics and hospitals. My visits focused on maternal health care. I helped launch the Community Midwifery Training Program at the Institute for Health Sciences (IHS). Sixty young women enrolled. The program was based on a new competency-based national curriculum and endeavored to upgrade the clinical skills of the 150 women already enrolled in the IHS' traditional, classroom-based curriculum. Until this program began, most program participants were selected by the Ministry of Higher Education and came from privileged and politically well-connected families in Nangarhar Province. The mandate for this program was that participants would be drawn from economically and ethnically diverse populations that represented four provinces in the Eastern Region: Nangarhar, Laghman, Kunar and Nooristan. The young women were selected by the Council of Elders—known as *shuras*—in each of their communities, based upon their academic preparation and their commitment to serving their community as midwives.

The girls selected for the new midwifery training program were thrilled at this opportunity for professional training, as they had been conditioned not to anticipate any training after high school. When I met with them shortly after the program began, they spoke enthusiastically about this chance to learn a profession. Each one had a story about a husband, a father, or a brother who encouraged and supported her after the elders had talked with them. The value that these women placed on completing this program was evident in their high rate of attendance and in the effort that they put into their studies and clinical training. Few dropped out, despite the fact that some of them came from remote provinces like Nuristan and Kunar.

These young women overcame the difficulties of getting care for their children and convincing their husbands, fathers, and other male relatives to let them live in a dormitory in Jalalabad five days per week. A few continued their training through pregnancy, childbirth, and postpartum care. They studied with each other, lived with each other, and supported each other through family difficulties and the rigors of clinical training. Finally, they encouraged each other as they attended a job fair together to submit their resumés to organizations that would help them find positions using their skills in their communities when they graduated.

During my tenure as Acting Country Director, I made a visit to a Comprehensive Health Clinic near several villages in Behsood District outside of Jalalabad. There, I learned how much the newly trained midwives were valued in the community. Six turbaned older men—some with long white beards—who were representatives of the *shura* that had been charged with responsibility for supporting the clinic waited patiently for nearly an hour while I toured the clinic with an evaluation team sent by our headquarters. The Program Manager who was our host informed me that the men had been busy overseeing the cleaning and painting of the clinic on the previous day in preparation for the visit. With this knowledge, I initiated the meeting, which was conducted in Dari, with the group of men by going through the usual exchange of greetings and thanking them for their support of the clinic. Then, we got to the main agenda item.

"I understand that you have a request for me," I said.

"Yes, we do," the old man who was the spokesman stepped forward and stretched out both hands in formal greeting. I acknowledged by putting my right hand over my heart and bowing slightly.

Then the man spoke in a strong voice. "We are happy that our clinic now has a delivery room and midwives to deliver babies. However, we want this service available 24-hours. We want a midwife here at night," he said with emphasis. As he spoke, the other men nodded in agreement.

The clinic staff had told me before the visit to expect this request.

"I understand your problem. You are right to make this request. We also want the women in your family to be able to have babies safely," I said as I gestured toward the clinic staff. "However, we have a security problem here. In order to have a midwife in the clinic at night, we need to have a little house adjacent to the clinic that is big enough for her and one of her male relatives. We also need to have two guards for the house. Can you help us provide that?"

"Yes we can," the spokesman declared. "We are poor and few of us have cars. It is too far and too difficult for us to take our wives to the hospitals in Jalalabad if they have problems in childbirth. We don't want them or our babies to die. We want the care for them here. We will provide those things so that our women can have babies safely."

The old man's colleagues nodded in agreement.

Within two weeks, the *shura* provided a house and guards, and the Behsood Clinic started offering 24-hour service.

The level of security on the outskirts of Jalalabad has always been more tenuous than in the city itself. Even in the times of Zahir Shah, the outskirts of Jalalabad—districts within neighboring Laghman Province— were marked by local armed conflict. In the daytime, the province looks deceptively peaceful. When your vehicle turns off the dusty road and away from the harsh, rocky landscape of the Jalalabad Road to cross the suspension bridge over the Surubi Dam, about thirty miles north of Jalalabad, you are treated to a refreshing sight. Lush green fields planted with fruits and vegetables and an elaborate system of irrigation canals fed by the Kabul River have made this valley one of the most important agricultural areas of the country. These pastoral scenes lead you to assume that this is a stable part of Afghanistan. However, family feuds, differences in religious practices, political allegiances, private land disputes, and rivalries among opium growers have provoked battles among Laghmanis since any resident of the province can remember.

Michael and I were caught in the midst of one such conflict in 1968 when we arrived at the rural home of one of the Peace Corps Volunteers one evening after dark. We had been warned to arrive by dusk, but we had been delayed in Jalalabad, so it was already pitch black along the country roads. We became more anxious as we approached the plantation where the Volunteer was staying because we saw bright flashes across the fields.

"Michael, did you see those flashes? Were those rifles being shot?!"

"I think so," he said in a worried voice. "They told me in Jalalabad that there was a feud going on between the families out here. I just hope we don't get caught in the cross-fire!"

When we pulled up to the checkpoint outside the plantation where the Volunteer lived, a fierce-looking, turbaned Pashtun man flagged down our truck, motioned for Michael to roll down his window, and shoved the barrel of a rifle into his neck. He challenged Michael in Pashtu and switched languages when Michael replied in flawless Dari.

"What is your business?" he demanded. "Why are you foreigners out here after dark?"

"We came to visit the home of Amir Khan," Michael explained. "He is housing one of our colleagues there—a young man named Dan."

The guard pointed his finger at Michael and said angrily, "Amir Khan told you to come before dark. Why did you not obey him? You could be killed out here. Don't you see the gunfire?"

"We saw the shooting," Michael answered, "but we had no way to let Amir Khan know that we would be late. We apologize."

The guard shook his head as if to say, "I'll never understand these foreigners." He motioned us down the drive until we approached a large

A New Culture in the Palm Springs of Afghanistan

house. We heaved sighs of relief at having escaped being shot as our host, a tall slender man wearing the Pashtun *kola* (cap) in lieu of a turban, bolted out of the house. He was at the door of the truck before we could get out. He was waving a pistol.

"*Salaam alekum,* Michael," he said. "You are late! It's very dangerous here after dark. That is why I told you to come before nightfall!"

"We apologize, sir," Michael said. "This is my wife, Suzanne."

Amir Khan placed his right hand on his heart as he addressed me. "*Salaam alekum, Khonum* Susan. Welcome to my house."

"*Salaam alekum,* sir." I answered as I modestly bowed my head and lowered my eyes.

Eventually, Dan made his entrance and joined us for the dinner that Amir had waiting for us. Michael's job that night was to graciously extricate Dan from the hospitality of Amir Khan, a well-known drug lord in the region. Hence, I retired to our room immediately after dinner while the men engaged in heated conversation.

I was asleep by the time that Michael arrived, so I did not hear the outcome of the negotiation. However, I woke later in the night with the realization that I needed to use the outdoor latrine. I was afraid of encountering armed guards, but there was no other option. I took a lantern, slipped out of our room, and was trembling as I approached the silent, tall guard with a rifle who stood in front of the outhouse. I prayed that he would not shoot me or attack me. He said nothing but stepped aside as I entered. I heard him return to his position in front of the door while I was inside. When I knocked to come out, he moved aside again to let me pass as I made my way silently back to our room on the second floor of the house.

When Michael and I came to breakfast the next morning, our host was already sitting at the head of the breakfast table. His pistol, with the safety latch off, was laying next to his right hand. Amir Khan motioned for Michael to sit to his right and for me to sit to his left.

Throughout the meal, he alternated between being overly gracious and charming toward me and coldly polite toward Michael.

"You Americans don't understand hospitality! I offered Dan a place to live. We feed him well and take good care of him here. Now your office wants to take him out of here. Why? This is an insult to our Pashtun culture!" As he said this, he picked up his pistol and waved it in the air.

Lessons of Love in Afghanistan

Michael acknowledged Amir Khan's hospitality for Dan but added, "We appreciate all that you have done for Dan, Amir Khan, but the Peace Corps wants him to live in Jalalabad where he is closer to his work and near some of the other Volunteers. We've been asked to take Dan with us to Jalalabad when we leave this morning."

"You're not taking him! You've insulted me. Maybe I won't let you leave either!" Amir Khan said. "You Americans are very impolite people. I stayed up last night to welcome you and had a nice breakfast prepared for you this morning. And now, you want to leave. People will think that you don't like my hospitality if you leave so soon. This is not good!" He held the pistol anxiously.

As my fear grew, I fought to remain calm and kept my eyes on the gun as Michael did the talking. Ultimately, Michael agreed to leave without Dan on the condition that Dan had permission to move within two weeks. This would allow Amir Khan to collect the full month's rent from Peace Corps and to communicate a face-saving message to the community about the reason for Dan's departure.

As we drove away from the house, the opium fields that were the cause of Amir Khan's battle with his neighbor stretched before us. They were not yet in flower, but their vast green expanse was impressive. We weren't tempted to stop to appreciate the scene, however. We drove directly back to the main road, relieved to be out of rifle range.

In 2005, I made several visits to Laghman Province to interview village women in three districts as part of assessing use of an interactive health education book. We conducted the study in this province for both demographic and political reasons. Villagers in this area were poor, uneducated, and conservative people living in an area consumed by ongoing fighting because of their province's political and strategic importance. Until they understood the value of health care and education, they would remain victims of any insurgent forces who took power in the area.

My visits started out well. At each village, we stopped the vehicle caravan and I met briefly with the elders to thank them for allowing us to conduct this study and to tell them about its purpose. My only disappointment was that I could not interview women alone, as I had hoped. Single interviews proved impossible in the crowded compound living situations that characterize village life. Moreover, Afghan women are not comfortable being visited by strangers when they are alone. On rare occasions, I was able to talk to women with only their children present. More often, however, I talked with several women from the same family in one sitting.

The male Pashtu interpreters who accompanied me on these trips were never allowed into the rooms of a home in which women were present. Hence, they had to remain in the garden once they obtained permission for me to interview, and I went in without them. I quickly worked out a way to speak to the women by finding an old man or a high school girl who knew both languages and who would join the conversation and translate my Dari questions into Pashtu.

We sat on the ground for nearly all of the interviews—either on dirt floors of humble homes, on porches outside those homes, or under trees in gardens. The Pashtu women were curious about me as a foreign woman, but more reserved and less likely to ask me questions than the Tajik village women whom I had interviewed in two districts of Kabul Province. The women in Laghman were serious and some bordered on somber. I did not hear any laughter among them. I also noticed that tea was not offered in the poorer homes of villages in two districts of this province, whereas it had been offered in virtually every home that I visited in Kabul Province.

In Laghman households, many families had designated a male relative to meet me at the entry of the house and speak on behalf of the women. While he was present, the women seemed willing to let him speak on their behalf. My challenge was to get the man to hover around outside and allow me some time alone with the women. Whether the group was large or small, most of the women watched in silence while a few women answered my interview questions. Because of the annual national immunization campaigns, the women knew about the importance of immunizing their children. However, they were less knowledgeable about other areas of health, including reproduction. They were also less likely to volunteer reproductive information about themselves than the women in Kabul Province.

I learned that the women who were in the intervention group were intrigued by the idea of using an electronic, interactive book as a learning tool. For many, this was the first book of any kind that they had seen. The school age boys and girls and the men in the family were more enthusiastic about the interactive books than the women. These women told me that they preferred learning from the local Community Health workers over learning from the book. Since most of the women interviewed were illiterate and few had any schooling, this response made sense. They were used to learning through oral instruction, observation, and emulation.

My last interview in the Alingar District of Laghman brought me closer than I had planned to the battles raging on the eastern border of this province. We reached the village home just prior to midday. I was told that we could not go to any villages further east because of skirmishes on the other side of the mountains. As I entered the compound, I saw that there was no water source nearby and that the children were dirtier than they had been in other homes. The family had placed a *charpoy* against a wall for me to sit on in a dark room with mud walls. They stood opposite me in a multi-generational group to answer my questions. I was struck by the fact that all of the women, who appeared to be many years apart in age, were pregnant. It was also unusual that several men were present in the room with the women. Normally, they would be in a separate room. Because of the demographics of the group, I wanted to take a photo, but my cultural awareness and a sense of the general uneasiness among the people in the room told me not to take out a camera..

As I was concluding the interview, three more men entered the room with stern expressions and whispered to the other men. Their combined seriousness made me nervous. I quickly put away my notebook, thanked everyone, and left the house. Just outside the door, I was met by six more men who stood between the house and the compound's exit door. They stared at me with open hostility. I saw that the agency Security Officer, Project Manager, and driver who had accompanied me to the site were all in the agency vehicle with the motor running. The security officer shouted at me to hurry and get into the car. I obeyed and the car drove away quickly without the usual gracious exchange of goodbyes.

I sensed tension among my male coworkers. Saleh looked particularly tense. As we drove off, I asked, "Saleh, is something wrong? Why were those men outside the house?"

"They came to report that on the other side of those mountains the American forces have just captured the commander who is from this village. They know that you are an American. We have to get you out of here!"

The other men said nothing, but emphatically nodded their agreement with Saleh's statement as the driver stepped on the gas.

We drove along in tense silence for a few minutes until we were sure that we weren't being followed. Finally, the project manager asked me, "Weren't you scared?"

"No, I wasn't scared," I answered. "When I saw those men in the compound, I knew that I needed to be cautious, but I wasn't scared. Afghans have always been good to me and they have given me no reason to be afraid. Besides, if I was scared, I couldn't do my job." As I said this, I felt the mood in the car lighten. We were all out of danger now.

"That's why we love working with you," Saleh answered. "We know that you love Afghanistan and that you are comfortable here. We can tell that you are not afraid like many foreigners are."

I smiled with pleasure at the compliment from these normally reserved Pashtun men.

Kunar Province in northeastern Afghanistan, is often in the news because of the ongoing battles still being fought there between the Coalition Forces and the insurgents. In 2005 and 2006, my agency opened several clinics in Kunar, including the first Comprehensive Health Clinic that has ever existed in Chawkee District. Due to security concerns, I wore a *chadri* as I secretly traveled in one of two unmarked cars to visit the staff and patients in two of our agency's clinics. Before we left the Jalalabad office compound, I gave my passport and identity papers to the Regional Director—a medical doctor—who was traveling in the other car. I knew that if we were stopped at a checkpoint, I would be asked to hand them over.

"What shall I say if I'm stopped and they ask me why I have these papers?" the doctor asked.

"Just say that you are my husband but don't like traveling with me so you put me in a separate car," I responded.

The doctor blushed as the Afghan staff members who had been listening exploded into laughter.

When I arrived at the first clinic, I saw 80-90 people lined up for treatment and was told that this was the typical daily patient load. I learned that ninety women had delivered babies in the three months that the Chawkee clinic had been open. Previously, home deliveries had been the only option. The Kunar Provincial Minister of Health was so pleased that I would visit the province that he cancelled his meeting with the newly appointed provincial governor to accompany me. At the end of the visit, the provincial minister thanked me and told me that I was the first INGO Country Director to visit their facilities.

As a result of enthusiastic telephone calls made by agency employees of clinics in the districts that I had visited, a major security concern on this trip was that the wrong people would learn of my identity. Hence, our return trip to Jalalabad was more dangerous than the trip to the area. In order to reduce chances of a problem on the return trip, we switched cars and changed our departure time. These proved to be good decisions, as we later learned that a bomb exploded near the road on the border between Kunar and Nangarhar Province at the time that we had originally been scheduled to pass that checkpoint. On the return trip, Dr. Akbari, a member of our program evaluation team, spoke emotionally about the importance of the Kunar clinics.

"Susan," he said, "the people of Kunar have never had health care like this in their entire history. The work your agency is doing here is very important."

"I am so happy to hear that," I replied. "I came here today because I wanted to let the staff in those clinics know how important their work is. What we are doing here is not only helping people live healthier lives, it is also our weapon against the insurgents who are trying to return this area to chaos and warfare."

"You are right," Dr. Akbari said, "The Afghan people want this. They want health care, education, jobs, and peaceful lives. We will prevail."

My last visit to Jalalabad to monitor health projects included a visit to the largest camp for Afghan returnees in the Eastern Region. *Sheikh Misri* was visible proof of how desperately Afghans want to return to their homeland. These returnees from the recently closed refugee camps in Pakistan were living in some of the harshest conditions that I have ever seen. Their tents were pitched on a desert scraped of all fertile soil by an ancient glacier, leaving only rocks. Water was scarce or non-existent. The government and NGOs were scrambling to establish water and sewer systems and to get food and improved shelter to nearly 18,000 people who had settled there by the time of my visit. Everyone was dirty, hungry, and thirsty. There was no health care available.

Hundreds of people instantly surrounded our two agency Land Cruisers when we arrived. The drivers, security officer, and my bodyguard were nervous. We sent a runner ahead to find the spokespeople for the group. The head of the male *shura* had gone to the bazaar and his substitute had little to say. The head of the female *shura*, a substantial, confident woman wearing a dusty but colorful cotton *chador* and long dress, had plenty to say.

"Yes, lots of women are dying in childbirth," she said in answer to my first question. "Women are dying and babies are dying because we have no doctors or midwives. People get sick and die because we have no health care."

I liked her immediately and grabbed her hand. "We will help you," I said.

My friend and colleague, Pashtoon, an accomplished Afghan Midwife Trainer had accompanied me on this trip. She asked more pointed questions about the health status of the camp while a male colleague took notes. The session ended with the three of us women—the head of the female *shura*, Pashtoon, and me—posing for photos with our arms locked together. Within a week of my visit, the Eastern Region Program Manager had reported our data to the Nangarhar Provincial Minister of Public Health and had made arrangements for our agency to deploy a mobile clinic to the site. Our agency also collaborated with other INGOs to develop integrated services for the camp.

Sheikh Misri continued to exist long after my visit, but conditions improved thanks to the work of INGOs that built shelters and brought water, sanitation, and a variety of social services and training to the site. Despite the services available to them, the daily lives of returnees who inhabit the barren stretch of land on the edge of Jalalabad are vastly different from the lives of the Kabulis who still spend their winters in gardens filled with roses and palm trees just a few miles away.

Michael Griffin - 1998

Gul Hassan - 1969 - Kabul

Suzanne with local school boys on a sheep farm - Spring 1968
Pul-i-Kumri

Women's Literacy and Health Class in Logar Province - July 2002

Boys at cracked window - July 2002 - Logar Province
sons of women in the Literacy and Health Program

Photography by Peter Bussian

Suzanne and Peter at agency office in Logar Province - July 2002

Gul Khana Palace, Kabul - August 2, 2002

(L to R) Sigurd Hanson, Christiane Amanpour, Liz Hume (Lawyer and agency expert on trafficking of girls, which Ms. Amanpour was reporting on), Suzanne, and Nina Papadopoulos, who developed the agency's Women's Literacy and Health program implemented in Afghanistan and Pakistan

Photography by Peter Bussian

Christiane Amanpour and Suzanne - August 2002

Masood's Memorial - August 17, 2002 - Panjshir Province
Suzanne with agency Engineer/Architect Wahid Ahad and his son

Girls School in Jalalabad - 2002

Suzanne and students in front of makeshift school - July 2002
Kabul Province, on the outskirts of Kabul City
below: Suzanne and girls at the same location

Girls School classes - August 2003 - Kabul
two students in the first (legal) post-Taliban girls school in Kabul

Women in Bamyan Province - 2003
agency small business project

Photography by Peter Bussian

Women in cart - 2002
Kabul Plains area, on the road going north to the Salang Pass

Kuchis in Kabul - 2003 - Khoshal Meena
near the camp for internally displaced persons

Photography by Peter Bussian

Truck drivers - 2003 - Jalalabad Road, Kabul

Girls assisting in street work - 2005 Shar-i-Nau District, Kabul

Photography by Peter Bussian

Girl - Karte Se - 2004

Photography by Peter Bussian

Woman and her young son in Women's Center - 2005 - Kabul

Family Business - 2007 - Pul-i-Kuhmri

Chapter 10

Freedom Fighters and a New Democracy

I struggled out of bed at 4:00 a.m. on my last Friday in Afghanistan in summer 2002 and mumbled a greeting to my housemates. We hurriedly sipped coffee in the guesthouse kitchen while we waited for agency cars to pick us up. We were going to visit the tomb of Massoud, an Afghan national hero for his leadership in the fight against the Russians. We would be on unpaved roads for over half of the trip, so we had to start early to make it to the Panjsher (five lions) Valley and back in one day. At that time, travel to the Panjsher Valley required special clearances from the Afghan government, but one of our Afghan colleagues, Engineer Ahad, was a finalist in the architectural competition to design the permanent shrine that would house Massoud's tomb. He had the clearance papers and invited us to go along on his site inspection.

Peter, Ruby, and I were in one car with Engineer Ahad and his son Yaya. Sam, Dan, and another Afghan colleague were in the other car with the government official who arranged our trip. Most of us dozed as our caravan traveled along the two-lane, paved highway through the Shamali (windy) Plains. At one point, I woke and found myself staring through the window into the faces of a de-mining team crouching over their work at the edge of the road. I reached for my camera but stopped. Who knew what restrictions there were on photographing this type of work, and what if my taking a picture caused them to lose concentration on their dangerous work?

"Peter, I know the red rocks mark the area that hasn't been de-mined and the white rocks mean that the area has been de-mined, but what does it mean when the rocks have red dots on them?" I asked.

Peter chuckled and gave me a wink. We'd both been in Afghanistan long enough to have encountered many practices that defied our Western logic. "Well ... they probably mean that they're uncertain about those areas."

"It looks as if they're uncertain about a lot of areas," I said. "And the uncertain areas are right on the edge of this road. I sure hope we don't get a flat tire."

"Yes, and you better not think of stopping and getting out along this road," Ruby added. "Those mines are *everywhere*."

Engineer Ahad was not an engineer but, like other college-educated Afghan men with professional occupations, had that title of respect. He was an excellent host. He had arranged for us to breakfast in a private room at a teahouse in Jabal Saraj, the town that marked the end of the Kabul Plains and the beginning of the climb into the mountains. We sat on red cushions on a carpet that had been swept of crumbs and enjoyed the warmth of morning sunlight through the dirty glass windows as we sipped tea and used pieces of fresh, hot bread to pull chunks of sizzling lamb off kabob skewers. Although the kabobs were delicious, my stomach was not used to meat in the morning, so I didn't eat much. As usual, the presence of two women in the teahouse caught the attention of many patrons, even though Ruby and I were modestly dressed in *shalwar kamizes* and—because of our dark hair and eyes—often passed for Afghan women. When we quietly excused ourselves to use the *tashnab* (restroom) dozens of pairs of eyes followed us.

Unfortunately, the paved road ended in Jabal Saraj. We turned a sharp right onto a graded road and went up a steep hill under Jewett's tower, a tall mud-and-brick structure that offered those who climbed it a panoramic view of the Kabul Plains. We bumped along the narrow, rutted road that climbed toward the mountains for two more hours—a particularly uncomfortable ride after a meal of bread, meat, and tea. On the way, we passed the outskirts of Gulbahar (flower of spring). As I gazed at the line of mulberry trees in the public gardens along the Panjsher River, I recalled the wonderful picnics that Michael and I had shared under those trees with our Afghan and American Peace Corps colleagues. Our cars slowed as they moved up the narrow road that clings to a rocky cliff in the Kwakh Gorge. As we looked down from the road, we saw the wreckage of Russian tanks—reminders of fierce battles that had been fought in the Panjsher over the previous decades. As the road climbed up the cliff, we looked down at the glistening waters of the Panjsher River and the fertile green fields covering the narrow valley floor along both sides of its banks.

"It's beautiful, Ruby!" I said. "I can see why Massoud and his freedom fighters fought so fiercely to preserve this place."

"Yes, look at all the trees!"

"Shamali Plains had a lot of trees before the battles against the Russians," Engineer Ahad explained. "They were cut down so that enemies couldn't hide behind them. The Russians also poisoned the soil and filled it with mines. Although the fighting has stopped, the soil cannot be restored until the area is de-mined. That's why the villages in the Shamali Plains are abandoned."

"So these trees survived because Massoud and his men kept the Russians out of the main part of the valley?" I asked.

"Yes, Suzanne. That's why this valley is so precious to us," Engineer Ahad answered.

It was very windy at the top of the gorge. Ruby and I had to hold our *chadors* firmly under our chins to keep them from flying off our heads. We were not allowed entry into the temporary dome-shaped wooden shrine for Massoud's tomb because workers were frantically trying to finish construction before the September celebration of Massoud Day. After Engineer Ahad had inspected the site for the permanent shrine and talked with the workers, he led us up a trail to the top of the bluff and into a cream-colored building. We grew silent as we sat waiting for tea, thinking about the tragedy that had occurred in this office. Two Arab men masquerading as journalists had concealed a small bomb in a camera that exploded and killed Massoud, the leader of the resistance whose battles we had followed through U.S. press reports.

It was approaching lunchtime, so Engineer Ahad led us up another hillside trail into the beautiful gardens outside Massoud's newly constructed private home—a modest dwelling that he did not live to inhabit. Massoud's grandfather had designed the gardens, which had both vertical and horizontal waterways to irrigate the flowers, plants, and trees. The sound of running water surrounded us as we strolled among the beautiful flowers—including many varieties of roses—trees, and vines. We stopped briefly by a large covered platform that served as a place for prayer and contemplation, as well as a place to rest while enjoying the panoramic view of the rugged cliffs of the Kwakh Gorge and the Panjsher Valley below. While we waited for lunch to be prepared, we sat in the shade of almond trees and visited with Massoud's cousin and one of his military officers, who patiently answered our questions about Massoud's leadership in battle and his assassination.

Our lunch was more rushed than we would have liked, as we needed to get back to Kabul before dark for security reasons. As we thanked our hosts, I received a warm handshake from Massoud's cousin—a rather unusual gesture for an Afghan man toward a foreign woman whom he does not know well. I also noted that he seemed to know more about me than I had revealed in the group conversation. The next day I learned that this man was a former classmate and friend of my colleague Walid. I had told Walid about the planned trip the evening before our departure. I later learned that Walid had contacted his friend and told him to make sure that I was well taken care of.

On the way back to Gulbahar, we remarked on the innovative ways that the Panjsheris had used the removable parts of the remaining Russian tanks. Tank treads were particularly versatile. Laid out flat and linked together, they served as bridges and sidewalks; turned on end, they became fences around vegetable gardens.

As our car was leaving the bazaar of the last town before entering the arid Shamali Plains, we had the flat tire that we all had dreaded. Luckily, one of the roadside tire shops in the bazaar was still open, but by the time our tire was replaced, it was dusk. By radio, we notified our office of our whereabouts and drove rapidly toward Kabul. It was dark when we entered the city's outskirts, and we worried about the occasional rocket fire that we sometimes heard. Unbelievably, we had a second flat tire on an unlit street in front of the Iranian Embassy. Since it was dangerous for a group of foreigners to be gathered on a public street after dark, one car took us to our guesthouse while our Afghan colleagues stayed with the disabled car until the logistics department arrived to help.

Each time I have visited Massoud's tomb after that first visit, the shrine honoring him has improved in design and increased in size. On my second visit to the Panjsher, I was accompanied by a Bangladeshi pediatrician and my sister-in-law's husband Larry, who spent two weeks in Kabul volunteering at Rabia Balkhi Women's Hospital. By then, a more permanent building for Massoud's tomb had been completed and we had an opportunity to enter it and stand beside the tomb as we silently paid our respects to the Afghan hero. When I visited Massoud's shrine at the conclusion of a Massoud Day celebration in 2010, an attractive, two story complex of marble granite buildings designed by Iranian architects was nearing completion. It completely covered the top of the hill.

In Spring 2013, I saw the finished complex. It includes a library, museum, indoor meeting hall, and outdoor amphitheater. A green space lined by yew trees extends perpendicularly from the façade of the complex to the hillside edge. The shrine's design immediately called to my mind the shrines of Iranian poets that Michael and I had seen in Iran. The hexagonal, one story, white marble building is surrounded by six marble pillars that support the lapis-blue dome, which rises three stories above the tomb. Natural light shines through bronze-framed, glass panes under the dome to illuminate the tomb and draw the gaze of visitors inside the building to the lapis lazuli star on the underside of the dome. Afghans and empathetic foreign visitors to the shrine are visibly moved as they contemplate the price that Massoud and thousands of other Afghan fighters have paid for the freedom of their country.

In December 2003, the people of Afghanistan began to experience political freedom for which Massoud and other brave Afghans sacrificed their lives. The *Loya Jirga,* a gathering of 500 men and women representing their fellow citizens, was convened on December 13th. My agency colleagues were pleased that the president of the *Loya Jirga* was from the politically powerful Mujadidi family, whose members had returned to Afghanistan after years of exile in Pakistan. A medical doctor from that family was helping us improve the medical training of doctors in a hospital in which a dozen of us worked. Despite a small bomb that destroyed a wall of the Inter-Continental Hotel near the ballroom where the *Loya Jirga* had been meeting, the group kept deliberating and the national media reported their progress on the evening news. Less than a month later, on January 4, 2004, they presented Interim President Hamid Karzai with the Constitution of the Islamic Republic of Afghanistan. The rights outlined in the 38 Articles of Chapter Two of that document include the right of both men and women to vote and to be elected to political office, the right to assemble and demonstrate, the right to free education through a Bachelor's degree, and the right to free primary health care for all Afghan men, women, and children.

In Autumn 2004, Afghans turned out in huge numbers to vote in the country's first presidential election. They waited patiently in long lines starting at 5:00 a.m. to cast their ballots. The pride of Afghan women who were voting for the first time was thrilling to see. Female physicians who worked with me at the women's maternity hospital were flush with enthusiasm as they told me about the number of women who had stood in line with them to cast their votes. They described a ninety-year-old woman who had someone push her wheelchair to the polling place so that she could vote. She told all who would listen, "I never thought that I would live to see this day!"

There were eighteen candidates representing four ethnic groups (Pashtun, Tajik, Uzbek, and Hazara) on the ballot, but Hamid Karzai received 55% of the more than eight million votes that were cast.

In Summer 2005, I got regular first-hand reports on the country-wide efforts to mobilize Afghans to vote in the parliamentary election, as I lived for several weeks in a private guesthouse where European and American election committees lived. The election workers bravely traveled to both secure and insecure areas of the country to hold community meetings in order to educate people about the responsibilities and duties of Parliament and to encourage both men and women to run for seats. Afghanistan had held parliamentary elections before (1949, 1952, 1959, 1965, and 1988), but these elections marked a new era in Afghanistan's political history because women were guaranteed 25% of the seats in Parliament.

Several female physicians from our agency were candidates for the seats that were reserved for women. Although none of them were elected, we were all energized by the fact that they were running. Campaign posters for both male and female candidates were plastered on every available wall in the center of Kabul, as well on the trunks and branches of trees that lined Shar-i-Nau streets. When the Afghan Parliament was convened in 2006, women's voices were heard in the deliberations of that body, in public speeches, and in news reports broadcast on daily radio and television.

While the Afghan central government is organized along democratic lines, its formal government structure coexists with the traditional *shuras* at the local level. Although women's *shuras* are steadily increasing in numbers, the vast majority of the *shuras* are composed of men. One of my greatest satisfactions in working with Afghan communities has been learning to work effectively with men's *shuras*. Mentored by my Afghan colleagues, I have learned that the support of local *shuras* is crucial to the success of nearly every project initiated by government and NGOs in Afghanistan. I now understand why Michael spent so much time talking with community members to get their opinions of planned Peace Corps projects in their areas.

My first personal experience of the impact of *shura* support occurred during the rapid assessment of the effectiveness of the interactive health book for 2,000 Afghan families who were using it for the first time. We were pleased to see statistically significant differences between the families who used the book and those who did not. The most meaningful indicator for me, however, was an invitation to have tea with a *shura* leader in Laghman so that he could tell me that this interactive book was like a dictionary of health for his family. In Pashtu, he gave me this example:

"One evening our children were arguing during dinner about the nutritional value of each of the vegetables they were eating. To settle the argument, one of the children went to get the interactive book and brought it to the table. He turned to the section on nutrition and tapped the stylus on the page so that everyone could hear the answer."

My most challenging meeting with a *shura* occurred in Qarabagh. An American woman who had lived in Afghanistan as a teenager returned to the country and visited some family friends in a village. She learned that the village needed a school and mobilized her Rotary Club, as well as the community of Falmouth, Maine, to raise the necessary funds. My friend Walid has an NGO that is dedicated to implementing training and literacy projects for women and building schools for girls. He was asked to assist with this project. In the process of negotiating with the village community elders on behalf of the donor, Walid learned that the village was divided between two families who wanted to build a school.

Walid decided that I needed to meet with the *shura* as a representative of the American donors. As we were leaving Kabul for Qarabagh, Walid

Freedom Fighters and a New Democracy

got a call from a community member reporting that a heated argument at the *shura* the day before had ended in a fist fight between representatives of the families that wanted to build the school. The other family had already contracted with an INGO to build the school, and the international representative from that INGO would be attending the meeting.

The entire *shura*—about fifty men—greeted us. As it was a hot day and the *shura* had no meeting room, we sat outdoors under the shade of large trees. Jeff, the expatriate representative of the INGO, Walid, and I were assigned seats on a large *charpoy* facing the semi-circle of men. As each side made their case for building the school, I noticed that classes were being dismissed in the temporary school behind the semi-circle of men. Only boys were exiting the school. I immediately addressed the school principal who was part of the *shura*.

"Excuse me, sir. Isn't that your school?" I asked in Dari.

"Yes, *Honum* (Madame)," he answered.

"Is that school only for boys?"

"Girls can go there if they want to," he answered as he shrugged his shoulders.

"Then why am I only seeing boys come out of that building?"

The principal looked nonplussed and had no answer. Educated men in Afghan society are not used to being challenged in a public meeting—especially by a woman.

I addressed the *shura* members.

"Do girls have a school in this village?

They shook their heads, to signify "no."

"So you are asking me, as a representative of American donors, to build a school that is only for boys, is that right?" I asked, my anger rising.

Some of them looked embarrassed as they nodded. I realized, then, that the men assumed there would be only one school built. The first priority for most villages is for boys to be educated so they can get jobs.

That did it for me. I had come here with the mandate to build a girls' school, not another school for boys.

"I am able to help rebuild the Afghan educational system because I received a doctorate degree in Education," I stated forcefully. "I got that degree partially because both my father and my husband supported my efforts. You are fathers and husbands and you are willing to sit here and not allow the girls in your village an opportunity to get an education. Not

Lessons of Love in Afghanistan

only are you wasting their brain power, which could help improve this village, you are denying their children opportunities that they might have if their mothers are educated. So if you think that I am going to tell the American donors to send money to build a school that is only for boys, you are wrong."

The group was silent after I spoke. Many men looked at the ground. The man who was sitting to my right, in the position of honor, leaned slightly toward me, looked at the ground and quietly asked me, "What do you want?"

I turned slightly toward him, but, according to the custom of Afghan women, did not look directly at him. "Let the International NGO build the boys' school on this site. I want land to build another school for girls," I said in a rather loud and defiant whisper.

Other ears perked up, listening to our conversation.

"Alright, you have it," he said in a voice that all could hear. "I will donate the land."

Relief registered among the *shura* members as their leader announced the decision: The other family would work with the INGO to build the boys' school and the family known to the American woman whom I represented would build the girls' school. In November 2007, the construction of the girls' school was completed and the school was officially handed over by Walid's NGO to the Provincial Education Director of Kabul Province. Over 350 children, almost half of whom are girls[3], are currently enrolled in grades 1-9 in this school.

My most recent experience with *shuras* was in the communities of Jawzjan and Sar-i-Pul Provinces, where teacher trainers from our project were trying to get community *shuras* to work with Parent Teacher Associations (PTAs) and school management teams—principals and head teachers—to develop School Improvement Plans. The success of this effort was remarkable. *Shuras* in these provinces (where agriculture is the main industry) supported the costs of digging wells and provided water tanks for drinking water, repaired damaged classrooms and tents, constructed latrines, built security walls around the school grounds,

---

[3] *This conservative community followed a common practice in Afghanistan—designating several rooms in the girls' school to classes for boys in primary grades, as they knew that Taliban would destroy or close a school that was solely for girls.*

Freedom Fighters and a New Democracy

bought fabric to have uniforms made for the students, and donated land for new schools to be built.

I attended one especially memorable meeting with the *shura* that supports one of the high schools in Jawzjan Province. Prior to that meeting, the *shura* had already paid for the renovation of five classrooms and had started discussing support for the half-completed library. The teachers came to the late-afternoon meeting prepared with lists of their needs. As it was another hot August day, chairs for the meeting were arranged in the school garden.

After introductions, I thanked the *shura* members for supporting the high school. I also thanked the school science teachers who had discussed with me the need for a microscope when I had visited the school the previous month. I told the *shura* and the teachers that as a result of their request, our agency would be buying a microscope for each of the 101 high schools in the two provinces. The teachers thanked me for the microscope, but added that they still needed reference books to put in their library.

"Do you have a library?" I asked in Dari.

"We are building one over there," one of the *shura* members answered as he pointed to a half-finished building.

"Okay, you complete the library and we will give you some books," I responded.

Then the bargaining process began. We negotiated a bit on the amount that the project would be willing to spend on the books. Although the teachers wanted more than I could allocate, they understood that I would have to spend the same amount for the other 100 high schools in the two provinces. Next, the teachers asked for laptop computers and a DVD player to use in teaching science.

"We cannot buy you laptop computers, but we can buy you a DVD player. Maybe the *shura* can buy you the laptops," I added, nodding toward the *shura* members.

"We will buy the laptop computers," one man said after consulting with his neighbor.

At the end of the meeting, everyone went away satisfied. We had formed a partnership—everyone was going to contribute something to improve the education of the children in that school.

Lessons of Love in Afghanistan

As I traveled back to the agency's Shiberghan office with the members of the training team, I flashed back to situations in which I had watched Michael negotiate with community members both in Afghanistan and in the United States. I now understand the satisfaction that he felt when completing a meeting in which everyone has spoken directly about what they want and what they can do, especially when the results of the discussion are tangible. How different these meetings were, I mused, from the long discussions at official meetings in Kabul which only seem to lead to another series of meetings that ultimately may—or may not—have tangible outcomes. Both the community *shuras* and the long official meetings have common elements, however. They are venues where individuals are free to express their opinions about how institutions should work. As long as they both thrive, there is hope for the success of a democratic government in Afghanistan.

Chapter 11

Moment of Decision

"Susan, it's time to go. We have to go now, dear Susan!" The sharp knock on the door and Naik's whisper roused me from deep sleep. I thought I was dreaming, but the white light of the full moon flooding through my window allowed me to see the crack of the partially opened door through the curtain that covered the doorway. The voice came from there. In my sleepy state, I had not immediately recognized the version of my name that so many Pashtuns use, but I was suddenly alert and knew that Naik was speaking to me. When I threw off the thick cotton quilts, freezing air hit me and my teeth began to chatter. I rose slowly from my cot and stumbled across the room toward the doorway. As I pulled back the thick curtain, I saw that Naik, our Operations Director, and the office driver Hakim were already dressed for the road. They greeted me in unison.

"*Salaam alekum, Khonum* Susan."

Since I was barely awake, I felt as if I'd been kicked in the stomach, yet I knew the Afghan expectation of a cheerful response to the first greeting of the day.

"*Salaam alekum*, Naik and Hakim. *Chiwakt ast* ("What time is it")?"

"Its 3:30," Hakim answered in Dari. "We have to start early in the morning while mud on the road is frozen. It's a six-hour journey. Our appointment at the clinic is at 10:00. We need to hurry to get there. When the muddy road thaws, the road will become impassable."

"Okay, I'll be ready in five minutes," I replied.

"We're waiting for you," Naik said and they both descended the steep stairs to the courtyard.

There was still lukewarm water in the metal tank in the shower room and I splashed some on my face before adding two more layers of clothing in preparation for our journey to western Bamiyan. The March snow melt had begun when the sun was shining, but night and early morning temperatures were still frigid.

We had arrived from Kabul by air on the previous day. After visits to the Bamiyan Hospital and nearby clinics, I had acted as a tour guide for Naik, who was of Tajik origin and was visiting Bamiyan for the first time. As we toured the former sites of the Big Buddha, the Little Buddha and Shahr-i-Gholgola (City of Noise), I described for him what these ancient landmarks had looked like before the Taliban had destroyed them with dynamite. I showed him where Michael and I had climbed up to the heads of both Buddha statues via interior mud stairways that connected the network of Buddhist caves inside the cliffs. Since the caves were off limits, I described to Naik how the walls looked with drawings and smoke marks that were thousands of years old.

As I recalled for Naik the expansive view of Bamiyan Valley that I had seen from the head of the Big Buddha more than three decades ago, I remembered that Michael had surprised me by retreating quickly from the place where we stood together on the Buddha's head. He explained that he was experiencing a sudden wave of acrophobia, which he couldn't understand because he'd never had that reaction to hiking on high mountain trails. I had remained on the Buddha's head alone, entranced by the pastoral scene below.

When Naik and I visited the site, rubble from the destructive dynamite blasts was still piled at the base of the empty niches that once enclosed the Buddha statues. The Japanese Government had begun its many years of renovation work to restore the statues. I was sorry that Naik could not experience the cave interiors or the bird's-eye view of the valley as I had. He was thrilled, however, to have his picture taken amidst these ruins so that he could show his family where he had been.

Naik and I also visited the ruins of Shahr-i-Gholgola where I told him a story of how Genghis Khan was able to destroy the city with the help of a tip from a young princess who wished to spite her father for taking another wife after her mother's death. As Naik explored the ruins, I sat in silence on a rock and recalled more details of the visit that Michael and I had made to this place on a freezing cold day in 1969.

Michael and I were marooned in Bamiyan City for four winter days because the six-seat plane that had flown there for a one-day site visit could not return after snow clouds moved in over the mountains.

Each morning after our arrival, Michael and I had packed our small overnight bag, walked out to the runway, and stood for several hours. Wind whipped around us as we watched for the plane to appear over the mountaintops that surround Bamiyan City. The fancy control tower built by the U.S. government was useless because it had no communications or tracking equipment, so the Afghans assigned to the control tower were unable to tell us whether the plane had left Kabul. All they could do was remain in their elevated position so that they could sight the plane's approach before we saw it from the ground.

After four days of shouting back and forth to the people in the control tower, Michael and I took the Afghan Post bus out of Bamiyan City, despite the fact that the previous bus to Kabul had gone over the side of the narrow mountain road, killing everyone aboard. My anxiety about our safety on that trip was rivaled by my concern about how I would be able to go to the bathroom when we had breaks during the eight-hour trip. All of the men got out and disappeared behind rocks and the occasional bush. Meanwhile, the women in the bus, all of whom wore *chadris* and skirts, passed around a tin cup into which they relieved themselves. Since I was wearing western-style pants, the cup was not passed to me. Ultimately, I had my own semi-private break with Michael standing guard in front of a rock while everyone in the bus supposedly looked the other way. As often happened when I took bathroom breaks in Afghanistan in the middle of a seemingly empty landscape, a shepherd appeared out of nowhere to observe the scene.

Among the passengers on the crowded bus was a young man who was studying his *Afghans Learn English* book and was eager to practice his new English language skills with Americans. The conversation proceeded along the pattern of his lesson. Both Michael and I knew the book and the format of the lesson dialogs, because we had taught English as a Foreign Language classes.

"Hello, my name is Yousuf."

"Hello, Yousuf. I'm Michael."

"And I'm Suzanne. It's nice to meet you."

"It's nice to meet you, too. How are you?"

Moment of Decision

"We are fine. How are you?"

"I am fine. Are you Americans?"

"Yes, we are. Are you a student?"

"Yes, I am. I am studying English in class eight."

We proceeded with this constrained dialog for over a half hour until Mohammad got a pained expression on his face and said, "This is end of page forty-four. I don't know any more English."

Yousuf was ecstatic when Michael continued the conversation with him in fluent Farsi. Yousuf spent the remainder of the trip quizzing Michael about America. Having far less skill in the language than my husband, I was only able to interject occasionally. That did not matter to Yousuf, however, because, like most Afghan men, he was far more interested in conversing with my husband than with me. Had we been in a house or office, I would have been dismissed to a separate room to interact with the women.

My trip to Bamiyan in early spring of 2004 was under entirely different circumstances, but the weather still had a major impact on the trip. Despite the early start and the prospect of many hours on a rutted road, I was excited about seeing the western part of Bamiyan Province for the first time. Before I got into the front passenger seat, Hakim, the driver, warned me about the discomforts of the twenty-year-old Russian jeep that served as our agency vehicle. Regardless, I was surprised by how much icy air came in through the leaky windows and roof. The back seats had been removed to accommodate two stretchers for patients who needed to be transported from our agency's clinics in the province's western districts to the hospital in Bamiyan City. Naik had to ride on one of the bench seats for stretchers without a seat belt. He ultimately regretted his generous offer that had given me the front seat: due to the jostling he took on the long journey, he succumbed to motion sickness. Although I empathized with his discomfort, I had learned to sit in the front passenger seat in order for my back to survive long trips over bumpy roads.

The six-hour journey took us over a frozen, muddy road so bad that the jeep was sometimes riding with only one set of wheels on the ground—usually the front and rear wheels on the driver's side. When the jeep tipped at a fifty-degree angle toward the hillside on the passenger side of the road, I was grateful to be strapped tightly in my seat.

I smiled gamely *up*—not sideways—at Hakim as he glanced over to see how I was doing. Naik had been propelled to the back of the vehicle. When the road leveled out, the three of us exhaled, glad that the most nerve-wracking part of the trip was behind us. As we relaxed, we silently observed the light of the full winter moon playing across a blanket of snow that stretched to the horizon. As dawn approached, the light on the snowy plains took on a surreal, faint pink glow against the dark blue sky. Crumbling red sandstone ruins of buildings emerged from the snow at odd intervals, the only signs that humans had once lived here. This peaceful landscape was still deserted because it had not yet been de-mined. This was the area in which, between 1992 and 2002, over 40,000 Shia Muslim Hazaras were slaughtered by the Taliban.

Shortly after dawn, we started seeing other travelers on the road: solitary young men pushing bicycles to the tops of hills and low moun-tain passes and riding them down the other side. Since the narrow tires of their road bikes could not negotiate the muddy, rutted road, the bike riders were traveling over the smooth, frozen landscape parallel to us and making better time than our jeep. I mused that there should be a big market for mountain bikes in Afghanistan.

We reached Yakalang, the district capital, around 9:30 a.m. The sun-warmed mud was soft now and our jeep was getting stuck more and more frequently. All three of us were worn and weary from the constant bumping. Hakim warned us that if the mud got much softer, we'd have to get out and walk. But he didn't say how far we'd be walking.

"How much longer, Hakim?" I asked.

"We're almost there, *Khonum*," he responded. I had been getting the same answer for two hours. Naik was nearly green. We had made a couple of stops so that he could get some air and smoke a cigarette. My guess was he'd rather walk than continue riding in the back of that Russian jeep.

Suddenly, Hakim steered the jeep to the shoulder of the road and parked it. "We can't go in the vehicle anymore," he said. "We have to walk."

We didn't protest. Naik and I slung backpacks over our shoulders and followed Hakim, who made this arduous trip three times each week. Walking wasn't easy either. The suction of the mud nearly pulled off our

Moment of Decision

boots as we picked our way across ruts toward the trail that led up to the clinic on the bluff above us. As we trudged through the mud, we noticed a man and boy coming down the trail toward us leading two horses.

"The clinic sent horses for you," Hakim announced. "Can you ride?"

To his surprise, I answered, "Yes."

I had learned to ride my cousins' horses as a child. It was one of the thrills of visiting their home in a southern Oregon logging town.

Naik, who was shorter even than me, was frightened of mounting and riding a horse for the first time—especially in less than optimal conditions.

I thrust my foot into a stirrup, hoisted my 5' 3" body up to mount the horse, settled into the saddle, and relished the surprised expressions of the Afghans. They had expected me to sit sidesaddle, like Afghan women. Had I been wearing my customary long Afghan skirt, sidesaddle would have been the only alternative. However, on the advice of other foreign women who had made regular trips to Bamiyan, I had worn jeans. Even though the son of the horse's owner walked a few steps ahead to guide my mount, the journey up to the bluff on the narrow zigzag trail was not easy for the large animal. I speculated about how many horses and mules must have tripped while carrying pregnant women sidesaddle up this same trail to the clinic. I was also aware of the stares of scores of Hazara patients and medical personnel sitting outside the clinic on the bluff above us, patiently awaiting our arrival.

We arrived at the Deh Sorkh (Red Village) Clinic a half hour later and waded through the crowd of patients—male and female adults as well as many children—to be enthusiastically greeted by the clinic staff. Few agency staff members from our Kabul office ever made it to this remote spot.

Men of every age wearing dark turbans and heavy wool jackets were sitting in a semblance of a line on the west side of the entrance to the male outpatient clinic. Their Mongol features, ruddy cheeks and dark eyes, made them easily distinguishable from other ethnic groups when you saw them in Kabul. In the capital city, Hazaras are a minority group, so it was a shock to see them here in a majority status. The older boys were sitting or playing near the male adults. Boys under six, however, gathered near the brightly clothed Hazara women sitting near the east door of the clinic which was where the females received medical care.

There were no blue *chadris* worn by the line of females that extended to the clinic doors from the opposite side of the building. Instead, I was delighted to see the women's faces framed by *chadors* in pomegranate red, Kelly green, hot pink, and sunflower yellow. I loved being able to see the women returning my smiles and greetings and immediately felt comfortable with them, even though I don't speak Hazara. Some were nursing their babies; others were minding their toddlers and young children. Among both groups of men and women, the noise level was far lower than what I had experienced with comparable groups of adults in Kabul. I wondered if their relative silence was a result of severe post-traumatic stress due to the slaughter of their neighbors that had ended only two years before. Or perhaps it was a habit grown out of respect for their environment, this beautiful wilderness of snow-capped mountains surrounding fertile valleys crossed by clear, cold streams, and rivers. I regretted these patients would have to wait longer than normal on this day because the medical staff would be meeting with Naik and me about the clinic's needs and our plans for expanding services.

The Deh Sorkh Clinic was unusual not only because of its remote location but also because it was supervised by a female physician, Dr. Mariam, whose husband, Mustafa, was also at the clinic that day. Mustafa explained that he was a businessman who worked in Dubai in the United Arab Emirates six months each year and spent the other six months supporting his wife in her work at the clinic. I had heard that Hazaras were more supportive of the education and professional development of women than most of their Afghan countrymen, and this was proof. At the time, I knew of few Pashtun and Tajik couples in Kabul who had such an enlightened arrangement that allowed both individuals to pursue their respective careers. In those groups, husband and wife were often of the same profession—both were doctors or both were teachers—and worked in the same location.

Shortly after our visit, President Karzai appointed a woman governor for Bamiyan Province—the only one of the thirty-six provinces in Afghanistan to have a female governor. Based on what I had observed in Afghan culture, this was the only province that would accept a woman in that position.

Naik and I toured the clinic facility, admiring the commitment of the staff to providing competent patient care in a converted Afghan house—a common arrangement for many rural clinics. Even though the floors were dirt and the walls were whitewashed mud, basic infection prevention practices were used in the cleaning of instruments, equipment, and linens. As we passed through the clinic, I was acutely aware that my every move and word was being carefully observed by both staff and patients. I was the first foreign woman that many of them had ever seen. As part of my assistance to Naik in assessing the logistical needs of the clinic, I helped him determine the dimensions of the waiting area that needed a roof to shield patients from snow, rain, and sun. When I paced off the space in approximately three-foot strides and called out the dimensions to Naik, who was recording them, there was considerable comment among the observers. They had never seen a woman performing a task normally assigned to a man.

Dr. Abdullah, the lead male physician, drew my attention to a hand-drawn wall map showing the six hundred villages that the clinic served. The two midwives on the staff noted that they could only provide prenatal care to the few women from these villages who could make a trip to the clinic. They agreed with me that this area needed a Community Midwife Education Program, and the midwives' efforts had to focus on home visits to provide prenatal care and to train village women on hygiene and techniques to ensure safer home deliveries. As we talked, I observed brightly clothed women descending from the bluff on foot and donkey for their long journey back to their homes. I wondered how many women in the developed world would be willing to undergo such hardship to get medical services.

It was unthinkable that we would not have lunch with the staff in Deh Sorkh before departing, even though it was an hour before the customary lunchtime. We ate our modest meal of rice and beans with the doctors in a more hurried fashion than usual because we still had a meeting at the Yakalang Hospital before starting the six-hour return trip to Bamiyan City. Naik and I descended the bluff on horses once again and, with the help of their handlers, guided our mounts through the thick mud on the road that led to our Russian jeep. Because the road was unusable for motor vehicles, there were no mechanical sounds—only the breath and footsteps of our horses and handlers, the distant voices of a gaggle of village women walking from the fields, and the gurgling sound of a nearby stream.

As I rode, I pondered a career decision that I was trying to make. It had been nearly two years since the community college district had approved my application to take a summer sabbatical to work in Afghanistan. The assumption was that I would replicate a study on literacy among Afghan women as a follow up to my dissertation and then return to academia. Instead, I became involved in program development with two different INGOs. I loved the work. Since summer of 2002, I had spent two quarter breaks and another summer as a consultant in Afghanistan. I finally signed a contract in October 2003 as Program Development Manager. My college had been very cooperative, granting me every kind of paid and unpaid leave to which I was entitled. After two years, however, they needed an answer regarding my future plans.

I reflected on how many times my family and I had driven hundreds of miles to find the kind of isolated beauty and peace that surrounded me here. We often visited wilderness areas and national parks in the United States. Scenes of a hiking trip with Michael to Half Dome in Yosemite flashed through my mind. I also thought of the discussions Michael and I had had about returning to Afghanistan as Retired Peace Corps Volunteers. If I did not have to earn a salary to support myself, I realized, I would be doing exactly what I had been doing today—working in the far reaches of Afghanistan to assist a people whom I loved with the rebuilding of their country. Since I now had a job that allowed me to do that, I could think of no good reason to return to my position as a community college dean. Although I missed my family and would have to work out ways to see them regularly if I stayed in humanitarian work, I knew the answer that I would send from Kabul to my college president: "I am not coming back."

When we reached the jeep, we dismounted from our horses, thanked their handlers, and sent them on their way. As we got into the vehicle, we spotted two female patients from the clinic and their children who were riding donkeys and walking on the road. We offered them a ride to Yakalang. At first, they were grateful and left older children to guide the donkeys along the road as they piled into the vehicle with their babies and toddlers. Soon, though, their faces showed fear at every major bump and their hungry babies screamed because the women could not nurse properly in the lurching vehicle. The women demanded to be let out. When we stopped the car, they quickly clambered out. As we pulled away, they seemed happy to sit motionless as they waited for the older children with donkeys to arrive so that they could resume their journey the traditional way.

Our return trip to Bamiyan City was difficult and dangerous. Outside of Yakalang, we were joined by an agency Land Cruiser from a clinic three hours west of Deh Sorkh. The Land Cruiser promised a more comfortable ride for Naik, who immediately grabbed the passenger seat in the other vehicle since we would be traveling in a caravan back to Bamiyan City. Naik was replaced in the bench seats behind me by two young Hazara staff members, one of whom was a doctor. Once again, the mud made travel difficult. I watched and provided encouragement at several stops as the male staff members took turns digging out wheels and using winches to pull the vehicles out of the soft mud and snow banks. At one point, I started to wander off the road to find a private place to relieve myself.

"Susan, don't go there!" Naik called to me. "Come back! The drivers say there are land mines there!"

As I turned towards the car, I found that the ground under the snow concealed a sticky mud in which I became mired up to my knees.

"Oh no!" I called to Naik. "I'm not sure I can get back." Now I was trying to extricate myself from the mud and get back to the vehicle without losing control of my bladder. I finally managed to free my stuck feet.

"Good, you're back!" Naik said in obvious relief when I reached the jeep. "We'll find you another, safer place." The faces of the drivers and other male passengers in the two vehicles showed that they were relieved as well. Such incidents caused mild panic among my male traveling companions. Their worst fear, I believe, was that they would have to physically rescue me from some dangerous situation.

Even after twelve hours at the wheel, Hakim managed to keep his focus as he negotiated the narrow, rutted roads after dark. The mud was freezing again, making the last two hours of travel a bit easier. The entire team was exhausted, hungry, and cold when we finally got to our guesthouse in Bamiyan City at 7:30 p.m. for a late dinner. We agreed, however, that the fourteen-hour trip had been successful and worthwhile. Despite his physical discomfort on the trip, Naik was enthusiastic. Late that evening, he copied all of the digital photos from my camera to his laptop so that he could share with his family his first experiences in Bamiyan. For me, the success of the trip went beyond the work we had accomplished. I slept well that night with the conviction that work on development projects in Afghanistan would be my new career. I have never regretted that decision.

Three years later, I traveled to Bamiyan to assess education programs our Japanese partner organization was about to hand over to the U.S. agency for supervision. Abdullah and Halima, both fluent English speakers who managed the Bamiyan programs, traveled with me to the northern portions of the province to observe girls' literacy classes they had organized.

I was surprised to see that most of the literacy teachers were teenage Afghan girls who had been educated in Iran while there as refugees. Although the classes were called "women's literacy classes," most of the students were teenagers—like their instructors—and some were much younger. When I asked Halima why young girls enrolled in the literacy classes were not in regular Ministry of Education schools, she responded, "Their families need them to help herd the sheep and goats and work the fields, Suzanne. They can't let them spend half a day in school, but they can spare the girls for two hours four days a week to come to places near their homes for literacy classes."

Halima's explanation was a sobering reminder of the pervasive poverty of Bamiyan Province, which is now one of the poorest of Afghanistan's thirty-six provinces.

My impression of wide community support for education among Hazaras received a reality check when I met with an assembly of four Parent Teacher and Student Associations (PTSAs) organized by our agency's Norwegian partners. Women and students were well-represented in these groups, I had been told, but there were only two adult women (besides me) and two female students in the group of nearly forty men.

The PTSA discussion turned to early childhood education. A middle-aged *mullah* stood to address me and started questioning why our agency was interested in educating young children "as we know they can't think yet." I asked my Afghan colleague for translation to confirm what I thought the *mullah* had said.

My colleague responded, "Please don't think that I agree with this man, Suzanne, but I will translate. He said that he doesn't know why our agencies should spend time and money educating little children when everyone knows that they cannot think. They are only two years old."

I was shocked and knew that I had to respond to the *mullah*, but I was acutely aware of the need to save face for this important man in the community.

I responded in Dari, looking to the translator for support when I realized that I was lacking some Dari vocabulary to complete my comments.

"Sir, many people have long thought that young children aren't ready for learning," I responded. "However, our ideas of what young children can do have been changing as a result of research on the brains of young children. Through the miracle of computers, we are able to see the brains of infants functioning. We now know with certainty that their brains are active and that they are capable of learning at birth. Since the information from this research is new to many people in the world and may not have reached Afghanistan, I hope that you will use your position to share it with parents in your community."

I held my breath and watched for the *mullah*'s response. He stood up, puffed out his chest, and faced the group, then he nodded toward me

"Thank you for this new information," he said. "And thank you for visiting Bamiyan." Then he scanned the audience, smiled and walked away as they all rose from their chairs out of respect. Later, I discussed the exchange with my Afghan colleague, Mustafa, from the Norwegian organization. He confirmed that I had been in a difficult situation but had not made the *mullah* angry nor had I caused him to lose face in the community.

"He meant it when he thanked you," Mustafa said.

The day before I left Bamiyan on this visit, I was pleased to learn that our hosts had planned a trip to Band-i-Amir—a string of five crystal-blue self-damming lakes located 75 kilometers (47 miles) west of Bamiyan City. The water in the lakes is very cold year round because of the high altitude (2,916 meters, or 9,567 feet) at which they are located. Because of improvements to the road from Bamiyan City up to the lakes, the two-hour trip was much easier than it was when Michael and I went there in 1969, but it was not without difficulties. Our two-car convoy experienced four flat tires during the half-day outing.

The lakes were just as breathtaking as I remembered them, though the commercialism around them is new. Now there are food stands and parking lots around the main lake—the two-mile long Band-i-Haibat (Dam of Awe). Water rivulets streaked with yellow sulfur flow continuously over the side of the forty-foot rock wall that forms the dam of the lake. After picnicking on kebabs in a shelter next to Band-i-Haibat, our group drove to one of the smaller lakes—Band-i-Pudina (The Mint Dam)—where we spread out a carpet and enjoyed the watermelon that we had brought along. Because this is a shallow lake, some male visitors were swimming, even though the water was very cold. Perhaps they were among those who believe that the lakes have healing powers because of the minerals in them.

As I watched the swimmers, I thought of my visit to Band-i-Amir almost forty years before when Michael and I briefly swam in one of the cold, shallow lakes in complete privacy. It was a romantic camping trip for us because few Afghans then visited this isolated site. The only people within our view were a small group of French campers who, like us, were car-camping for the night. As they were up on the bluff, we had the valley to ourselves. The water was so clear that photos we took of each other that day clearly show the colors of our bathing suits, even though we were standing in water up to our necks.

Luckily, we decided not to pitch our two-person tent next to our vehicle that night and slept, instead, on the folded-out back seat of our International Truck. During the night we felt a small earthquake and woke to find the earthquake had caused a significant stream of water to start flowing over the side of "our lake." The hubcaps of our truck were half submerged. Despite the earthquake and the lack of any amenities at the lake, Michael and I were reluctant to leave Band-i-Amir. We had experienced twenty-four hours of total privacy there—one of the attractions of wilderness camping for many young couples. Since Gul Hassan, our gardener Majid, and the street guard seemed ever-present at our little house in Kabul, and hotel employees were constantly knocking at the

Moment of Decision

doors of our room when we traveled, total privacy was a rare luxury for us in Afghanistan. As we drove away from Band-i-Amir that day, I was very happy. I had no idea then that I would be coming back to this amazing place more than three decades later without my wonderful husband.

My 2011 trip to Bamiyan was far more comfortable than all the others. The international agency that asked me to consult on their adult literacy project insisted that the female program director and I stay in the famous Silk Road Hotel. It was the only hotel that met their security standards. Spacious rooms beautifully furnished with traditional Afghan furniture and tiled, modern bathrooms were sheer luxury after my previous stays in spartanly furnished guesthouses with outdoor toilets. I started and ended each day at the Silk Road Hotel gazing out my window at the still-empty niches in the red cliff where the Buddhas had been and knowing that Michael would have shared my sadness over their loss. He would also have expressed satisfaction, though, that the once-barren fields between the hotel and the Buddhas were again being cultivated and were the light green color of plants starting a new growing season.

Chapter 12

The Khyber Pass

The modern reputation for danger in the Khyber Pass stems from Afghans' slaughter of British soldiers and civilians fleeing through the rugged mountains in the northwest frontier that separates Afghanistan and Pakistan. That occurred in the winter of 1842. Only one British soldier lived to tell the story. However, foreign armies feared the fierce Afghan warriors here hundreds of years before colonial Britain occupied the country.

Adventurous travelers to Central Asia remain fascinated by the history and nefarious reputation of this famous route. For that reason, they include it in their itinerary despite the danger and uncertainty of the trip. As you cross the Afghan border with Pakistan at Torkham, you are in the company of smugglers, highway robbers, refugees, truckers, ordinary Afghans and Pakistanis travelling for business and personal reasons, and a handful of foreign travelers.

As Michael negotiated the narrow roads and switchback curves of the Khyber Pass in the Peace Corps' 1968 pickup truck, he shared with me his reflections on the history of the place and regaled me with accounts of battles between the British and the Afghans. I scanned the mountaintops for places where Afghans probably posted lookouts for British troops making their way along the road and imagined how they felt as they marched through the pass realizing that there was no chance of escape. Afghans still celebrate the routing of the British every August 19th, which is Afghan Independence Day. The signs announcing the headquarters of the Khyber Rifles near Torkham are reminders of that period of history.

After Michael reminded me of the possibility of highway robbers, I started checking roads down the sides of the craggy mountain for signs of turbaned bandits riding toward us on their steeds at full gallop. Despite warnings from other travelers who had been victims of these random attacks in this lawless region known as the Northwest Frontier, we felt slightly invincible and lucky.

I was focused more on the weekend ahead than the threat of highway robbers, as Michael and I headed to Pakistan from Jalalabad. We were planning on a weekend of "R and R" in a city with more Western amenities than Kabul could provide. Peshawar offered us the civility of Jan's and Dean's Hotels. In these British colonial establishments, we could expect clean bathrooms, white walls, lacy curtains, comfortable beds, large ceiling fans, and gracious room service that included a menu of British and Pakistani fare and cardamom tea. We were also eager to visit the Air Force base where we could shop at the PX and get a hamburger and beer at the Officers' Club. The knowledge that we would face the threat of robbers on our return trip did not stop us from loading the truck with soft drinks, beer, and other goodies from the PX to carry back through the Khyber Pass into Jalalabad and then through the Tangi Gaur Gorge to Kabul, where we shared our booty with our Peace Corps colleagues.

In the 1960s, intrigue on a different scale was going on within Peshawar itself. On a visit to Peshawar Air Force Base, I entered into conversation with a couple who were my parents' age at the Officers' Club restaurant while Michael was ordering our drinks at the bar. The Soviet Union had shot down an American U-2 spy plane that had been flying missions within their borders, capturing its pilot, Gary Francis Powers, on May 1, 1960. That was big news, so I asked the couple if the fact that the plane had flown from the Peshawar base still caused concerns for those stationed there. The woman looked shocked, and her husband, who was in military uniform, said simply, "We cannot talk about that. It was nice meeting you, Suzanne. I am afraid that we have to be going now." With that, they paid their bill and left.

When Michael returned to the table and found me alone, he asked what happened and I told him.

He shrugged and said, "This base is carrying on a number of sensitive military operations. I am not surprised that they didn't want to talk about the U-2 incident. They are not particularly happy that it made the news."

Lessons of Love in Afghanistan

In 2002, I was eager to make the trip through the Khyber Pass again but security conditions did not allow it. Instead, I would be flying over the pass. As I planned my journey from Kabul to Pakistan, I mused about what might have changed in Peshawar. Were the Jan's and Dean's Hotels still there? (I discovered that shopping malls bearing their names had replaced these gracious establishments.) Would I find, in the shops and Sardar Bazaar, consumer items not available in Kabul? Was the furniture bazaar still there? Was the hotel my agency booked for me anything like places I had stayed with Michael?

From a professional perspective, I was eager to visit the office and project sites of my new employer. As I was now helping design medical training programs and managing a women's hospital training project in Kabul, I wanted to find out from Afghan and Pakistani colleagues at the Peshawar Office what they had learned from providing medical services to thousands of Afghan refugees still in camps along the city's outskirts. I felt that we could replicate some of their systems and practices in clinics and hospitals in Afghanistan.

That trip was successful, and I was able to return to Kabul, by airplane, with constructive information for the programs I served. I made several more trips between Kabul and Peshawar over the next two years, but all of them were by air. By 2004, road security was finally good enough for foreigners to travel through the Khyber Pass.

As I prepared for that trip, I suddenly got cold feet. An agency driver and a guard whom I had just met were driving me to the border in Torkham. At the border, I would transfer to a car from our Pakistan office, with a driver and guard whom I had never met. Knowing that anything could happen on this trip, I badly wanted someone with me whom I knew and trusted. I contacted Walid, who was then working at the UN. I knew that he was making occasional trips to Peshawar to work on his Master's degree at a private university there. I asked if we could travel in the same vehicle across the border. He readily agreed.

At Torkham, the agency driver from Jalalabad let us out of the car and Walid walked with me across the border. The Pakistani driver and guard were waiting for us with a minivan, but first I had to get an entry stamp in my passport. Since Walid is Pashtun, he was able to cross the border at that time without either a passport or a visa. However, he went to the border office with me and told me to sit off to the side with several other women while he took my passport to the desk. I was briefly surprised that the officials allowed him to do this, but then remembered where I was. In many Afghan families, men handle all dealings with strange men while women sit out of view wrapped in ample *chadors* or completely covered in blue *chadris*.

We got in the agency minivan, and I breathed a sigh of relief. Nothing had gone awry. As we passed out of Torkham, however, the van stopped to allow two armed Pakistani soldiers carrying rifles to get into the seat behind me and Walid.

"Why are those soldiers here?" I asked, in alarm.

The driver, guard, and Walid all laughed.

"They are here because you are a very important person," Walid said. "The Pakistani government provides armed guards for all foreigners who travel through this pass. These guards will travel with us to the next checkpoint. Then they will get out and others will get in. The guards will change at three different checkpoints before we get to Peshawar."

I was satisfied with this explanation but was uneasy through the entire trip because men with automatic weapons were directly behind me. Despite my unease, I soon became mesmerized by the rugged terrain, which I remembered from trips through this pass thirty-five years before. The road was just as narrow and the climb through the mountains just as dramatic. Walid broke my reverie when he pointed to a mountain peak.

"Look at that mountain, Susan."

"I see it, Walid, have you been there?"

"Yes. My classmates and I fought against the Russians on that mountain."

"You did?! How old were you?"

"Seventeen."

"Oh! You were in high school! Did anyone in your class get injured or killed?"

"No, we were lucky. None of us got killed." He pointed to the opposite mountain and added, "Many students who fought on the mountain over there were killed."

"That's terrible," I said. "They were so young."

"Yes, they were. But that is what happens in war, Susan."

Lessons of Love in Afghanistan

I was still imagining the battle when Walid pointed out another mountain.

"See that mountain, Susan? That is where my family and I crossed into Pakistan."

"I don't see a road there," I said. "Did you go on foot?"

"Yes, we did. It was very difficult, especially for the old people and the children, but it was the only way to get everyone out. The Pakistanis would not let us cross on the main road through Torkham, as we did today."

"I'm sorry," I said, feeling the inadequacy of that response.

"Thank you, Susan, but that is just life. Sometimes it is hard."

Yes, I thought to myself. It's harder for Afghans than I ever imagined. It seems that everyone in Afghanistan has stories of difficult times. Yet they have survived, and they still manage to be gracious and take care of us foreigners. We have a lot to learn from them.

Walid and his brothers, all of whom were in their teens, had made five trips over the mountains on foot to bring the rest of their family members over the border. After hearing Walid's stories, my previous trips through the Khyber Pass seemed frivolous in the face of the journeys that he had made. I decided not to describe those trips to him.

Over the next two years, I travelled to Peshawar several times with my Afghan colleagues from our agency's Jalalabad office. A number of them had families living in Peshawar, so we travelled there for the weekend on Thursday afternoons. Because I was in the van, we had to add armed Pakistani guards to our entourage after we crossed the border. My colleagues never complained about the inconvenience of multiple stops to change guards, even though it added extra time to our journey. I never got comfortable with the idea of armed men whom I could not even talk to, as I don't speak Urdu, sitting directly behind me.

In Peshawar, I visited several refugee camps where Afghans have lived for decades. They had moved from tents to mud houses and had developed small bazaars where the residents could buy basic goods. The clinics our agency had developed in those camps were impressive for their organization and quality of care. I was particularly impressed by records on pregnant women and the system that made certain each woman had a Community Health Worker or midwife accompany her on prenatal

The Khyber Pass

clinic visits. A female doctor reminded me that all of these systems were possible because the camps are self-contained communities.

I also visited a wide range of hospitals in the city. All had well-developed systems compared to Afghan hospitals. However, there was a striking difference among facilities. Women who could afford the high-end maternity hospital got private rooms, elective laparoscopies, and clean sheets. In isolation delivery rooms—where women with infectious diseases delivered their babies—sheets were burned after being used. In contrast, the large public hospital that treated Afghan refugees didn't even have a separate unit for women with infectious diseases.

During my visits to Peshawar, my agency usually booked me into the Celebrity Guesthouse or the Rivoli Guesthouse. The Celebrity featured cheap copies of Rococo furniture with gold paint detailing. The lacy curtains and ceiling fans, however, reminded me of Jan's and Dean's. The Rivoli had a completely different look. The staff liked to book me into what they described as "the honeymoon room." Everything in the room was green—including the oversized bed with fake gold leaf decor on the headboard, the matching love seat, and the emerald green triangular bathtub. On my first night there, I learned why honeymooners rarely (if ever) booked this room. The loudspeaker from the mosque on the other side of the hotel driveway broadcast the call to prayer into my room at 4:30 a.m. The sound was so loud that it seemed like the *muezzin* was next to my bed yelling into my ear. Despite my protests, the Rivoli staff booked me into that room for two more visits. I survived by putting in earplugs before I went to sleep.

Three years of occasional weekend road trips to Peshawar following field visits to Jalalabad came to an end in 2006. Pakistani officials at the border seemed to inspect my passport more carefully as I entered and exited the country. On one occasion, the agency security officer and I had to go to the Ministry of Interior Office in Peshawar before leaving the country, in order to get a letter of permission—with my photo attached—which allowed me to travel in the agency car through the Northwest Frontier back to Afghanistan. On another occasion, I was detained in the passport control office by an official who insisted that I did not have the proper entry stamp and that I had, therefore, been in the country illegally. Finally, a Pakistani colleague from our agency's Peshawar Office intervened and persuaded the official to stamp my passport so that I could exit the country. Once outside the office, I showed my colleague the entry stamp that the official said was missing.

"Suzanne, he saw it too. He just tried to frighten you so that you would give him a bribe."

I subsequently learned that my border experiences were minor compared to those of other colleagues. My friend Peter recalled being stopped at the border as he was fleeing Afghanistan during the Taliban era because his Pakistani visa had expired.

"They wanted to send me back to the Taliban!" he exclaimed. "I just kept walking and hoped they wouldn't shoot me in the back."

Another colleague, a Pakistani who worked in Jalalabad and had been making weekend visits to his family in Peshawar for over a year, was suddenly detained at the border in our agency vehicle as he was returning to Afghanistan. He was accused of being a spy. Although our agency was able to negotiate for his quick release, it took two weeks to get our vehicle back. After this incident, strong restrictions were established on all staff regarding overland travel to Peshawar. Expatriates from Europe, Australia, and North America were no longer allowed to make the road trip and could only enter Pakistan by air.

In the years since then, foreigners, high-ranking Afghan and Pakistani officials, and lesser-known Afghans driving their private vehicles have been kidnapped as they travelled between Peshawar and Jalalabad. Some have been held for ransom for several weeks. A few have been killed. The Khyber Pass is, once again, a very dangerous place. A few miles north of the pass another war is being fought. In an attempt to keep insurgents from re-entering Afghanistan, NATO troops are fighting them in the Northwest Frontier both on the ground and in the air.

Until 2008, many international humanitarian workers in Afghanistan were required to have valid Pakistani visas in the event of the need to evacuate from Afghanistan if armed conflict escalated. Following the increased number of criminal incidents in the Khyber Pass, the war in the Northwest Frontier, and the explosions targeted at places where foreigners gather in Islamabad and Peshawar, international agencies in Kabul finally realized what many of us had been thinking: Evacuating from Afghanistan through Peshawar would be like jumping from the frying pan into the fire.

The Khyber Pass

Chapter 13

Shiberghan

In 1968, Michael and I made two trips to the northern provinces. Rather than ending our second trip in Mazar and returning to Kabul, we were asked to continue west to Shiberghan and assess that city as a possible new site for Volunteers. The sixty-mile trip in late February took us seven hours, because the unpaved road was like a washboard. Thick dust sifting through the windows of the jeep turned our hair nearly white. We looked like a couple in their sixties instead of young newlyweds.

"How much longer before we get there?" I asked Michael as we jolted along.

"I think we're almost there. Look, I think we're coming into the city now."

This provincial capital "city" looked like a small town. The caravan *sarai* at the entry to the city was vacant, though we learned that it was full of camel caravans on market day. There were only a few streets, and they were lined with cheaply constructed shops and bazaar stands. The Shiberghan Hotel was not hard to locate, as it was the only visible hotel in the city center. We were grateful to be able to wash off the dust and change clothes before our dinner at the mayor's house.

The mayor greeted us warmly, even though we arrived later than he expected, and escorted us into his modest home. The rest of his family was waiting for us to join them for a simple meal that was served in traditional Afghan fashion, to which I was becoming accustomed—on a plastic tablecloth on the floor. We sat around the cloth on *toshaks* and used pieces of bread to pick up our food using our right hands, as left hands are considered unclean in this part of the world. After two months of practice, I was gaining confidence in my ability to eat Afghan food in this manner. However, the greasy fried eggs were a real challenge.

The meal seemed more rushed than I'd become accustomed to. Rather than the usual break between the meal and the serving of tea, our plates were whisked away as soon as we finished our main course and the tea and fruit appeared immediately. The mayor announced that we were to be his guests at the Shiberghan Cinema, where an Indian film was showing soon. Moments later, we were escorted to the mayor's car and were driven with his family to the cinema. There we were joined by the family of the chief physician of Shiberghan Hospital.

As we entered the theater, we were escorted to balcony seats. All of us were dressed in Western-style clothing and none of the women were veiled, so our arrival caused quite a stir. We quickly realized that the balcony seats were the only seats in the theatre. The patrons—all men—on the main floor sat on mats and small carpets. As I looked down at the scene below, I thought, "This was what an Elizabethan theater looked like when Shakespeare's plays were being performed." The groundlings were below us, and we were seated in the location that elite members of society used in Elizabethan times.

The Hindi movie (which was three hours long) seemed to go on forever, but the Afghan audience was engaged throughout. Just as it was near conclusion, uniformed soldiers came into the balcony area and whispered into the mayor's ear. He shook his head in agreement and turned to Michael.

"Mr. Sharifi is in town," he told Michael in Dari. "He has been trying to get in touch with you and wants you to come and see him. My driver will take you."

Hassan Sharifi, who was of Uzbek ethnicity, was the president of the Afghan Gas Company. He was in Shiberghan to check on the progress of the gas line that was being built to carry natural gas from Shiberghan to the Soviet Union. Hassan had attended the University of Texas and made a point of befriending the few Americans who came through the northern provinces.

As Michael was engaged in leave-taking comments to the mayor in Dari, he didn't have time to explain to me why we were being led by the soldiers from the theater to the car. As we drove out of the city into pitch darkness, I became concerned. Michael was sitting in the front seat with the driver and I was alone in the back seat.

"Do you know where we're going, Michael? I asked with some anxiety.

Michael turned around and tried to give me reassurance, but in the pitch black, I couldn't read his face. "We're going to see Sharifi. He's in town. The driver appears to know the way to where he is staying. I can't ask him, because I don't speak Uzbek and he doesn't speak Dari or Farsi. I've tried a little bit of Turkish, but he doesn't know that language either." Michael sighed and I could tell he was uncomfortable.

"I don't like this," I said. "We don't know these people and we don't have any idea where we're going."

Suddenly we saw the lights of a compound. As we got closer, we realized it was the Russian Compound.

"Oh no! I said in a loud whisper. "We're not supposed to go in here, Michael! We are going to be in big trouble with the U.S. Embassy!"

As we approached the gate, Michael turned around again. The floodlights shown on our car and I could see that Michael's eyes were dark and worried. "I know, but we really have no choice. We'll have to trust them and see what happens."

The Russian guards seemed to know the driver and waved us through the gate after asking him some questions. We hoped that the driver had not revealed that we were Americans. We drove through and stopped in front of a small dwelling that resembled a unit in military barracks. As we stopped, the screen door flew open and Hassan Sharifi, whose stature was closer to mine than Michael's, came bounding out.

"Michael! Suzanne! Welcome to Shiberghan!" he shouted enthusiastically. "I was going to see you tomorrow, because I wanted to have you travel with me back to Mazar on a different route than you took to get here. But then three of us here started talking about our college days in the U.S. and our evenings of playing bridge there. We wanted to play a game tonight, but we needed a fourth player. I remembered that Suzanne said she'd played bridge in college so I sent my guys to get you."

Michael and I laughed both out of relief and out of affection for this man who constantly surprised us with his spontaneous plans.

"Only an avid bridge player could understand why someone would go to these lengths to find a fourth for bridge," I thought. I was hoping the U.S. Embassy would not find out we'd come here. Russia was regarded as our enemy, and Embassy personnel were very concerned about the

Shiberghan

communist cells forming among Afghans who lived in northern cities. I was concerned that the Embassy would consider us communist sympathizers because of our visit to this compound. I wondered how Michael would explain this evening in the Russian Compound to the Peace Corps Director and the American ambassador.

A decade later, it turned out that the American Embassy had good reason to mistrust the motives of Russians in Afghanistan. This compound housed Russian military officers who led the Russian invasion of Afghanistan in 1979. In that year, Russian soldiers began a war that ultimately involved 100,000 Russian soldiers who killed tens of thousands of Afghans. By the time the Russians retreated a decade later, more than 14% of the occupying soldiers had died.

I had barely settled into my chair when the portly head of the Afghan bank started dealing the cards. To his right was the head of the Afghan cotton company, who was, like his two companions, in his forties. We played bridge for several hours while Michael alternately watched Russian volleyball games on a black and white television that hung on the wall above our bridge table and joined our conversation as we played. Sharifi's pleasure in having our company and introducing us to his important Afghan colleagues offset, for a while at least, our concern about the grilling we might get from the Embassy when we returned to Kabul.

After we completed our site review in Shiberghan the next day, Mr. Sharifi had another surprise for us. He wanted to take us back to Mazar along the pipeline because it ran through a favorite bird hunting area. The private road was also a shortcut that saved three hours on the return trip to Mazar.

"We can shoot some marsh birds and take them to my house in Mazar, where my wife will cook them for lunch," Sharifi announced enthusiastically. He had us meet him at the site where the Russians were laying the pipeline. The driver of the large Russian pipe-laying machinery nearly fell out of the cab when Sharifi led me right up to the side of his rig and gave me an animated explanation of the process in English, while Sharifi's colleague was giving Michael an explanation in Dari. I am sure that the last people the Russian workers expected to see at the site were two Americans.

After we visited the pipeline, we started driving east toward Mazar through the Amu Darya. Once we got to the bird hunting area, Sharifi pulled out two 12-gauge shotguns and handed one to Michael and one to me. I blanched, because I had never held a gun in my life. Since many young women whom Sharifi met at the University of Texas were experienced gun users, he assumed that all American women knew how to use guns.

"Suzanne has never used a gun, Sharifi," Michael said.

"Oh, I didn't know that. In that case, I'll show her how," Sharifi said.

Since I weighed just over 100 pounds and did not have a lot of arm muscle, the rifle felt heavy as I hoisted it and tried to hold it steady. The first time I fired, I almost fell backwards because the butt of the rifle kicked into my stomach. I wasn't a good match for the force of the kick. Sharifi and Michael were kind enough not to laugh and showed me how to adjust my stance to gain more stability while I held the rifle and fired.

Having survived the target practice, I felt prepared to do some shooting but not from a moving vehicle, which was the method for these Afghan men. Sharifi sent a staff member out onto a plain where flocks of birds had gathered. He threw a small rock into the center of the flock, which caused a large number of them to take flight. While he did that, the drivers positioned our jeeps on the edge of the flock. When the birds suddenly took flight, we pointed our guns into the flock and fired. There were so many birds that we were bound to hit a few. Since I was sitting in the seat behind Michael, I was more concerned about accidentally shooting him or the driver than I was about shooting the birds. I was relieved when the hunt was over.

Once our catch—sixteen small grey marsh birds—had been collected into bags, Sharifi got into his jeep and led a caravan back to his house, where his wife had a delicious lunch waiting for us. She had thoughtfully cooked birds that had been shot on a previous hunting trip so that we wouldn't have to wait to eat while she cleaned and cooked our fresh kills.

Michael described the hunting expedition in an aerogram to my parents. In his characteristic way of reporting events, he focused on the positive aspects of the day, including his observations on my target practice.

Shiberghan

Dear Mom and Dad,

…. Wish I'd had a movie camera. We were going cross-country on a huge plot of nationally protected land—all oil and gas fields. The game is plentiful—grouse, pigeons and birds not found in America, plus fox, gazelle, deer, wolves and lots of prairie dogs. Our friend Sharifi brought along a couple of 12-gauge shotguns for us and we stopped in the middle of nowhere.

For Suzanne, he set one rock the size of your fist on another and told her to shoot it off. She did with the first shot at 30 yards, which doesn't make her Annie Oakley, but it's not a bad start. I surprised myself by shredding an old partridge box with one shot skeet-fashion. The gun bearer risked his life nobly by getting out in front of me to heave it up in the air.

Soon after, we came upon a flock of small, thrush-like birds. With Suzanne and I at the guns, we gave them a broadside from the jeep and got about ten in the first volley of three shots. (Suzanne was so surprised she couldn't find the trigger for her second round.) Another time we got about six more and then called it quits.

It was a great time for both of us and Suzanne took to the new sport like she'd been hiding a long ranching-hunting background from me. It was really a thrill.

I visited the Russian Compound for the second time in August 2006, a few days after I arrived in Shiberghan as Senior Program Manager for Education for an INGO. Sharifi and the trip that Michael and I took to Shiberghan were on my mind as the agency car drove my new colleague, Lynn, and me to the abandoned compound on the edge of town. Fields immediately adjacent to the compound sat neglected and weeds grew high around the building where I had played bridge.

"This is a favorite picnic spot for Shiberghan families," Lynn said. "They find a little privacy among the buildings and some shade from the sun."

"Had anyone told me that this compound would become a weekend picnic spot for Afghan families, I would have thought they'd lost their minds," I said. I watched in amazement as families made themselves at home in the compound which, to me, represented the beginning of a very dark time in Afghan history.

Lessons of Love in Afghanistan

I would have been equally incredulous if, in 1968, someone had predicted that Shiberghan would become my base of operation for two years while I supervised a demonstration teacher training project for 625 schools in the provinces of Jawzjan and Sar-i-Pul.

We arrived in the compound that included our INGO's offices and living quarters. Lynn had been living there alone for a year and seemed pleased to have another American woman join her.

"We just completed renovating your unit," Lynn said. "Lucky you! You'll have a Western toilet!"

"Thank you," I said, in a matter of fact manner. I did not yet realize how unusual it was to have a Western toilet in this part of Afghanistan.

As Lynn talked, I noticed the sparseness of my living space and how few amenities I would have. My shower room was just that—a room with a small window, a wood-fired water heater and two buckets. The shower-head in the wall worked some of the time.

The "marvelous Western toilet" and a small sink were in a separate, unheated room painted periwinkle blue and located on the opposite end of the unit from the shower room. The door to the toilet room had an old-fashioned hook and eye lock. Between these two convenience facili-ties were two adjoining parallel rooms.

My bedroom was furnished with a double bed covered with green mosquito netting—the mosquitoes would be active for at least another month—a chest of drawers and an office desk and chair. The living/dining room had *toshaks* covered with red corduroy on the floor, a low table, a television set on a portable stand, and a small refrigerator. There was a space for a wood-burning stove near the door to my bedroom. Both rooms were painted "creamy," which seems to be Afghans' favorite color for home and office interiors—followed closely by baby blue, light green, and pink.

The living room windows were adorned with heavy red corduroy drapes tied back with gold ropes affixed to plastic golden hooks. Floral-patterned white sheers also covered the windows.

"The sheers allow light to come in during the day, and the heavy corduroy keeps out the cold and gives you privacy at night," explained Tamim, the logistics manager, who was beaming with pride at my appre-ciation of his decorating job.

Shiberghan

While doing my best to recognize Tamim's efforts, I was trying figure out how I could offset the dominance of red in the room and make this space more comfortable. This was to be "home" for two years!

Shiberghan offered none of the expensive restaurants for foreigners or weekend parties that filled many INGO workers' non-working hours in Kabul. However, I learned on my first day in the Shiberghan office that hours of leisure would be few. Lynn and I were the two international staff members in a regional office of twenty Afghan staff members that supported program activities in the northern provinces and supervised two other provincial offices.

Since our offices were a five-minute walk through the compound from our living quarters, Lynn and I routinely worked from 8:00 a.m. to 7:30 p.m., six days a week, with a half-hour break for lunch and a late dinner. Field visits to program sites and meetings with staff members in Shiberghan, Sar-i-Pul, and Andkhoy fully occupied us between 8:00 a.m. and 4:30 p.m. When the Afghan staff left, we spent several hours responding to queries and tasks assigned by the Country Office in Kabul, from our respective project partners in Health (Lynn) and Education (me) and occasional requests from our headquarters office in the United States. Because of the nine-hour time difference between Afghanistan and the Eastern United States, the e-mail from headquarters started arriving at dinner time in Shiberghan.

After our dinner, which was prepared by the office cook in the late afternoon and left for us to reheat in our kitchen, which was adjacent to Lynn's room, we either returned to our offices to continue answering e-mail or carried our laptops to our respective rooms to respond to messages from family and friends and participate in Skype calls. We needed to retire before 11:00 p.m., as staff would start arriving in the office side of the compound before 7:30 a.m. the next morning. We worked Saturday through Thursday at noon. Our only day to sleep late and have time to ourselves was Friday, the Islamic world's day of rest and worship. On Fridays, the only Afghan staff members in the compound were the guards at the gate.

During the months that road travel was possible, Lynn and I were nearly inundated with visitors. When the snow started falling, we had no visitors for weeks.

Lessons of Love in Afghanistan

Visits from our Kabul Office colleagues were a mixed blessing. We were very glad to be able to discuss big issues with them in person, rather than exchanging strings of e-mails or trying to overcome bad connections and abrupt cuts in service involved in having a lengthy conversation by mobile phone. We were also glad for social conversations over dinner. On the other hand, our colleagues often arrived with a packed schedule of activities that taxed the logistics of the office and required Lynn and me to rearrange our schedules to support them.

Virtually all of the international and Afghan program staff who came from Kabul also visited our office in Sar-i-Pul Province. Our INGO had established nutrition programs for children and PTSAs in the schools there. The program office in Sar-i-Pul City had no Western amenities. The Eastern toilets were outdoors and meals were cooked in a traditional Afghan kitchen that was separate from the office building. We ate our meals sitting on *toshaks* on the floor, arranged around an oilcloth "table." After meals, the dishes and cloth were removed and the dining space resumed its function as a meeting room.

Supervision of teacher training for over 7,000 teachers who taught in 625 schools meant that I spent a lot of time on the road. I was usually the only foreigner traveling with male Afghan provincial managers (only one of whom spoke some English) and several male trainers who only spoke Dari or Tajik. Nearly all the female trainers worked in provincial capitals, so I was usually the only woman on long distance trips between cities. These trips facilitated the development of my Dari, because there was often no one available to translate.

Since the provincial capital of Sar-i-Pul Province was nearly eight hours' road travel time from the eastern border of that province, I had to establish a satellite office for the project in Tukzar, which was a 4½ hour drive on unpaved roads going east from Sar-i-Pul City if the weather cooperated. On days that it rained or snowed, the trip took much longer.

We rented a newly constructed house across from the main mosque in Tukzar and converted it into an office space and sleeping rooms for the trainers. Construction of the kitchen portion of the house was incomplete when we rented it: the owner's cows were sheltered in the space next to the outdoor kitchen until the kitchen was finally enclosed and renovated. An average of seventeen male trainers slept in one wing of the house. The only female trainer—a mother of nine—and I occupied

Shiberghan

a tiny room with an attached shower room in the middle of the house, next to the project office.

When I travelled to Tukzar to observe the progress of teacher training, I was expected to stop first at the District Governor's office, which was opposite one of the schools where we conducted the training. On one trip into town, I was running late and went directly to the school with the intention of visiting the governor later. However, the governor's head guard—a seven-foot tall man who wore a bandolier of bullets across his chest and carried a large rifle—had seen me arrive. One of the governor's staff arrived at the classroom door with the message that I was supposed to report to the governor immediately.

"Why didn't you stop in my office when you arrived?" the governor asked sternly in Tajik.

My provincial manager translated the words, but the displeasure in the governor's body language needed no translation.

"I'm sorry, Governor," I answered. "I was late because we had a flat tire and I needed to see the class before it ended."

"Well, you need to know that security here is not good right now," he remarked, "but my guards will protect you."

I was about to ask, "Protect me from what?" when I remembered that I'd seen four times as many money changers in the bazaar that morning as I had seen in my last visit. I had wondered what had prompted this increase.

"You understand, don't you, that the opium from Helmand travels through this town after the harvest?" the governor continued.

That explained all the money changers: we were surrounded by drug dealers!

"Thank you, Governor, I didn't realize that before I planned this trip," I said. "I am only here overnight and will leave tomorrow."

"Good!" the governor said. "Thank you for helping make our schools better."

I took my leave and returned to the school to continue my observations. We had discovered that the female primary grade teachers were illiterate and could not read the training materials in their language. I was too busy observing and advising trainers to spend time worrying about drug dealers.

Lessons of Love in Afghanistan

The return trip from Tukzar to Sar-i-Pul City was difficult because of bad roads, but I had been prepared for trips like this by all the trips Michael and I made across the Amu Darya, where there was no road at all along many parts of the route. The rewards for enduring those trip were scenes of the agricultural life at the heart of the Afghan economy.

As we made a sharp turn in the road descending from the hills, we would come upon women arranging harvested grapes on mats on the sides of low-lying hills. The grapes lay in beautiful patterns of green, red, yellow, and purple. They would dry to form the most delicious raisins I have ever eaten.

Scrambling down a hill on the other side of the road, we'd see herds of sheep of multiple varieties being guided down to green pastures by boys and girls whose seriousness of purpose was remarkable for their young ages.

On the flat stretches between Sar-i-Pul City and Shiberghan, our eyes feasted on vast fields of wild red tulips *(lalah)* in lush green fields (sometimes offset by tiny bright-yellow star-shaped flowers) that would appear in early spring after the rains. We would sometimes stop to pick some *lalah* and take pictures of each other in this setting, which could be the pastoral backdrop of a romantic movie scene.

I frequently wanted to stop and photograph scenes of baby animals grazing with their mothers in the same fields during spring: ewes with their lambs, goats with their kids, mares with their foals (both horses and donkeys), cows with their calves, and mother camels with their long-legged babies whose curly haired bodies remind me of teddy bears. Whenever I saw these grazing animals, I had flashbacks of childhood visits to my paternal grandparents' farm.

In Shiberghan, I learned that one's appreciation of springtime's warm breezes and lush green fields sharpens after enduring months of bitter cold. Although I had experienced long months of snow and cold during the five years that I lived and went to school in Indiana, snowplows cleared the streets and I could expect to study in warm classrooms and live in a warm house.

Shiberghan has neither snowplows nor centrally heated buildings. After a night of heavy snowfall, the guards would dig through the drifts

Shiberghan

that had formed right up to the edge of my porch and make pathways for me to get to the office and the kitchen. Ski underwear was my second skin for four months. The heaters and stoves in our offices were only able to heat the areas immediately around them, and I made frequent trips outside throughout the day to go to offices across the compound. I wore four layers of clothing to ward off the cold when going offsite to visit school buildings or meet with public officials. The sawdust stove in my living space could only keep two rooms warm. When the two extra sawdust cores that the office guards left next to my front door ran out in the middle of the night, I put on my coat and boots and retrieved additional cores from the storage space across from my unit rather than brave the cold and icy path to the guardhouse gate for help.

Monthly trips to and from Kabul in winter were sometimes as hair-raising as my first January trip through the Salang with Michael. We still experienced whiteouts, and the roads were even more dangerous because of heavy traffic both directions through the 12,000-foot pass. Huge snowplows struggled to keep the pass clear to prevent thousands being stranded on the road. Despite their efforts, hundreds of travelers die in accidents on the Salang Pass road every winter. There are still no guard-rails to prevent a vehicle from pitching over the side of the mountain on the approach to or exit from the long tunnel through the mountain.

Chapter 14

Addiction to Afghan Carpets

Collectors of carpets from Central Asia know that some of the best are made in northern Afghanistan. The sheep raised in that area grow thick, strong wool to protect their bodies from the extremely cold weather. During my time in Shiberghan, I was able to observe the first part of the carpet production process: the shearing of the sheep in the spring, the transport of the wool in bags on the backs of camels to the carpet makers, and the sorting and carding of the wool.

Two Turkoman brothers who own Shiberghan's best carpet store arranged for Lynn and me to spend an afternoon observing the rest of the process in their compound. They left the store under the supervision of a male relative and directed our driver out to their huge family compound in the country. Several families had dwellings inside the compound and all the buildings involved in carpet production were contained inside the compound walls.

"I've seen rug weaving demonstrations for tourists in the bazaar, but I've never seen the whole process. Have you, Lynn?" I asked in wonderment at the concurrent carpet-making processes underway.

"No, I've been asking to see where they made their rugs for a while because I've bought so many from them. I think this is their going away present to me."

"It's an appropriate gift, Lynn. That whole trunk of carpets is proof of how much business you gave them. They're really going to miss you ... and so am I," I added wistfully as I pictured the empty rooms that would be across the courtyard from mine in a few days.

Since neither Lynn nor I spoke the family's language—Turkoman— the brother who spoke English explained all the processes as he guided us through the steps from one side of the compound to the other. Since he knew that we were most interested in seeing the women doing the weaving, he took us first to the huge weaving room, which was in a mud building of its own. Open doorways opposite each other at the front and back of the building and windows on either side provided ventilation for about ten women who were working there. They were weaving two carpets on large side-by-side looms. The work had a measured but continuous pace. We saw the paper "cartoons" (designs or patterns) for the rugs that they were weaving and learned which women in each team were responsible for ensuring that the patterns were accurately followed.

After observing, asking questions, and talking to the women for a half hour, Naeem took us to another part of the compound where we followed the processes that led up to the weaving of the carpets. First we saw some of the sheep that they were raising. Then Naeem showed us a bag of freshly sheared wool. We moved on to the place where the dyes were being made—ground lapis for the famous lapis blue, ground roots of vegetables for the browns, pomegranate seeds for the reds, and saffron for bright yellow. Those brilliant colors were boiled in large pots that were embedded in a cement platform. Using wooden spatulas the size of six-foot shovels, two tall Turkoman men with strong arms dipped and stirred shopping bag sized bundles of yarn in the pots of color.

"Look at those colors, Suzanne, aren't they brilliant?" Lynn asked.

"Yes, I like lapis blue the best. I can't believe they are grinding up those beautiful lapis lazuli stones that could be turned into lovely earrings, necklaces, rings or even bowls!" I imagined how the jewelers on Chicken Street in Kabul would feel if they saw these precious stones being ground up.

On the way back to the compound, Lynn and I talked about what we had seen. We were thrilled to have witnessed the processes that created the carpets that we had been admiring, inspecting, and purchasing for years.

When I was alone in my room that night, I reflected on how I had come to be so taken with Afghan carpets. It started with Michael's Iranian carpet—a 3' x 4' red Mauri Turkoman. It was one of his possessions from Iran in the trunk that made it back to America. Another trunk, which contained his clothing and personal belongings, never arrived. I was fascinated by this small red carpet and found the color and pattern a welcome relief from the bland, earth tone wall-to-wall carpeting that I had grown up with.

Lessons of Love in Afghanistan

When Michael and I saw the beautiful Afghan carpets in Kabul and Mazar, we knew that we needed to take one back to the United States for our first home there. We spent a long time looking for a good quality room-sized carpet that we could afford. I enjoyed climbing onto the ten-foot stacks of carpets that filled nearly all the space in modest shops in the bazaar and peeling carpets one at a time until we saw one that interested us. If we showed interest in actually buying a particular carpet (or if we were regular customers), the shopkeeper would call for tea and we'd sit and have a friendly conversation with him before closing the deal. Topics ranged from the weather and politics to his family concerns, depending on how well we knew the shopkeeper. After that break, we'd return to the discussion of the carpet and arrive at a price. Initially, the dealer would name a price that was much higher than he expected to get. Our job was to start the bargaining at about half that amount. He would lower the price and we would raise our amount until we struck a deal.

Over time, we settled on the kind of carpet we wanted for our first house in the United States—a room-sized Daulatab carpet with the *Fil Poy* (elephant foot) design from Balkh Province—but we could not afford it. One day, an eighth-grade Afghan boy in my English class heard me mention that we were searching for a carpet.

"Mrs. Griffin, why don't you come to my father's store in Shar-i-Nau?" Abdullah asked, looking mildly offended. "You know that one reason I am learning English is to help my father with the English-speaking customers."

"Abdullah, we know that your father has a very nice shop, but the carpets in his shop are expensive. My husband and I are in the Peace Corps and we have just finished our studies, so we don't have much money."

"No problem," Abdullah, said. "We will take care of you. Please tell me what kind of carpet you want."

"We want a ten-meter red and black wool *Fil Poy* design from Daulatabad in Balkh Province, but I'm sure it's very expensive if your father's shop has it," I replied.

Abdullah beamed and replied, "We can get it. I will tell my father. Come to our shop on Saturday. I want my father to meet my teacher."

Michael and I visited the shop on Saturday. Before we entered the shop, we agreed that we could not afford to pay more than $300.

Addiction to Afghan Carpets

Abdullah greeted us at the shop door with a huge smile. "We found your rug!" he said triumphantly. "There were only two like you described and a German wanted both of them, but we convinced him to only buy one and saved this one for you."

As he spoke, he guided us into the spacious shop and over to a beautiful deep-red wool carpet with the *Fil Poy* design. As we sat on the floor to feel the warp and weft of the carpet, we exchanged glances that said, *"Yes he found it, but we can't afford it."*

"You listened carefully to my description, Abdullah," I said. "Yes, you found a beautiful carpet."

Abdullah's father finished business with another customer and joined us just as tea was brought to us on a tray.

"Father, this is Mr. Michael Griffin and my teacher Mrs. Griffin," Abdullah announced. He followed the Afghan tradition of saying my husband's name first and adding my title of teacher *(Ustaad)*, which is a term of respect.

"I am pleased to meet you, Mr. and Mrs. Griffin," Abdullah's father said in Dari, as he placed his hand across his heart and bowed slightly.

After exchanging additional pleasantries and sipping tea, we got to the business of the rug.

Michael started by asking, "How much is this carpet?"

Abdullah's father countered with a vague statement, "A very reasonable price for this quality carpet."

"No doubt it is a good quality carpet," Michael responded, "but I am not sure that we can afford the price."

"How much do you want to pay, Teacher?" Abdullah asked me.

"I am afraid that all we can afford is $300," I said.

Abdullah translated my statement to his father and they had an animated conversation that Michael quietly translated for me.

"The father told Abdullah that $300 was what he paid for the carpet. This carpet was one of a pair made that year in Daulatabad and he sold the other one to a German man for twice the price that we are able to pay. He added that they would make no profit," Michael said.

Michael then translated the conversation that was going on between Abdullah and his father: Abdullah pleaded on our behalf, "Father, she is my teacher. Because she taught me English, I can help you sell carpets to many foreigners." The father reluctantly agreed. Then, Michael broke into a smile and whispered, "They're going to sell it at our price!"

"Okay, Mr. Griffin. The carpet is yours for $300, a very special price for you because your wife is my teacher," Abdullah said in clear English. "My father asks that you please tell other foreigners about our shop. But don't tell them about this special price, because we can't offer it to others."

"I understand, Abdullah. We are most grateful to you and your father for finding this carpet for us and for giving us a special price," Michael said, as he turned toward the father, bowed his head slightly, and placed his right hand on his heart in a gesture of thanks. "We will definitely tell other foreigners about your shop!"

Abdullah was delighted. As Michael paid his father and a worker wrapped up the carpet for us, Abdullah said, "See Teacher, I told you we'd take care of you!"

"You did, Abdullah. Thank you and special thanks to your father," I said as I also gave a slight bow and placed my right hand on my heart.

Abdullah continued to beam at us as we walked out the door.

We took the carpet home and immediately rolled it out on the living room floor. We were thrilled to own a carpet that we had never thought we could afford. In the course of our married life, we bought other carpets, but the *Fil Poy* was always the one on our living room floor. We have spent many happy hours sitting around that carpet. Our daughters learned to crawl on it and grew up wanting carpets of their own.

I was unable to find Abdullah's father's store when I returned to Afghanistan in 2002, but thanks to my return to Afghanistan, and my discovery of Rauf's Carpet Shop in Kabul, the floors of my daughters' homes are also covered with beautiful Afghan carpets.

When in Kabul, I make bimonthly visits to the carpet shop of my friend Rauf, a tall, brown-haired, solidly built native of Herat. Unlike many Afghan men who look at least a decade older than their age, Rauf looks younger than his fifty-six years. His handsome face with light olive skin and ruddy cheeks has aged well. His brown eyes light up with a twinkle when he sees friends enter the shop, and he greets them with a sincere smile and a firm, warm handshake.

Addiction to Afghan Carpets

I became a customer of "Rauf Carpets" in 2002 on the first weekend after I returned to Afghanistan. I had brought cash with me from the United States to buy carpets for myself and my daughters. The day after my arrival, I was alarmed to hear that serious government upheaval was predicted by our security officer and that we might be evacuated from Afghanistan within days. *If I have to evacuate,* I thought, *I at least want to leave with some carpets!*

Most of the clothes that I had with me could easily be stuffed into the "run pack" recommended in the agency orientation manual for a quick evacuation if needed, so I had room in my luggage to carry rugs. Not fully comprehending that you cannot take major amounts of luggage in an emergency evacuation, I envisioned myself taking my suitcase full of carpets on the evacuation flight, as I had done when I evacuated from Isfahan with my daughters.

Linda, the area finance officer for our INGO, had visited Kabul before and bought carpets from Rauf's shop. She wanted some more carpets to take back to Australia to sell to her friends. I was already primed for a carpet-buying expedition when she invited me to join her on a visit to Rauf Carpets.

Rauf had owned his small shop on Chicken Street for twenty years when I met him. It consisted of two rooms. The first room was full of mediocre carpets that were sold to novice buyers and tourists who simply wanted a souvenir carpet at a cheap price. The doorway to the second room, which was reserved for serious and knowledgeable buyers, was so low that I had to stoop to go through it. When I straightened up, I was delighted to see the colors, textures, and smells of the quality carpets piled to the ceiling against three walls of the room. I was thrilled to once again be able to get down on the floor to examine carpets as I had done so many times with Michael in the bazaars of Afghanistan and Iran. I love the process of determining the age of the carpet by feeling the softness and flexibility, establishing tightness of the weave by running my hand over the back of the carpet, tracing the intricate designs on the carpet with my fingers, counting the borders, walking around the perimeter of the carpet to evaluate the mellowness of the colors in different lights, and examining the design to determine which area of Afghanistan the carpet comes from.

Between my use of Dari and my approach to examining the carpets, Rauf figured out that I had been in Afghanistan before. In breaks in our conversation that related to the purchasing of the carpets, we exchanged enough information to know that this conversation would not be our last. I left his shop that day enthusiastic about the two carpets that I had bought and pleased that I had a new Afghan acquaintance who might become a friend.

As Linda and I walked into the guesthouse with our rugs, we were met by John, our security officer, who was wearing a very stern face.

"Where were you, Suzanne?! We have been looking all over for you and calling you on your radio! Don't you have it with you?"

"Yes, I do. But I had it off."

"You're not supposed to have it off. Why did you turn it off?" John asked impatiently.

"Because we were bargaining in the rug shop and it made too much noise," I said.

"It made too much noise because we were calling our staff members to tell them to return to the guesthouse. We're in 'lockdown' because the Vice President of Afghanistan has been assassinated! You have a radio for these kinds of emergencies, but it won't help us reach you if it isn't on!" John's face was turning red and he was nearly shouting.

"I'm sorry, John. I'll keep it on in the future," I said, feeling slightly annoyed at what I considered an over-reaction to the situation. However, I was slowly beginning to realize that these security procedures might be important. After all, assassinations are pretty rare in countries that are at peace.

After apologizing, I went up to my room and packed my rugs into my suitcase for the evacuation order that never came.

Since that first trip to Rauf's store, I've bought dozens of carpets and saddle bags from him for myself, family members, relatives, and friends who are thrilled to receive these lovely products of Afghan weavers. I have also taken scores of new friends and visitors to Rauf, all of whom have come away as delighted with their rugs as I was with my first purchases.

Rauf's original shop on Chicken Street is now a storage place for his vast carpet inventory. He has a bigger store in a spacious ground floor

Addiction to Afghan Carpets

location that opens onto the square of a three-story mall set back from Chicken Street. He also maintains a small street-front store to attract the casual window shoppers.

On Friday and Saturday afternoons, Rauf's shop is bustling with activity. Rauf's oldest son Hameed, 28, and Hameed's younger brother, help their father serve several groups of foreigners who are in the shop at the same time. Whenever possible, I try to visit the shop on quiet weekday afternoons when Rauf has time to visit and welcomes the company. He knows that I like green tea and orders it as soon as I enter the store. Only after we have inquired at length into each other's health and the status of our families do we get down to the business of purchasing carpets.

During our conversations, I have learned Rauf's life story. He was born in 1956 and is the oldest of ten children. His siblings include five sisters and three brothers who live in Herat. He and one younger brother are the only two family members who have left Herat to live in Kabul. Rauf makes frequent trips back to Herat to visit his mother and other siblings as well as to check on the activities of his rug workshop. The weavers at the workshop are turning out new designs from various regions in Afghanistan out of Belgique (from Belgium) quality wool, which European and North American buyers have begun to demand. Because of the finely spun quality of the wool, these new rugs have a crisp clarity of design that is found in traditional rugs that are made of silk or of a mixture of silk and wool. Some of the workshop production is also dedicated to making new carpets with old Afghan designs that are rarely seen in the markets of Kabul. If Rauf spots a rare design among the aged, threadbare rugs that old men bring to his shops in Herat and Kabul, he will take it to his workshop to be copied before he makes it available to his customers.

Rauf started his rug business during the reign of Zahir Shah, when Rauf was still in the eighth grade. His father had retired from his job as a teacher and Rauf wanted to help support the family. When the schools closed in Herat due to a teachers' strike, Rauf took a carpet from the family home and walked through the bazaar to sell it. After two or three days, he found someone who would pay him 2,200 Afghanis—$70 U.S. at the exchange rate of that time—for his carpet.

Six months later, Rauf was sitting on the street with three more carpets from his family when a bus full of young hippies from Amsterdam came through Herat. When the bus stopped, he took his carpets onto the bus and asked if anyone wanted to buy them. The young people on the bus were so eager to buy carpets that Rauf went into shops owned by his friends and neighbors and got as many as he could carry. At the end of the afternoon, he had sold twenty-five carpets and made a profit of $1,300. This sum was more than three times the monthly salary of an Afghan university professor or an attending physician at a government supported hospital. He had become a carpet merchant.

Throughout his high school years, Rauf spent half of his day at school and the other half selling carpets. He fondly recalls his Peace Corps English teacher at the high school, "Mr. Joe." Rauf was highly motivated to learn English because it helped him communicate with foreign customers. He also learned some English from his brother-in-law who had studied English in Hawaii. Rauf finished high school in 1975 and formally began his own business by renting a small shop on the second story of a building in Herat's commercial district. He had only twenty carpets to sell. In order to attract business, he walked the streets carrying some of his merchandise and invited foreigners to come to his shop to see more carpets. After three months, he had sold enough carpets to afford the rent of a street-level shop that attracted foreign visitors who were walking around the city.

In 1982, when battles with Russians had grown intense around Herat, Rauf came to Kabul and set up the same small shop on Chicken Street where I met him in 2002. He continued to sell carpets to foreigners. He remained in that location through the period of Russian occupation, the conflicts with the *Mujahadeen,* and the repressive reign of the Taliban. He noted that there were a surprising number of foreigners on Chicken Street during these turbulent periods.

"There were lots of foreigners here with the UN and with ICRC (International Red Crescent Society). They even came during the *Mujahadeen* fighting in Kabul. During the Taliban time, some came at night in *chadris* to buy rugs from me," he said proudly.

In the mid-1980s, Rauf began making trips to India, Russia, Hungary, and Bulgaria to sell his rugs. His best markets were in India and Hungary. Now, Rauf's main trips out of the country are to his shop

Addiction to Afghan Carpets

in Dubai. Rauf's son Hameed makes rug-marketing trips abroad, having recently participated in rug exhibitions in China, Spain, and India. So far, Hameed has not been able to get a visa to participate in rug exhibitions in the United States. However, Rauf's rugs have made their way into the American market through Americans who were Rauf's customers in Kabul. An American midwife, whom I brought to Rauf's shop in 2003, now sells his rugs to residents of her Colorado community as well as to other customers online. Another customer who formerly lived in Kabul sells Rauf's rugs in Spokane, Washington.

Rauf has ten children—seven daughters and three sons—who range in age from Hameed to his nine-year-old son Farid and six-year-old daughter Sayrha. Four of his daughters are married and have given him two grandchildren. In 2005, Rauf shared with me his concern over the effectiveness of the treatments that his wife was getting for breast cancer and his plans to take her to India for more treatment. When they returned from India, he was relieved that her cancer was in remission. However, the cancer returned.

One Friday in 2006, my friend Mike and I found both of Rauf's shops closed with no explanatory sign on the doors. We returned on Saturday and learned from the employees that Rauf's wife had died. Two weeks later, I visited Rauf and shared with him my understanding of his deep grief, as I had experienced intense grief after Michael's sudden death. Rauf's sorrow was compounded by his anxiety over who would help him raise his two youngest children. In those first months after his wife's death, Rauf could not manage a smile for his customers. However, the birth of his third grandchild, Hameed's son, finally brought him some joy, and Rauf's smile started to return.

Two years later, I noted that Rauf seemed more relaxed and his smiles were coming more readily. I soon learned that he had remarried. His new wife was a widow who is older than he is and who had happily taken on the role of stepmother to his two youngest children.

My conversations with Rauf these days often focus on his concerns about the education of his youngest son and daughter. Like many middle class parents in Kabul, Rauf has given up on the possibility of his children getting a good education in a government-operated school. Instead, he pays 5,000 Afghanis ($100) per month for each child to attend a private international school. He is particularly pleased with how rapidly his young children are learning English. I was delighted to be in his shop the first time that Sayrha came to visit. Without any sense of self-consciousness, she responded to his request that she sing "Twinkle, Twinkle, Little Star" for me and my friend Lisa. In her clear, high-pitched voice, she got through the entire song without a mistake, pausing only to take a breath between verses. Her smile of accomplishment when we applauded was matched by the smile of her proud father.

Rauf is content with his home life now. Three of his daughters and all three sons—including Hameed and his wife—still live with Rauf and his second wife. He says that he has enough children now and just wants to enjoy his youngest children and his grandchildren. When asked to reflect on the success of his business, Rauf proudly stated that he has forty years of experience dealing with foreigners and showed me several of the thirteen large leather address books that contain the names and addresses of all his customers, as well as descriptions of the rugs that they bought.

"I know what they like," Rauf said. "When rug sellers come into this mall with rugs to sell, I select the ones that my customers want. I love this job. I enjoy this business. It's a very clean business. If you like a rug, you pay for it. If you don't, you don't pay the price."

Rauf's regular customers can cite many other reasons for his success. We think that his inventory of rugs is the best in Kabul. Through his many connections, he can also acquire specific rugs that we are looking for, which no other dealer has been able to find. Most remarkable to many of us is the fact that Rauf does not forget the rugs that his regular customers have bought. Without consulting his notebook, he can describe to me the specifics—size, color, and design—of rugs that I bought from him three years ago. A trip to Rauf's shop doesn't feel like a business errand. Instead, it's like a visit to a friend. For those of us who are sometimes away from Kabul for months at a time, a visit to Rauf's shop is like a homecoming.

Chapter 15

Terrorism Up Close in a Luxury Hotel

January 16, 2008

"Bye, Frederick! I'm going up to Shiberghan on Wednesday, so I'll see you in a week," I said as I headed for the ladies' locker room. It was 6:00 p.m. I'd have to move quickly to get through the shower and change into street clothes before the car came to pick me up outside the hotel at 6:30 p.m.

I took off my tennis shoes, stripped off my sweaty clothes, grabbed the neatly rolled, blue towel from my locker, wrapped it around my body, and made a beeline for the showers. As I was checking to see which shower had an unclogged drain, I jumped at a loud rumbling sound coming from the other side of the wall. It sounded like a huge, heavy piece of machinery followed by a plastic-sounding *BLAM!* Other women in the locker room screamed, but I was stunned into silence.

This was a different sound from the *BOOM!* I'd heard and felt on Christmas morning in 2003 when an IED exploded in front of a UN apartment opposite our guesthouse on a main thoroughfare in Kabul.

"The explosion is inside the building!" shouted a woman near the makeup mirrors.

Marina, the woman who'd been in the shower stall next to mine shouted, "It's an IED explosion!"

No, I thought to myself. That's a grenade. And it came from next door in the men's locker room!

As I pulled the towel around me and ran toward the lockers to get into my clothes, I heard a second, louder rumbling and then a deafening, *BLAM!* that shook the walls. All eight of us women in the locker room screamed and covered our ears.

"No, it's a grenade!" I shouted.

197

As I finished my sentence, the machine gun fire started.

We heard men shouting in the reception area outside the door to the women's spa. The walls shook again and all of us began to panic. The door leading from the ladies' locker room to the gym area flew open briefly. I saw a jumble of men pouring out the door of their locker room trying to escape the gunfire. They were waving their arms, shouting, and heading toward the outdoor pool.

Marina and I ran toward the changing area. As we passed the glass-enclosed relaxation area, we instinctively crouched low. We expected glass shards to start flying at us any minute. Plaster dust was already flying from the walls and ceiling.

"Get away from the glass!" Marina shouted. This was not easy to do, as the wall of mirrors over the sinks was perpendicular to the glass-enclosed lounge. A bullet would shatter the mirrors just as easily as it would the glass doors of the lounge.

We braced ourselves against the opposite half-wall and moved toward the locker area.

One woman screamed, "What'll we do?!"

Another screamed "Where can we go?!"

Gia, a middle-aged Filipino woman who was the head masseuse, said in a loud whisper, "You stay here! I'll get help."

"Don't go out there!" three of us pleaded with her. "You'll be shot!"

"I must go. It's my duty!" Gia shouted back as she pushed past us.

"Gia, there's nothing you can do! They'll shoot you!!" I tried to grab her arm.

Without another word, Gia disappeared through the heavy door that led to the Maisha Spa reception area.

"Get away from the glass!" Marina shouted. "Get to the lockers! They're all wood."

All eight of us, some in their coats because they'd just arrived and others of us who were dressing to leave, crowded into the U-shaped locker and changing area and crouched between the wooden benches and the three walls of lockers. Marina and I grabbed our clothes from the lockers and pulled them on as fast as we could.

We'd barely gotten dressed when the man whom Frederick had been training moments before burst into our area. In a loud whisper he reported, "They're KILLING PEOPLE IN THERE!! THREE ARE

ALREADY DOWN!" He moved toward the farthest corner of the changing area and, with his back against one of the wooden lockers, sank to the floor and pulled himself into a fetal position.

We arranged ourselves on the floor with our backs against the wooden lockers.

The women immediately got on their cell phones and started calling their drivers, security officers, and significant friends.

"Quiet! We have to be quiet!" I whispered.

I moved to the far end of the changing area, opposite the man in the fetal position, and wrapped my red scarf around my phone to muffle the sound of my voice. I called our Deputy Director of Finance and Operations, who lived in the same compound as I did.

"Umair, this is Suzanne," I whispered.

"Hello, Suzanne. How are you?"

"There've been two explosions and gunfire here at the Serena!" I said.

"I'll tell the drivers," Umair said. He didn't get it.

"No!! Tell them NOT TO COME!!! I'll call later," I whispered.

The spa had a rule that our phones had to be on silent mode while in the spa area, but the phone of a woman who had just arrived rang. Then another phone rang.

Marina pointed at them and ordered in her loudest whisper, "TURN OFF THE RINGERS!"

For the moment, the shouting and gunfire from next door were masking the noise of the phones.

I sent short text messages to the Country Director for my agency and to my housemate, Mike.

"We should call the American Embassy," Marina whispered. "Who has the number?"

"I do," I whispered. "I know someone there."

I called my Afghan friend in the Consular Section. After several rings, I got a Dari recorded message saying that the person wasn't available.

Bitterly disappointed, I dialed the American Embassy switchboard and hoped for an answer. My hands shook. Finally, someone picked up. Relieved to hear a voice on the other end, I rattled off the information in a whisper, "I'm Suzanne Griffin. I'm in the women's locker room of the gym at the Serena Hotel. There are eight women and a man here.

Terrorism Up-Close in a Luxury Hotel

There've been two explosions, gunfire and shouting in the men's locker room next door."

"We heard there was trouble at the Serena, but we had no details. In what area are you?" asked the operator in a calm, business-like voice.

"We're in the women's spa next to the gym, the *Maisha*."

"And what are the names of any Americans there?"

"Marina, Roshan, Tatyana, and me."

"Thank you. I'll pass this to our Consular Section and we'll be back to you."

As soon as she hung up, my phone vibrated. It was my Afghan friend in the Consular Section.

"Suzanne! I heard the report about explosions at the Serena and then saw your name on my phone. Are you are there?!"

"Yes."

"Are you alright?"

"For now, yes, but there's still shooting next door. We don't know if they'll try to come in here."

"Okay, you'll hear next from my boss, the Consul. She'll tell you what to do."

The phone vibrated again and the Consul was on the phone. Once again, she asked me to name the Americans in the group, including their family names, and to tell her how many others were there.

"We can't take other names now," she said. "We're primarily responsible for the Americans."

Lilly, the Country Director for my agency, called in response to my text. I told her what was happening and that I'd called the Embassy. She didn't get the gravity of what was happening.

"Why did you call them?!" Lilly asked.

"Because there's a lot of shooting and they're the only ones who can get us out."

"Suzanne, you don't have to do what the Embassy tells you and you don't have to evacuate in their cars. I'd rather that you came out in our agency cars with our drivers."

She didn't seem to understand that a gun battle was going on outside the hotel, that the road in front of the hotel was probably sealed off, and that the drivers of any cars approaching the scene were likely to be shot.

Lessons of Love in Afghanistan

"Lilly, our drivers will never get in here! Only soldiers can get us out of here. There's a lot of shooting! I have to hang up now!"

By now, there were shouts from lots of men in the spa reception area and more shooting. Either the Afghan army had arrived or reinforcements had come for the initial shooters.

Another man tore into our locker room from the gym area. He was an American that I knew named Alfred. He shouted, "THEY'RE KILLING PEOPLE IN THERE! TWO OF THE GUYS THEY SHOT FELL ON ME!! I think I'm gonna … PUKE!" As he said this, he sank to the ground next to me.

Alfred was bad news. It was always about him. I was angry that his need to shout might get us all killed.

In a firm voice I said, "Sorry you went through that, Alfred. If you're feeling sick, toilets are over there. If you're planning to stay here, get yourself under control and be quiet! You're endangering all of us."

Alfred looked shocked, but he quieted down.

Then we heard Afghan voices next door. They were asking in Dari if anyone was in there. There was no lock on our door, but they didn't try to open it. We trembled in terror. Were they Afghan police and army people here to help us, or were they the bad guys?! Were we going to be shot or be rescued?! We could only wait.

The Consul called again. I told her that there were now ten of us— eight women and two men. She confirmed that we were doing the best thing by keeping quiet and not responding to Afghan voices from outside our door.

We didn't know how many shooters were out there. We also didn't know that there had been three suicide bombers in the hotel.

At 6:45, the hotel staff came through the area and called out in English, "Is anyone in there?" Then they opened the door and found us. They looked surprised and relieved. I think they were expecting to see dead bodies.

"Come on, we have to get you out of here!" one of them said. There's still a suicide bomber in the hotel. We don't know where he is. We're going to take you to the basement until we find him."

Those who had their coats on were already out the door. The manager of sales for the hotel stayed behind with me while I put on my coat

Terrorism Up-Close in a Luxury Hotel

and grabbed my gym bag. As we exited the women's spa, we saw blood, damaged Plexiglas, and bullet casings all over the floor of the reception area. Gia had gotten through the reception area to the hallway door that led to the lobby. Her body blocked the doorway. Her eyes were open and stared blankly at the ceiling. Her face was grey. I sobbed as I had to step over her to get out to the lobby. It was very difficult for us to leave her there. She died because she ran outside to get help for us. I wanted to stop to whisper, "Thank you, Gia!" but the staff were urging us to hurry to a safer location. She was their co-worker. I couldn't imagine how they felt leaving her there.

We found out later, from the medics, that Gia was not dead when we stepped over her body. She still had a faint pulse when they attended to her. She died shortly afterwards, at the hospital. If only I had known! I don't know what I could have done to help her as we rushed out, but I might have at least provided her some comfort.

As we crossed through the lobby, we saw lots of blood and more damage from explosions and bullets. I couldn't run as fast as the others, because I'd had surgery on my right hip eight months before. The hotel sales manager stayed with me as we followed a trail of blood through the kitchen. As we emerged from the kitchen and rounded the corner, we couldn't determine which way the group had gone to get to the basement.

We passed some guest rooms. The manager whipped a plastic room key card out of his pocket.

"Go in here!" he said. "You'll be safe here and we'll get you later. Don't open the door unless you are sure who is on the other side."

I entered the room and immediately went to sit at the desk by the room phone. As I sat down and got ready to call the Consul, I was both relieved and nervous. I was out of the gym, but was I safe in here? Would that one suicide bomber come down the hall? I didn't know which room I was in, so I went to the door and opened it carefully to see the room number 220 in large wooden letters. Then I settled down at the desk and mechanically punched the numbers into my cell phone. First, I called Mai at the Consular section to tell them where I was.

"Mai, I got separated from the group because I couldn't run fast enough. They're all in the basement of the hotel, but I'm alone here in 220. I don't know whose room this is, but there are some men's clothes draped on the chair."

Lessons of Love in Afghanistan

"Okay, Suzanne. Are you alright?"

"Yes, but I'm worried about how I'll get out of here."

"Don't worry, we'll get you out. There are people on the way. Just don't open the door until you hear an American voice."

I was glad that Mai gave me that advice because after I hung up there were loud Afghan voices in the hallway. I froze in the chair as someone beat on the door and tried to force it open. The double lock held. I sat quietly until the voices went away.

Lilly called and asked where I was.

"Why are you alone?" Lilly asked. "Why aren't you with the others?"

I repeated to Lilly what I'd told Mai about getting separated from the group.

"Okay. I have a call in to our Security Coordinator at Head Office. He'll be calling you with some instructions," Lilly said.

"Alright, I'll wait for his call," I said.

"Suzanne, it's about 7:00 a.m. on the west coast now. This is already on the MSN news page. Do either of your daughters read it in the morning?"

"Yes, Rachael does. Sarah and her husband are in Hawaii right now, so they're still sleeping."

"Well, I think you should call Rachael, or do you want me to call her?"

"No, I'll call her."

I dialed Rachael's number and, amazingly, got through on the first try. From the sound of her voice, I had awakened her.

"Hi Rachael, this is Mom."

"Hi, Mom, where are you?!"

"I'm in Kabul in the Serena Hotel. You'll see on the news that there's been an attack on the hotel. I was in the gym when it happened, but I'm okay. I'm in a hotel room waiting to be rescued by American soldiers."

"Oh Mom!!"

I'll never forget the sound of Rachael's voice as she uttered those two words. Her tone clearly conveyed to me that this situation was raising her worst fears for me.

"Are you really alone?!"

"Yes."

"Mom, I'm worried that you are a hostage. I'm going to ask you some questions."

Terrorism Up-Close in a Luxury Hotel

Rachael proceeded to ask some of the same questions that Lilly had asked. I assured her that I'd call when I was out of the hotel. At the end of the conversation, she asked for Lilly's phone number. I learned later that she called Lilly and asked if I was a hostage.

After that call, another bunch of men banged on the door and asked in Dari if anyone was inside. I froze again and sat silently as they rattled the door. Then they moved down the hallway banging on other doors.

The agency security officer, Matt, called from the head office and gave me the same advice that I'd received from the Embassy Consul. As he was speaking, I heard American male voices calling loudly, "Ma'am, we're from the U.S. Embassy. Are you in there?"

"Matt, there are American voices out there! Shall I open the door?"

"Be cautious, Suzanne. Open the door part way and hand the phone out to one of them."

I did so, and one of the Americans gave his name to Matt and told him that I was okay.

When the man gave the phone back to me, Matt said, "Okay, Suzanne, you can open the door now."

When I opened the door completely, I was confronted by three heavily-armed American men, two of whom had automatic weapons pointed at me. One man was on one knee bracing his weapon in a firing position. The man who had talked to Matt was standing and had his gun pointed over my head. The third man was checking the hallway, his back to me. In retrospect, I realized that they also thought that I was a hostage and were prepared to fire at whoever was holding me.

My rescuers were from a private security firm hired by the U.S. Embassy. They placed me between them and moved slowly down the hall. They also added another hotel guest to our group—a Nicaraguan man who was wearing shorts, a T-shirt, and flip-flops. He was staying in the hotel while waiting for permanent housing and had just returned from "R and R."

When we got to the hotel lobby, it was swarming with soldiers— Afghan Army, ISAF, and American. The crowd was so dense that the Nicaraguan man and I could no longer see the damage to the lobby. Our focus was on trying to understand the orders we were being given while also trying to respond to calls coming in on our cell phones. Ultimately, the twenty-plus of us civilians who were in the hotel were divided into groups of four, surrounded by armed men, and moved slowly across the lobby.

For me, the move from the lobby to the vehicles waiting outside was the most frightening part of the ordeal since the shooting had stopped. After remaining relatively calm throughout the three hours since the shooting started, I started shaking and breathing rapidly as we were escorted through the crowded lobby. We filed along the covered walkway and out into the street, where armored cars from the American Embassy were waiting. I heard someone say that the lady in the red scarf (which I was wearing) was the one who had been talking to the Embassy. I felt exposed and couldn't breathe normally until we got into the car.

As I got into the car, the man behind the wheel seemed to know my state of mind. In a deep Southern drawl he said, "Good evening, Ma'am. You're okay now. Just make yourself comfortable until we get everyone out. Then we'll take you to the U.S. Embassy."

"Are you from the military?" I asked,

"No, Ma'am," and he named a security contractor I knew was legitimate.

As I waited in the car for the other hostages to get out of the hotel, my cell phone rang. I was surprised that it was an Associated Press reporter who said she'd gotten my number from one of Lilly's friends. I mistakenly assumed that Lilly had given permission for me to talk to the press. The woman asked my name, age, and agency affiliation. Then she asked me what I had seen. As I responded to her questions, my voice shook. I don't remember what I said, but I saw my words in print over and over for the next week. Apparently, my simple statements were of interest to many media people because they appeared in major newspapers and news magazines around the world. Some friends later told me that they heard my live interview on National Public Radio. The statement that was most often quoted appeared in the *Verbatim* section of *TIME* Magazine on January 17th.

> "There was blood on the floor all the way to the kitchen. There was a lot of blood in the lobby. There were empty shell casings outside," SUZANNE GRIFFIN, a Seattle resident, on suicide attacks that killed six people in Kabul's upscale Serena Hotel on Jan. 14. Griffin was in the hotel gym's locker room when the violence broke out.

Terrorism Up-Close in a Luxury Hotel

It was nearly ten at night before our convoy started moving slowly through the almost-deserted streets of Kabul toward the American Embassy. We were escorted to the brightly lit cafeteria in the basement of the Embassy, where we were greeted by a well-organized group of staff members. Our group of evacuees included several men whose pants were completely covered with blood. They had tended to some wounded victims in the hotel lobby before the ambulances came. Their faces showed the emotional impact of their heroic efforts.

Each of us was interviewed several times, first by a person who wanted factual information—our names, passports and/or identity cards, etc. While we waited for medical check-ups, we were also interviewed by a counselor, a chaplain, and a man who was coordinating our transportation back to our respective agency guesthouses. While all of these interviews were going on, we were fielding phone calls from our agency colleagues and eating snacks, our "dinner" provided by the Embassy. At one point, the Ambassador arrived to tell us that we were welcome to stay overnight at the Embassy if we didn't want to travel on the Kabul streets until daylight. We thanked him, but most of us just wanted to go to our guesthouses and be with our colleagues.

The man who was coordinating our transport insisted on talking directly to the people who were picking us up and specified that an American had to be in each car that was picking up an American evacuee. At 11:00 p.m., we were individually escorted to the gate by a heavily armed American soldier and handed over to the colleagues taking us home. My colleagues were quite a remarkable pair: Mike came in his most American outfit, including a Boston Red Sox baseball hat. Umair wore a *shalwar kamize* and a *pakhol*. Their rationale was that Umair would be able to handle the late night checkpoints of the Afghan police and Mike would be recognizable to the American Embassy guards. I was relieved and grateful to be welcomed by them and taken to our guesthouse compound. Once there, I suddenly realized that I had not had a meal for almost twelve hours and gratefully accepted the food and drink that my housemates had waiting for me.

While I was communicating with concerned family and friends over the next few days, I heard the story of the horrors experienced by three women—one of whom was my friend—who'd been caught in the gun battle between the terrorists and the hotel guards at the outside entrance of the hotel and in the lobby. One of the hotel guards fell on the hood of their SUV as he died. The women crouched on the floor between the front and back seats while their driver tried to flatten himself on the front seat floorboard. I felt lucky to have been spared such horror.

Friends and acquaintances in Kabul wondered why I did not seem more traumatized by the Serena experience and why I did not feel the need to immediately flee the country. I replied that the ordeals related to my evacuation with my daughters from Iran prepared me for some of this.

I added, "If I and others like me leave because of this, the bad guys win. I can't abandon the Afghans who need our support and live with this situation every day."

The Serena event caused me to reflect on the last days Michael and I spent in Iran with our daughters. It was 1979. I had completed graduate school, and Michael and I had both gotten jobs in Iran. We wanted our two young daughters to become acquainted with life in countries we loved, besides the U.S.

When the trouble started in Iran, we thought it was a temporary situation. On previous assignments in Iran, Michael had been through at least one *coup d'état* that lasted a few weeks, and then life had returned to normal. But that didn't happen in 1979.

In mid-January 1979, exactly twenty-nine years before the Serena attack, my daughters and I had wept as we waved goodbye to Michael in the dark early morning hours. We were aboard a bus of evacuees, pulling away from the InterContinental Hotel in Isfahan and headed to a military air base outside of the city. We would board a Pan American Airlines flight arranged to take the American dependents of U.S. government employees and contractors to the United States. Michael was one of the "essential personnel" who, because of their technical, diplomatic, and linguistic skills, were to remain in Iran until the evacuation of Americans from Iran was complete.

The turbulent events that led to our evacuation had begun a month earlier on *Muharam*, a day of mourning for Shiite Muslims. Our family, the U.S. Consul's family, and several other Americans were trapped inside the U.S. Consulate while an angry mob of thousands of Iranians

chanted, "Death to Americans!" across the boulevard. A massive traffic jam prevented them from crossing the boulevard and burning down
the consulate. Instead, they marched down the far side of the boulevard
and burned the Savak (Security Police) building. A few days later, my
daughters and I were nearly caught in gunfire on Char Bagh Bala Street
in Isfahan as I walked them home from school.

In the weeks following, daily life was stressful, but we encountered
many Iranians who welcomed and aided us. I will never forget an old
woman who helped me as a group of men on strike marched down
Charbagh Bala just as the university bus let me off. I dodged into a phone
booth to call Michael. "Go to Julfa (the Christian quarter)," he advised.
But it was too late. I could already see the eyes of the men at the front
of the march. The old woman silently walked up to the phone booth and
stretched her *chador* across it until they passed. I thanked her in Farsi and
she was gone. My tears upon hearing that we would be evacuated were
partly for the many good people like that woman, who we would leave
behind.

For six weeks after our evacuation, the girls and I waited anxiously
for the return of Michael, who had to stay behind to evacuate other
Americans out of Iran before he could join us in San Francisco. During
those weeks, our greatest fear was that he would become a victim of the
pre-revolution violence. To calm myself, I recalled instances of Michael's
resourcefulness and survival skills during our last two, difficult weeks in
Iran. For several days, armed soldiers and Khomeini supporters blocked
intersections in different sections of Isfahan. I remembered how angry
faces pressed against our windshield and guards shouted loudly in Farsi
as Michael rolled down the window. I was frightened, but Michael had
figured out the game. He had photos of both the Shah and Khomeini
face down on the dashboard. As we approached each intersection, he
evaluated the men stopping the cars. The Shah's soldiers had automatic weapons. The Khomeini followers had both guns and baseball bats,
which they used to smash windshields. Michael calmly selected the appropriate picture to display on the dash and ran his windshield wipers in
a vertical position—the expected sign of support. The guards grudgingly
let us pass.

We rejoiced when Michael came home just before Valentine's Day and spent the next seventeen years being a loving, dedicated father and husband.

After surviving dangerous situations in Afghanistan as a couple and in Iran as a family, it seemed a cruel irony that I had suddenly lost Michael while in the safety of our peaceful Seattle home. He had a massive heart attack one morning in 1999, while taking his shower. Immediately after he died, I wondered how I could survive life without him. During my first year as a widow, I kept replaying in my head the conversations we'd had about the heart history of males in his family and his instructions to me to "move on" after he died. With daily reminders around me of his presence in my life and of what might have been, I wondered if I could ever move on.

My determination to survive the Serena attack confirmed for me that I had moved on. At the time of Michael's death, the outpouring of love from my daughters, my sisters, my widowed father, the large Griffin clan, my own extended family, and many dear friends and colleagues kept me afloat. A similar outpouring of concern and love followed the Serena event and reminded me that I still have a large support group and much to live for. My support circle is bigger now—it includes many Afghan and expatriate friends and colleagues in my "second country."

Chapter 16

This Isn't the Place That I Remember

"Abdullah, what's the Dari word for traffic jam?" I asked my driver one day.

"*Mirabar*, Susan," he answered.

"That's the same word that I use for the sweet fruit spread for bread, isn't it?"

"Yes, Susan, it's the same word."

"Do you know that *mirabar* means 'jam' in English, Abdullah?"

"Now I do, Susan."

"'Jam' is also the English word for the sweet fruit spread for bread," I added.

"Really?"

"Yes, *mirabar* is the direct translation of 'jam.'"

While we talked, I instinctively cringed as Abdullah maneuvered through traffic that left only inches between our SUV and vehicles on either side of us. As usual, I was grateful that he was the driver, and not me.

Amazingly, there are few car accidents in Kabul serious enough to tie up traffic. Minor fender benders are so common that drivers get out, check the damage, shake their heads and get back in their cars. When serious damage occurs, drivers get out and argue loudly, a crowd gathers, and sometimes the drivers come to blows. Then traffic jams, as everyone stops to gawk until police arrive to calm the situation and get everyone moving again.

When stuck in traffic, I remember scenes from forty years ago, when bicycles were the main form of transportation in Kabul and cars moved smoothly down the wide boulevards. In those days, when the city's population was only 750,000 (compared to 7 million today), Michael and I whisked across the city in ten or fifteen minutes, occasionally stopping to make way for camel trains from the provinces on market days.

Today, the city's gridlock traffic comes to a complete halt almost daily to allow the entourages of high government officials (including President Karzai) to move through the streets at high speed. Heavily armed men in vehicles around VIP cars are constantly scanning the streets for snipers and vehicles that might contain IEDs.

Traffic can also be blocked by demonstrations, but the timing of some of those can be anticipated. At the end of every month, Afghan Army veterans demonstrate in the morning outside the Ministry of Defense to protest the cut off or reduction of their benefits. The banning of street vendors from popular shopping areas can trigger protests from the vendors. Students at the universities stage several demonstrations a year because of their dormitory conditions, their lack of success in passing university entrance exams, and their overcrowded classrooms. These events disrupt traffic for a couple of hours in the morning until the police and army restore order. Longer protests generally break up at noon for lunch and midday prayers.

Serious security incidents can occur when traffic stops in deference to parades that memorialize military or religious leaders. The annual Russian and British Victory Day celebrations and the tenth day of *Muharam* procession of Shiite minority groups have high potential of erupting into violence. Heavily armed soldiers line the parade routes to prevent the rituals from devolving into ugly riots.

Violent demonstrations caused by political or military events that harm Afghan citizens or insult their religion are less predictable and more dangerous for all of us traveling on the main streets of Kabul. Hundreds of cars can suddenly be brought to a stop at a four-way intersection because the roads have been cordoned off while police try to contain the demonstrators. You pray that demonstration will not escalate and there will be no gunfire, as there is no possibility of escaping the area to take cover.

In the 1960s and early 1970s, in Zahir Shah's time, only a few thousand Afghans had cars. Many foreigners, including some women, did not require a driver. They drove their own cars because traffic was light, parking was easy, and in fifteen minutes, they could drive from Karte Se at the south end of the city to Shar-i-Nau, just north of the city center. Now

Lessons of Love in Afghanistan

agency drivers dodge bicycles, pedestrians, horse-drawn carts, herds of goats and sheep, buses, military vehicles, and other cars.

Rides through Kabul's streets are bumpier than streets in many of the country's provincial capitals. During the civil wars fought in Kabul, armored tanks constantly moving across the city destroyed the city streets. Army tanks still move daily across the city, but heavy construction trucks and lorries carrying freight from Pakistan do greater damage. The street repair efforts of city workers simply cannot keep up.

An agency driver who is a veteran of nineteen years with the traffic police made an observation that represents the opinion of most drivers in Kabul.

"Do you think that the city will ever repair these streets, Din Mohammad?" I asked.

"No. Kabul streets will never be smooth," he answered.

His wistful response reflected the sorrowful resignation that I have often heard from Kabul residents who remember a better time. The tone borders on despair for residents who have come to Kabul because they could not find jobs to support their families in the more peaceful, less crowded provincial cities they prefer.

The influx of millions to Kabul from the provinces has added to the already inventive ways in which Afghans adapt ordinary forms of transport to meet their needs in this crowded city. When my car is stopped in traffic, I envy the Afghans on bicycles, many of whom share their bikes with passengers who sit sidesaddle as the bike weaves in and out among cars and trucks.

Competing for space are vehicles of every conceivable type: wooden carts pulled by Hazara strong men, horse-drawn *gadis*, tiny Pakistani taxis that look like decorated golf carts, yellow taxis with white doors (scrambled eggs on wheels), mini-buses carrying the names of defunct European tour operations, and dump trucks filled with soil, rocks, metal pipes, and construction equipment. Ever present are overloaded public buses, one of which I saw recently weaving through weekday traffic fully loaded with people inside and bearing two flattened passenger cars strapped to the top of the bus.

My favorite vehicles are the large, ornately decorated lorries. They rumble toward you looking like large Christmas trees overburdened by ornaments. The lorries are often tilting to one side because of the unevenly distributed human cargo and because the shocks and struts are ruined. The bodies of the trucks are usually bright green. The detailing includes anything silvery and shiny, with pink and red being the favored accent colors. When I am stuck behind lorries, I marvel at the details in idyllic scenes painted on their sides. These pastoral landscapes, dream houses, trees and flowers remind me (and probably the painters of the landscapes as well) of the "more peaceful and attractive other Afghanistan" that lies outside the city limits of Kabul. As soon as spring arrives, thousands of Kabul residents begin the migration to this "other Afghanistan" every weekend for picnics, fresh air, and the quiet of an afternoon among trees.

Toyotas—especially Corollas and Forerunners—are overwhelmingly the most popular passenger cars in Kabul. Other models range from new Mercedes Benzes and Land Rovers to dented and rusted "vintage" American cars with long fins. Some of the new cars are demonstrator models with "LAND CRUISER" painted in large black letters on the side doors. I wondered if I was supposed to feel special when I got to ride in "ROAD STAR."

Directing this traffic circus are policemen wearing formal gray uniforms offset by white cotton sashes and matching gloves. They stand regally on round, raised daises in the traffic circles, waving their red and white signs, blowing their whistles and holding back lanes of traffic with their white-gloved palms. When friends pass, the police break into smiles and shout *"Salaam-alekum"* before resuming the serious business of ordering the chaos before them. Sometimes, when they see a former colleague at the wheel, they force an opening in the jams at traffic circles so their friend's car can pass. There have been several attempts to control some busy intersections with the traffic lights common to most modern cities. However, these lights are ignored by many drivers since they do not respond to the changing traffic conditions and don't work for several hours per day when the city is without publicly generated electricity. Hence, the traffic police in Kabul have more job security than their counterparts in most other big cities of the world.

As security incidents in the city increase in frequency, traffic police have been joined at nearly every major intersection by baby-faced soldiers with fingers on the triggers of their machine guns. During the day, there is often incongruity between the soldiers' equipment and their personal affects. They get public reprimands from their superiors for smiling too much. At night, however, it is all business. The agency drivers who transport expatriates to restaurants and other social engagements after dark are stopped at checkpoints at least a half dozen times every evening. Police are searching for suicide bombers, kidnappers, thieves, and other criminals whose activities are increasingly threatening the stability of life in the city that Kabul residents thought would be returning to "normal" by now.

Four years prior to the life-changing attack on the Serena Hotel, there was evidence of the deteriorating security in Kabul. On Christmas Day, 2003, an IED explosion was detonated from a speeding car on Shash Darak Street just two blocks from an Afghan Ministry of Defense facility. The windows of every building on the street (including a school, a clinic and our agency's two guesthouses) were shattered in the explosion. Because of escalating kidnapping threats against both foreign and Afghan humanitarian aid workers, most international aid agencies and contractors started traveling in unmarked cars in 2004. Until then, all the vehicles of international aid agencies were prominently marked with logos and acronyms. These markings allowed police and military forces to easily identify them and let them pass through official checkpoints. Another sign of an increasingly unstable city were the guards armed with machine guns that first appeared outside restaurants where foreigners dine, then outside stores where foreigners shop and in front of the houses in which they live.

Apparently oblivious to the changes in the security situation for vulnerable Afghans are the farmers and herdsmen who come from outlying areas and continue to move through the city's side streets with livestock, just as their fathers, grandfathers, and great-grandfathers did before them. Although traffic police have attempted to ban herds of livestock from city streets, animals still manage to mingle with vehicles—especially in the morning and late evening hours. A few months ago, I saw a multi-hued flock of longhaired sheep being herded by Afghan men down the side streets around our Karte Se district office, wandering through the upscale residential area of Wazir Akbar Khan and occasionally on the sidewalks in Shar-i-Nau. On early mornings—before the traffic gets heavy—donkeys loaded with saddlebags of grain, rice, or other food bound for bazaar stalls still plod along the edges of the roads and horses pulling carts loaded with fresh fruits or vegetables still arrive at the markets. At the end of the day, laborers often ride home in the back of large carts that have hauled wood and produce into the city. Both the workers and the horses pulling the carts often look ready to collapse from fatigue and thirst.

One afternoon, an Iranian colleague and I saw traffic slow for four large black water buffaloes coming toward us. Two of them were pulling an old wooden cart. The other two were following behind and were being beaten with wooden canes to keep them close to the edge of the road so they wouldn't bump into the vehicles whizzing by. I mentioned to Annette that I missed seeing the camel trains stop traffic in Kabul the way they did thirty years ago. I recalled the sight of a long camel train that became frightened by blaring horns. The bells around their necks jangled wildly as several broke free of the train and galloped across four lanes of rush hour traffic along the Kabul River.

"You are not likely to see them now," Annette remarked. "Many camels were killed for their meat when people were starving."

Her explanation jolted me into realizing the many differences between the Kabul of today and the Kabul of Zahir Shah's time—the Kabul that I fell in love with. I silently mourn for the clean air, slower pace, and friendlier tone of the Kabul that I once knew. Even the open sewers were more tolerable when the sidewalks weren't so full of people that you stand a real chance of being pushed into one by passersby who are fighting through the crowds to get to their next destination. The hardships of living in Kabul today have, like the smog that perpetually hangs over the city, obscured some exotic aspects of this place. The camel trains that have always symbolized this side of Afghanistan for me are gone from the urban scene, and with their disappearance some of the magic has been lost.

During the first summer of my return to Kabul in 2002, post-Taliban summer rubble was still being cleaned from the streets of Shar-i-Nau and other business districts in the center of Kabul. A number of buildings had survived the warfare, but most—especially the government buildings—bore the holes and chipped surfaces of repeated strikes by mortar shells and bullets. Portions of many buildings had collapsed from rocket attacks. Since 2008, most of the unsalvageable buildings in Kabul have been replaced by new construction, making every district of the city a hodgepodge of brightly painted and highly decorated new three- and four-story buildings adjacent to crumbling single-story mud bungalows. In some business districts, the contrast is even greater: ten-story glass office buildings and shopping malls are just around the corner from ancient open bazaar stalls and street vendors.

The cement barriers, sandbags, and razor wire that I saw around the compounds of foreign embassies and expatriate guesthouses in the summer of 2002 were symbols of wartime. I expected then that these barriers would gradually be removed as Kabul "returned to normal." But that has not happened. Because of the constant threat of insurgent attacks on any buildings that represent government, progress, or foreign influence, the cement barriers, sandbags, razor wire, and soldiers armed with automatic weapons have proliferated. Now, the barriers and armed men are not only around the compounds of embassies. They also protect the compounds of Afghan government buildings, banks, restaurants, and homes where government officials, well-known business leaders, and foreigners live. It makes me very sad that so many of us live behind fortified walls now, and that soldiers have to protect our dwellings and places where we do our work. When the fortification of public buildings began, the Italians attempted to add color to the omnipresent olive green, khaki, and gray oilcans filled with cement that barricaded their compound by painting the containers with red and white stripes and planting red geraniums, purple petunias, orange zinnias, and tomato plants on top. The plants thrived in the hot summer sun and brought a smile to many passersby. However, increased threats against that embassy required the building of another bulwark of tall cement barriers in place of the colorful cylinders. The geraniums and tomatoes now grow inside the Embassy compound.

For Americans, a significant change in the Kabul security situation is the escalation of visible and invisible security barriers in our Embassy. In 2002, I searched for the American Embassy that I remembered from 1969. I knew that the Embassy had been attacked during the many battles fought outside its walls for three decades, but I wasn't prepared for the barren ground, razor wire, sandbags, and cement barriers that I saw where the lovely two-story white building surrounded by well-tended grounds had once been. In order to register with the Embassy, I first

This Isn't the Place that I Remember

stood outside a ten-foot metal gate and slapped my passport up against a peephole for the heavily armed soldiers to see. Once inside the gate, I filled out a form at a makeshift guard shelter that was blocked by barbed wire from the pathway to the Embassy.

I'd hoped that the rebuilding of the Embassy would include restoration of the gardens, but I was disappointed. Heavily guarded gates and huge concrete barriers now surround the multi-storied fortified buildings that fill the original American Embassy site. The heavily fortified embassy buildings now cover both sides of the two block stretch that extends from Massoud Circle to the entrance to the ISAF compound and the old Ariana television building. When I walk the sidewalk along that stretch of buildings in order to attend meetings at the embassy, I am aware of the snipers in guard stations above my head and the potential for incoming rockets, explosive devices, or gunfire to hit the area at any time. The state of alert is so high that the Afghan woman in the shack inside the entrance gate who checks my bag and wands me for metal devices now wears a flak jacket and helmet. My program officer has advised me to remove my veil when I enter the compound and wear American-looking clothes like blue jeans so that I won't be detained because I look so much like an Afghan woman.

Ironically, the biggest security risk taken by Americans whose humanitarian activities are funded by the United States government is attending meetings at the USAID and U.S. Embassy compounds. In order for us to make these visits, we must get advance clearance for ourselves, those who accompany us, and our cars. If our cars don't get clearance before the meetings, we are dropped off at one of the most dangerous intersections in Kabul. We walk unescorted and without body armor to the first checkpoint to display our passports so that the guards can see them. Once past the first checkpoint, we are conscious of armed guards in watchtowers with guns trained on us. Large tanks and armed vehicles observe our every move as we walk toward the heavily guarded iron gates at each side of the compound. Though none of us who live outside the compound would trade our freedom of movement and daily interaction with Afghan society for the restricted lives of Americans who live inside this compound, we cannot help but feel like second-class citizens when, after we have risked our safety to visit our own embassy, we are regarded with suspicion until one of those "on the inside" greets us at the entrance.

The imminent danger of visiting the Embassy literally exploded one day when two American colleagues and I were leaving the USAID compound after our weekly meeting.

BLAM!! A huge explosion from the direction of Massoud Circle, just 500 meters away, went off as we were stepping onto the walkway through the Embassy complex. "Ugh!" I exclaimed.

I felt as if I'd just been punched in the stomach. Norm and Scott were several paces ahead of me on the sidewalk, and I saw the hair on their heads literally stand on end.

"It's an IED!" I yelled, "We can't go out there, but our driver's right near the explosion! What'll we do?!"

We were all afraid that our driver, Khanaga, had been hit by the explosion. Concern for him overcame our shock at the power of the explosion.

"Can you reach him on your phone, Suzanne?" Norm shouted as they came back toward me.

"Yes, I think so," I shouted back.

The aftermath of an IED explosion is always noisy and chaotic. There was some gunfire from Afghan guards outside the compound shooting in the direction of the explosion and a lot of noise from emergency vehicles at Massoud Circle. There were also American soldiers inside the Embassy compound yelling instructions at us. My hands shook as I punched the buttons on my cell phone. "He's answering!" I shouted, in relief.

"Khanaga, where are you?! Are you okay?" I asked.

"Yes, I'm behind a building—one of those shops near my parking spot. The windows of the building are all broken, but I'm okay."

"Good! I'm so glad to hear your voice, Khanaga! We thought … How about your car?"

"I can see my car and its windshield didn't break. Don't worry. You stay there awhile, Dr. Suzanne. Come when it's safe."

"Okay, Khanaga. I'll call when we can leave here."

As I was talking to Khanaga, two Marines ran onto the sidewalk from the USAID compound and frantically motioned us back into the building.

"Get back here! Get back here!" they shouted. "We don't know if there will be any more of those!"

We followed their orders and got back into the USAID reception area. The people there were in a quandary. They couldn't let us back into the compound because we had turned in our security badges, but they couldn't send us back outside because the Marines hadn't declared it safe.

After a half hour wait in the reception area, we were cleared to walk to the intersection where our car and driver were waiting. Khanaga broke into a relieved smile when he saw us. As we all got into the car, we were just thankful that none of us were injured. We later learned that six Italian soldiers in the targeted military convoy and ten Afghan civilians were killed, and scores of others were injured in the explosion just 1,000 meters away (500 meters beyond Massoud Circle).

No wonder some of the American Embassy personnel seem slightly paranoid to me. They live and work in this environment every day!

Their fortified environment provides Embassy personnel protection, but the grounds don't give them much relief from the harsh exterior of the compound. The small plots of grass and small flowers planted along the sidewalks and around the perimeters of some buildings don't offset the marble, glass, and metal facades of modern buildings around them. The gleaming marble plazas are so bright in the blazing Afghan sun that wearing dark glasses is a necessity if you are walking between buildings.

The residences in Shar-i-Nau that were abandoned by the American Ambassador and the embassy staff in the 1970s, however, have retained the gracious old gardens that Afghan gardeners managed to keep alive even during the drought years. The old pine trees are among the tallest trees in Kabul and screen out the ugliness of the damaged or half-constructed buildings that rise above the walls of adjoining compounds.

The fifty-year-old former compound of the American Ambassador's family housed humanitarian aid workers until 2010. I was one of them. We gladly put up with the inconveniences of buildings that needed repairs, noisy plumbing and ugly wiring for the spacious gardens filled with old rosebushes and newly planted perennials, as well as the huge pine trees that break the force of strong *shamals* (windstorms) which occasionally blow across Kabul in the afternoons and shade the houses from the scorching summer sun.

For me, these gardens were also filled with pleasant memories of a more peaceful Kabul. On summer evenings, I strolled around and remembered the parties that the ambassador hosted there. Live music from a trio or quartet sitting in the far corner of the *chaila* (grape arbor) filtered over the attendees while Michael and I mingled with guests from the American and Afghan communities. In 2007, a former Peace Corps colleague asked to visit my compound so that she could see the three marble steps separating the dining room from the sunken living room where she and other members of her group had stood as they waited for the ambassador to swear them in as Peace Corps Volunteers. In both her memory and mine, the former ambassador's house and gardens were bigger than they actually are. Now, the compound is dwarfed by ornate, three-story Dubai-style houses in nearby neighborhoods.

By the time the Taliban left Kabul, the twelve-year drought had eliminated any sign that this was once the Garden City of Central Asia. In 2002, most of the trees that had lined the wide boulevards were gone. Many had been cut down during the Russian occupation so that insurgent Afghans could not hide behind them and snipe at government officials. The remainder had been cut down by the city's occupants in order to heat their homes during brutally cold winters. Scorched brown leaves clung to the brittle branches of the few deciduous trees still standing. The only visible signs of dormant greenery were the dusty evergreen trees that rose above the compound walls of private residences. In Shar-i-Nau Park and many private gardens, leaves of prized rosebushes alluded to in poems and stories about Afghanistan and Iran looked like brown paper. The roses that had managed to open were covered with dust. Each day, Afghan gardeners around the city dribbled some water onto the plants and trees to try to keep them alive for one more season.

Their optimism was ultimately vindicated when the drought finally broke in 2003. In spring of 2004, vendors returned to the banks of the Kabul River to sell sapling trees and rosebushes to thousands of Kabul residents who planted them in their private compounds, while government agencies proceeded to replant the public gardens. Seven years later, Kabul's weather pattern returned to the weather we knew in the late 1960s. Rains started in late fall and heavy snowfalls resulted in drifts that covered the ground from December through February. Kabul is green again! At last, trees create a green canopy in Shar-i-Nau Park, shade the paths on the campus of Kabul University, and line the streets in the residential areas of Karte Char and Karte Se. In the spring and summer, roses bloom in gardens all over the city and create a spectacular display in Babur's Gardens—my favorite place in Kabul. Thanks to the work of the United Nations, the Agha Khan Foundation, and other agencies, Babur's Gardens have been restored to their former glory and the tree-shaded grounds are once again settings for Afghan family picnics.

As I stroll through Babur's gardens observing the gatherings now, I am carried back to the days when Michael and I shared picnics here with our Peace Corps colleagues. Even then, the gardens offered welcome respite from the noise, dirt, and traffic of this busy city. The crush of people on Kabul streets is here to stay, but here I find hope that the nightmare of fortified buildings guarded by armed soldiers in this post-war city will someday transition to the more civilized, peaceful Kabul that I once knew.

Chapter 17

Adjusting to a New Normal
in Afghanistan

"What's wrong, Michael? The jeep is wobbling worse than ever."

"It's the axle. This road may have done it in. Whoa! There it goes! We're not going anywhere for a while."

"What'll we do?! The nearest villages are ... well, where?!"

"It's about two kilometers to Samangan. I'll have to walk there for help."

"Are you sure? Can you get there okay? What about me?"

"I'm going to have to leave you here in the jeep, Suzanne. We have the Volunteers' mail here and lots of supplies for the Mazar office. We can't leave the stuff unguarded. Do you have a book?"

"Yes. I'm reading *Brothers Karamazov*, but ..."

"I know this isn't comfortable for you, but I think it's best if you stay here and read for an hour or so while I go for help. Keep the car locked. If the local people come to inquire, just keep the doors and windows closed and stay calm. They'll stare, but no one will harm you."

I was used to being alone in the car for short periods of time, but this time, we were in the middle of nowhere. That meant that Michael could be gone for quite a while, and I'd be on my own if something went wrong. I knew, though, that staying in the jeep was probably my best option. I'd attract more attention if I walked to the next village with Michael. I was a little scared about this new situation, but Michael didn't seem overly concerned and he needed me to be brave.

"Okay, Suzanne, I'm going now. I'll be back as soon as I can bring help."

With those words, Michael kissed me on the cheek, got out of the car, and locked it. As he walked toward the village, I wondered how I would do without him if local people showed up. My Dari was still rudimentary. There was nothing to do but follow his instructions and hope that he could find someone to fix the car before the afternoon was over.

For a while, I was alone, but no one is alone for long in Afghanistan, no matter how remote the area seems to be. First a shepherd, then his friend and some travelers came along the road, saw the jeep, and gathered around to peer in the windows and stare. I behaved like an Afghan woman would: I didn't look at them, drew my headscarf more tightly around my head, and kept my eyes on my book. They continued to stare and discuss what they saw.

An hour later, I was immensely relieved to see Michael return with a mechanic and a truck with a chain to tow our jeep. By now, there were a dozen men gathered around the vehicle. Michael and the mechanic explained the problem and a few helped them connect the vehicle to a towline so that we could get the jeep to the mechanic's garage.

When Michael and I made trips to northern Afghanistan, we worried about dangers related to bad roads and weather conditions, but we didn't worry about our personal security as we traveled north through Baghlan Province on our way to Mazar in Balkh Province. We could rely on the local people to help us out if we had difficulty.

Forty years later, I was making monthly round trips (8-12 hours each way) from Kabul to Shiberghan through the Salang Pass for a year and a half to guide the progress of our INGO teacher training activities in the provinces and consult with the project leaders in the capital. Because of my road trips with Michael during our Peace Corps service, I was less concerned about my safety than my international colleagues were. When I resumed those trips just two weeks after the Serena attack, my main safety concern was driving in the snow and ice. Although the road is now paved all the way from Kabul to Shiberghan, the road between Mazar and Shiberghan is treacherous in the winter because it is not salted or plowed regularly. Flying is not an option, either, as fog and snow during winter months often ground the small planes used for domestic flights.

A year after I finished my assignment in Shiberghan, the monthly road trips were no longer safe. By 2010, the security for both Afghans and internationals on road missions through Baghlan Province became unpredictable. Of particular concern was the town of Pul-i-Kumri, which was the normal rest stop and refueling point for INGOs and contractors who operate programs in Afghanistan's northern provinces. Highway robbery, locally initiated checkpoints, and kidnapping attempts caused many INGOs to limit or completely eliminate road trips for international staff. Other agencies ordered their drivers to stop only when absolutely necessary, and some agencies added armed guards to protect their drivers and passengers.

Given the deteriorating security in Afghanistan, I answer questions about my safety and the accomplishments of U.S. efforts in Afghanistan every time I return home.

As I answer these frequent questions, I often forget that I've been experiencing security incidents in Kabul since 2003 when we saw rockets landing near the large ISAF compound that was across the street from the guesthouse I lived in that summer. Perhaps that's because the Afghans in our guesthouses have worked so hard to protect us and, when they were unable to prevent an incident, to repair the damage and reassure us that they would take care of us.

Even my memory of the shock of the Christmas morning explosion in 2003 is mitigated by the tremendous efforts of Afghan staff in our agency to keep that event from ruining the foreigners' Christmas. Carpenters and glaziers worked all day to repair the windows in two guesthouses in time for our Christmas dinner. Meanwhile, the staff of our two guesthouses joined forces to prepare our Christmas dinner. They killed and dressed the two turkeys that we'd been raising and consolidated the cooking in the kitchen that had suffered less damage in the blast. While they were preparing our meal, three of us women who had collected information about the children of our house staff distributed packages of children's clothing to them to take home as our gifts to their families. Throughout the afternoon, our cook Najilla asked me why I insisted that she make a meal for twenty when only seven of us (including our two male colleagues who were returning from a road trip to Jalalabad) would be eating dinner. Her answer came when our dinner table was being set.

"Now it's time for you and the rest of the staff to have dinner, Najilla!" I said with a smile. "You've made us a delicious dinner and the rest of the staff have worked very hard to put our two houses back together. Go and join the others in the kitchen. We'll be fine on our own for the rest of the evening."

As we foreigners enjoyed our Christmas dinner in the front of the house, we heard laughter and references to "the foreigners' *Eid* (celebration)" from the rooms at the back of the house.

"Do you feel safe there now?" is a question that I am constantly asked.

"No, it's not totally safe, but we take whatever measures we need to take to be reasonably safe in an insecure environment. I am realistic about the dangers, but I do what I can to reduce the risks. If I felt afraid, I wouldn't be there."

"Do you really feel that our efforts there are making a difference?" is one of the most distressing questions that I receive after eleven years of effort in Afghanistan.

I used to answer this question with anecdotes about the difference that developed countries were making in Afghanistan. Now, I answer with statistics like these:

In 2002, fewer than 800,000 children—all boys—were enrolled in government-supported schools. The small numbers of girls who did attend school were taught in secret locations or in privately funded institutions. In 2012, just ten years later, over eight million Afghan children were in government-supported schools—nearly 40% of them were girls. By 2008, a teacher training project funded by the U.S. government reached over 77,000 teachers in eleven provinces. Four years later, virtually all thirty-four of the provinces were implementing this teacher training project and expected to impact most of the estimated 160,000 teachers of grades 1-12. The percentage of female teachers has risen from 22% in 2006 to close to 40% today.

Despite the efforts of radical conservatives to prevent girls from getting an education by burning down girls' schools, shooting female teachers, or attacking school girls directly with horrible tactics like throwing acid in their faces (as happened in Kandahar in early 2009), parents keep sending their daughters to school. Even though vocal advocates (including many Afghan men) for girls' education are potential targets for extreme conservatives, we cannot give up now. We cannot lose the hard-won gains made by getting more girls' schools built, more female teachers into the classroom, keeping more girls in school after sixth grade, and getting high school girls interested in the teaching profession. From this collective perspective, my answer to why I continue to return to Afghanistan is, "I need to keep supporting the Afghan government's education efforts—especially those for women. I don't want the Taliban and their terrorist allies to win. The Afghan people deserve better."

On January 15, 2009, a year after the attack on the Serena Hotel, I was in that same hotel for a lunch meeting regarding my transition from work with INGOs to leadership of a large contract supporting higher education. During that visit, I reflected on how much that attack had altered my view of the security situation in Afghanistan. Until the attack on that hotel, there were times that I could almost forget that I was living in a conflict zone. I had slipped into a comfortable after-work rhythm of exercising at the hotel gym and swimming laps in the pool before joining friends for dinner at a nearby restaurant. I now understood that beneath the "normalcy" of daily life in Kabul, the deadly struggle for political control of Afghanistan was ongoing.

The attack on the Serena also marked a change in tactics of the terrorists that caught security advisors to international agencies by surprise. It happened in the evening. Until that event, most terrorist attacks had happened in the morning. The Serena attack was also the first of a series of targeted attacks on places where foreigners gather—foreign embassies, hotels, restaurants, and supermarkets. These attacks are reminders that there are people in Kabul who resent the presence of foreigners in their city and the way that we live there. Like many others, I did not realize that the resentment of the conservative terrorists extends to those who collaborate with foreigners. The Serena Hotel was targeted because it is owned by Agha Khan, a member of a minority sect of Islam whom extremists resent because of his toleration of Christian coworkers and employees.

While daily life in Kabul appears normal to the casual visitor, foreigners who have resided in the city for years have learned to expect spectacular, large scale attacks at least once a year. In the years following the 2008 Serena attack, Kabul residents experienced the bombing of the German Embassy, the British Council, ISAF Headquarters, and buildings near the American Embassy. There were bombings of several hotels in which most of the guests are foreigners, as well as supermarkets—especially those operated by Hazaras—and multiple suicide bombs targeting convoys of NATO forces on Darulaman Road and Jalalabad Road.

Daily security reports now include an extensive glossary of acronyms used to describe the various kinds of incidents that have occurred. When you live with continuous reports of kidnappings and suicide attacks you almost forget that Kabul wasn't always this way. My friend Ruby, who returned to Kabul after six years in the United States, saw the situation more clearly. In 2002 and 2003, she noted, the threats were general— rockets fired into this or that portion of the city. By 2009, the attacks were targeted at individuals and groups—kidnappings, suicide bombs, robberies, and attacks on individuals. Those kinds of crimes are far more dangerous to civilian aid workers and contractors.

More alarming for Afghan residents of Kabul are attacks on government agencies and high profile government leaders by extremists who oppose their policies. High profile Afghans are constant targets. The motives behind these crimes vary. Some are personal vendettas, others are politically motivated, some are solely for money, and some are the work of extremists. Whatever the motives, Afghans who are seen as having more possessions, privileges, and/or power than their neighbors need to worry about their security and the security of their extended family.

The escalation in security incidents forced me to re-evaluate my purpose in Afghanistan and whether my work was important enough to continue to put my family through the anxiety of listening to news reports about the worsening situation. Because I was able to make a significant difference in education when I began working at the national level, I ultimately decided to continue working in the country, but to change the way I work. I returned to my original intention in coming here—to work within Afghan education ministries and institutions and make collaborative decisions with them on how to develop their educational systems. My efforts to follow that intention brought me back to my professional and personal roots in higher education.

My path back to the universities started with a temporary faculty assignment as an outreach instructor with the American University of Afghanistan.

"Hello Teacher!"

One of my students at the Roshan Telecommunications Headquarters greeted me as he entered the conference room where eleven young managers and I met two evenings a week. It had been a long time since I had been addressed as "teacher." I was delighted to be back in that role, despite the energy drain of teaching three hours after working a challenging eight hour day at the INGO office. The eleven Afghan students (ten men and one woman) made me think of community college students whom I had taught in Seattle. Like the evening community college students, these Afghans were highly motivated, intelligent, keenly aware of the outside world, and eager to learn the English language skills that would get them better jobs. I responded to their energy and enthusiasm for learning by offering fast-paced participative activities that centered on communication challenges they faced as mid-level managers in their work place.

"Great report, Sayed, you really analyzed the problem well."

"Hameedullah, what do you think of Sayed's recommendations for addressing the problem?"

"Nassima, that was a very good explanation of your department's accomplishments. I think you are ready to present it to your colleagues."

"Shabuddin, can you identify the biggest customer service challenges that Roshan is facing now?"

"Keramuddin, how would you handle this customer complaint?"

These young Afghan managers—all in business attire that one sees in Western offices—are never seen on international news reports. However, they represent thousands of employees in their late 20s and early 30s who support government and private sector offices in Kabul. They are the post-conflict generation of Afghanistan. One cannot help but feel hopeful about Afghanistan's future after spending a few hours with them.

The program at Roshan Telecommunications is one of many offered to corporate offices in Kabul by the Professional Development Institute of the American University of Afghanistan (AUAF). My visits to the AUAF campus felt like a homecoming after five years away from working in higher education. I didn't realize how much I missed the rhythm of the academic year and the interaction with faculty and students that characterized the decade that I had been a community college dean.

In the last two months of 2008, I worked with twenty Kabul University professors to develop competencies for teachers that would become the basis for a certification system for teachers in Ministry of

Education schools. As I entered the conference room full of male professors at the Ministry of Education Teacher Education Department, I knew that I was on trial. When they individually introduced themselves, each man emphasized his overseas graduate studies and years of experience in his discipline. I followed their lead and saw the look of surprise on their faces when I told them that I had a Ph.D. in Education from the University of Washington. They were even more surprised that I had spent as many years in the classroom as many of them had. During our months of working together, we grew in mutual appreciation and respect. As it turned out, this assignment was good preparation for full-time engagement with Afghan universities in my next position.

I was on the brink of leaving Afghanistan permanently in 2009 when Washington State University (WSU) offered me the opportunity to take over the leadership of a project to improve the capacity of the Afghanistan higher education system. The woman who had initiated the project needed to return home for health reasons. After considering the security precautions I would need to take while moving about the city and noting that the Kabul University campus appeared to be a safer environment than an INGO office with multiple foreign staff members, I decided that the opportunities to make a difference outweighed the risks, so I signed up for three more years.

The opportunity to use both my doctoral training and the skills acquired while working for state education agencies in order to make a difference in Afghanistan's higher education institutions was too good to pass up. Both the U.S. government and the Afghan government finally recognized that Afghan universities would play an important role in preparing the next generation of the country's leaders, and I wanted to be part of this effort.

Chapter 18

Kandahar

The last computer lab that the WSU higher education project opened was at Kandahar University. The donor agency representative had been reluctant to allow our project staff to open a lab at that location because "it was too dangerous." However, we persuaded her supervisor that Kandahar would remain dangerous until the people got the aid that other provinces were getting. Syed Muzaffar, the Afghan deputy of our project, was familiar with Kandahar from his years as a refugee in Quetta. He and I both felt that it was urgent for us to open the lab before the scheduled military surge in the summer of 2010, so we travelled together on a Pamir Airlines flight to Kandahar to open the computer lab in June of that year.

In order to reduce risks for me on this trip, Muzaffar and I spoke in Dari from the time that we arrived at Kabul airport where we sat among turbaned men from Kandahar (there were no other women) as we waited for our flight. Muzaffar treated me as if I were a female member of his family. I wore a modest black *shalwar kamize* and veil onto the airplane but carried my blue *chadri* in a leather bag to wear as soon as we got to Kandahar Airport. As we entered the middle of the terminal, I asked Muzaffar for guidance:

"Just tell me when to put on the *chadri*," I said.

Muzaffar scanned the terminal. "Do it now," he said in a decisive voice.

Once I had on the *chadri*, we walked briskly to the terminal door where a fleet of mini-buses—all crowded with men—were waiting. Muzaffar picked out a vehicle that had a front seat reserved for a female passenger and told me in Dari to get in. Aware that the eyes of ten men were focused on me, I silently obeyed and sat hunched forward with my eyes lowered as the minibus travelled to the main road. There, Muzaffar and I got out and tried to identify the university car that was to pick us up.

"What color is the car that is supposed to pick us up?" I asked.

"I don't know," Muzaffar replied as he dialed the phone number of our project team leader.

As I scanned the cars lining the road, I thought of the many photos of destruction caused by vehicle-borne suicide bombs on this road that I had seen on Afghan television. Before Muzaffar could complete his call, I saw a familiar face in a white car. The manager of our e-learning center got out and ushered us in.

On the drive into Kandahar, I warily scanned the streets for signs for danger. I was surprised at the well-paved wide boulevards with opposing traffic lanes separated by traffic islands filled with rosebushes, grass, and benches. Most of the buildings looked new. Then I remembered why: most of the city had been destroyed in all the fighting that had taken place the decade before this visit.

We passed the intersection near the main square where there had been a shootout between the Taliban and NATO forces the day before. The Taliban had decided to bait the NATO troops by organizing an informal meeting during which they occupied the benches in one of the traffic islands. Our two Kabul-based technical team members, Shams and Noorullah, who had installed the computer lab were staying in the hotel across the street from the site of the battle and were quite shaken when we met them.

"You should have seen it," they said in unison.

Shams said, "The NATO troops were over there and the Taliban were sitting right there. When the NATO troops started moving this way, all the Taliban pulled out the guns they'd been hiding."

"Then the shooting started," Noorullah added. "We just tried to stay away from the windows so the bullets wouldn't hit us."

We learned that the reasons the streets seemed empty of traffic was that the entire city had gone on lockdown after the gun battle. They expected more shooting to follow.

Our car finally came to a heavily secured street with no outlet. Our INGO guesthouse was there. Once inside the guesthouse, I changed quickly from the *chadri* to a black skirt and tunic over which I wore a black *abaya,* a long coat similar to those worn by some Arab women in the Emirates, with a matching veil. It was over 90 degrees Fahrenheit, so I knew that the rest of the day would be uncomfortable.

We travelled by car to Kandahar University, where the Vice Chancellor greeted us enthusiastically. Like all the other men present, he was dressed informally in a white *shalwar kamize*. The Kandahar Education Officer for the donor agency arrived with three armed American soldiers as her bodyguards. She and I were the only visible females in a room of over 100 men who participated in the ceremony. She agreed to remove her flak jacket and helmet for her speech, during which she expressed the belief that having this computer lab would open many educational opportunities for the Kandahar University students. I, of course, had no guards and wore the black *abaya* and matching veil when I made a speech about the responsibility of students to share with others—including members of their families—the computer skills and English language skills they would be acquiring in this new lab.

The Vice Chancellor made the first cut in the ribbon across the doorway to the lab and insisted that I make the second cut. In doing so, he was acknowledging me as the most important guest present, which was quite a compliment in a mostly male gathering. The Vice Chancellor then indicated the order in which other special guests—including the donor Education Officer and Muzaffar—should also make cuts in the ribbon. A student stood inside the door of the lab with a tray of wrapped candy, which everyone took as they entered the lab to inspect it. After all the special guests were in the room, the students were welcomed and encouraged to take seats at the computer workstations for the first time. They were clearly thrilled to be sitting at computers so new that foam covers were still protecting the screens.

After the ceremony, our project team members (all young men) asked why I was talking so long to the smallest of the three bodyguards for the Education Officer. They were shocked to learn that the guard was a female soldier who was also a veterinarian. The women they encountered at the opening ceremony, two in military uniforms and one in an academic leadership position, certainly challenged their traditional views of women's roles in society, which is exactly why we participated in the event.

The director of the learning center at the university invited Muzaffar and me for lunch at his family home.

Kandahar

"My family would like to meet you, Dr. Griffin," Sharif said," especially my mother."

"I'd like to meet her, as well, Sharif," I said. After the last few hours of being in male environments, I was looking forward to being in an Afghan home in which I could converse with other women. I was also dying to take off at least the outer layer of my clothing on this sweltering, hot day.

Sharif's brother greeted us at the door of his nicely decorated, middle class home in a quiet section of the city. He settled Muzaffar in the main living room while Sharif escorted me to the family entertainment space where I met his mother and father, as well as his lovely young wife and daughter.

Sharif's father and mother greeted me in Pashtu and he translated.

His father said, "Dr. Griffin, welcome. We are honored to have you and Muzaffar visit our home. Our family has always supported education, and we appreciate your support for our university and for our son."

"Thank you, sir," I answered in English. "I am honored to be your guest. You have a lovely home and I'm sure you are proud of your son, Sharif. Without him, we could never have gotten this learning center with the computer lab established."

Sharif's mother took one look at my flushed face under the black veil and said in Pashtu, which Sharif translated, "Dr. Griffin, its summer and it's very hot in Kandahar at this time. That black veil is too hot for this time of year. I have something else for you to wear." Then she excused herself and went to another room.

While I was meeting Sharif's wife and little three-year-old daughter, his mother came back with a lightweight yellow veil.

"Here you are," she said. "This is much better for you, especially in the house." As she was speaking, Sharif and his father discretely slipped through the doorway to join Muzaffar and Sharif's brother while I changed my veil.

Sharif's mother was right. The yellow veil was much cooler. I only wished that I could also replace the black cotton tunic that I was wearing, as well as the black cotton pants that I had to wear under my skirt according to the tradition of Pashtun women in the provinces. However, my head was cooler.

Somehow, Sharif's family had been able to keep their living room cool. Being able to enjoy a delicious lunch in this cool room was a wonderful respite after the morning ceremony at the university. Finally, however, it was time to leave. Muzaffar and I thanked the family for their hospitality and took our leave.

We were picked up in an unmarked INGO car that drove Muzaffar and me back to the INGO guesthouse. It was so hot that we could do nothing but retire to rest in our respective rooms until the sun went down. The house cook served us and two other guests in the house a light dinner outside in the garden at dusk. In such a lovely atmosphere, we could almost forget about the shootout in the middle of the city just twenty-four hours before.

The next morning, we were to pick up Shams and Noorullah at their hotel and go directly to the airport. Muzaffar and the driver saw no need for me to wear the blue *chadri*. They said the *abaya* and veil would be fine, as I wasn't getting out of the car until I got to the airport. What we all forgot, however, was that because there would be three male passengers, they would all sit in the back and I would be in the front seat with the driver. Since I was sitting in front, my face would be fully visible to all who cared to look at the occupants of our car.

We'd arranged for Shams and Noorullah to meet us at the corner of a major intersection to save us from the time consuming process of going through security at the hotel parking lot. Unfortunately, they were late. As we waited at the corner, large numbers of Pashtun day workers who were lined up along the street waiting to be hired, began to show a lot of curiosity toward this woman in the front seat.

"I never thought I'd want to wear the *chadri*, but I wish I had it now!" I said to myself. I was increasingly concerned that the men would figure out that I was a foreign woman. If they guessed I was an American, there could be trouble.

Muzaffar and the driver were also concerned. When the two young men finally arrived, he motioned to them to get in the car quickly. As the driver accelerated, he said, "You know it's dangerous to be sitting on this street in an INGO car, even if it's unmarked. And it's extremely dangerous for Dr. Suzanne."

As the conversation continued, I decided that the only thing I could do to minimize the potential danger of being identified as a foreign

Kandahar

woman was to literally keep my head down. I rode most of the way to the airport looking at my lap instead of the road.

Since the INGO car had a gate pass at the airport, I was spared another ride to the terminal in a minibus full of men. Once through the security stations, I was thrilled to be able to remove the *abaya* and veil and throw the lovely yellow veil from Sharif's mother over my head. I didn't care that I was one of a few women in the airport, and the only one wearing a yellow scarf. I felt safe for the first time in twenty-four hours.

As we settled into our seats in the departure area, I spotted a large photograph of the Kandahar Airport high up on the opposite wall. The photo was from the end of the 1960s, so it showed the airport as Michael and I had seen it when we traveled to Kandahar. I looked around and remembered how much Michael admired the architecture of this terminal, even though few people were flying in and out of this airport in its first years of operation.

"USAID sure knows how to build airport terminals," I said to Muzaffar. "Look at that photo! Now look around you. The airport hasn't changed much in all these years, despite all the fighting that has gone on around it. These beautiful high parabola-shaped arches with floor to ceiling glass windows between them still look pretty modern and they are in good shape!"

"They do, Dr. Suzanne," Muzaffar agreed. "It's reassuring to know that some parts of Kandahar made it through all the warfare in this area. Kandahar used to be a great city. It was the capitol of Afghanistan long ago."

"I know, Muzaffar. I really couldn't feel that my work in Afghanistan was complete until I'd done something to help the people in Kandahar. It was a bit scary coming here, but I'm glad we did it."

"So am I, Dr. Suzanne. Thank you for making this trip."

At that point, our flight was announced and we flew "home" to Kabul.

Chapter 19

A Girl Becomes a Bride

When I came to Afghanistan in 1968 as a new bride, both men and women were perplexed that I was not eager to prove my fertility by having children immediately. They were even more perplexed that Michael did not seem concerned about demonstrating his fertility right away by following the usual Afghan custom of fathering a child within the first year of our marriage. When we were out of earshot of men, Afghan women quizzed me incessantly about why I didn't want to have babies right away and what drugs and methods we used to delay having children. One of my motivations for learning Dari during our Peace Corps days was to be able to respond to the women's questions without involving Michael or an interpreter.

When I returned to Afghanistan as a grandmother, I did not expect the issue of childbearing to be raised again. However, Afghans remain curious about Americans' decisions about their children.

"How many children do you have, Suzanne?"

"Two daughters."

"No sons?!"

"No, but I have grandsons."

"That's good. How many?"

"Three."

"How old are they?"

"They are eleven, nine, and three."

"Very good, but you have no sons?!"

"No."

"That's too bad. If you had sons, they would take care of you now that your husband is gone."

"I know. But my daughters help me. Sometimes their husbands also help."

"Do you have brothers?"

"No. I have three sisters."

"No brothers and no sons! Why did you stop having babies after two daughters? Why didn't you try to have some sons?"

"Because two children were enough for us and we were happy with two daughters."

"Even your husband was happy without sons?!"

"Yes. He loved his daughters. He also knew that it would be hard for me to manage taking care of more than two children while I was teaching at the university."

"Oh. But couldn't your mother or mother-in-law help?"

"My mother and my mother-in-law were also teachers. My mother and father did not live very close to us when our daughters were little, but they sometimes took care of them on weekends. My husband's mother lived thousands of miles away."

"Oh!"

At this point the conversation usually stops. Most Afghans—both men and women—cannot comprehend these types of family dynamics. From the perspective of Afghan culture, my present life situation is as bad as can be imagined. I am a widow with no brothers and no sons. Hence, the Afghans were particularly concerned when my father recently passed away. In their minds, I am in a precarious position because there are no family men to protect me either in Afghanistan or in the United States.

The strong commitment of Afghan men—particularly Pashtun men—to protect the women of their families is at the root of many cultural practices that govern gender relationships in Afghanistan. One of them is the early marriage age for Afghan girls. Afghan boys are raised with the understanding that they are supposed to protect their sisters, and Afghan fathers are expected to protect their daughters. The domain of this protection includes both guarding the girls from physical harm and guarding their reputations. When girls reach puberty, fathers and sons get nervous about making certain that their daughters remain "good women" so that they will have the best chance to have a good husband. The mothers, aunts, and grandmothers, most of whom married in their early teens, also get anxious about protecting the virginity of the adolescent girls in their family, so they start pressing for engagement or marriage.

This family pressure for engagement or marriage often becomes overwhelming for girls once they enter their teens.

There is also discomfort among family members over the fact that most of the teachers in the high schools are men. This staffing situation is particularly true of areas outside of the major cities and provincial capitals because few female teachers in non-urban areas have the Bachelor's degree that is required to teach high school subjects. Since Afghan families are concerned about having men who are not related to them in power positions over their daughters, they are not comfortable having their daughters in classrooms with male teachers.

The combination of family pressure to marry, the scarcity of female teachers in middle schools, and rudimentary facilities in high schools causes three quarters of Afghan girls who have enrolled in school to drop out after sixth grade. Teenage girls who remain in school after grade six encounter an environment which is hostile or, at best, not welcoming. Unless they are lucky enough to live in cities where there are girls' high schools, they must enter a world of men to get a high school education. Girls who manage to remain in school after seventh grade are usually there because their fathers and/or other strong males in their family are supporting their education.

Sometimes, even fathers of girls who want to continue in school have to make compromises with other family members to keep their daughters in school until they graduate from high school. This was the case with my colleague and friend, Walid. All family members, including his wife (whose schooling ended with fifth grade and who married Walid when she was fifteen) pressed for the marriage of their oldest daughter Sayma to her first cousin once she turned fourteen. Although Walid helped select the young man as his daughter's future husband, he wanted Sayma to finish high school before marriage. During months of negotiations between Walid and his family members on this issue, he would not discuss the possibility of Sayma's marriage with her "because she is still a child." Finally, Walid agreed to allow the family to hold an engagement party for Sayma and her cousin when she turned fifteen. However, the future husband was not allowed into his house again until just before their wedding, which took place when she was sixteen.

Although I was honored to be the only foreigner invited to Sayma's engagement party, I accepted the invitation with some misgivings because of my opposition to her marrying so young.

At 9:00 a.m. it was already hot—too hot, I decided, to wear the traditional bland overcoat over my lapis blue and sea green embroidered party dress. I tried to ignore the stares of early morning shoppers as I swept into the best sweets shop in Karte Se to buy boxes of traditional cookies and *halvah* for the family.

When the agency car delivered me to the front gate of Walid's NGO office, a small group of men—some of whom wore special occasion turbans—greeted me warmly. I have known most of the male relatives in the immediate family for several years. However, this office was soon to be the gathering place for over two hundred male relatives and friends of the engaged couple, so Walid was anxious to move me to the place where the female relatives had started gathering. He escorted me to the SUV that was standing by, motioned me into the back seat and explained that his cousin would drive me through this conservative neighborhood to his home.

As soon as I was through the door to his home, Walid reappeared behind me and, in a low tone, reminded me of the identities and names of the half dozen women gathered there. I hadn't seen some of them since his younger son's naming party that had been held four years previously, so he guessed that I would have forgotten some of their names.

"Susan, this is my sister, that is my mother, over there is my wife's mother and her sister."

Before he could finish these introductions, Walid's fifty-year-old unmarried sister, who is mentally challenged, came into the foyer, gripped me in a warm embrace and kissed my face a dozen times. I hadn't seen her for more than a year, and she was delighted when I congratulated her on having completed the *Haj* trip that year.

I entered the main salon where female family members were waiting for the big event to start. Walid's mother sat on a cushion by the window in the central part of the room. She was dressed in a tasteful black and red paisley *shalwar kamize* with a matching veil. Though I had been told about her failing health, I was shocked at the lines of pain and age that were etched on her strong brown face. Her lovely grey eyes had turned milky and betrayed the pain that she was enduring even as she greeted me. Despite her pain, her hands were still strong enough to firmly hold my face as we exchanged five or six kisses on each other's cheeks.

Walid's mother-in-law looked even more fragile. Her white *shalwar kamize* and long silver braids accentuated her ill health. I sensed that my kisses of greeting to her had to be delivered gently. Walid's sister-in-law, who sat next to her mother, was as handsome as I remembered her from our first meeting. In height, bearing, and facial features, she looked like an older version of Walid's wife. Her brown face now had more wrinkles than when I last saw her and her hair had turned completely grey. However, beautiful brown eyes, strong features, a dignified smile, and straight posture called to my mind the faces of movie stars who have retained their good looks as they aged.

As I finished this initial round of greetings, Walid's wife entered the room. She is a tall woman—and looked more slender after the birth of her seventh child than at any time in the five years that I have known her. She also looked slightly anemic.

"Tabrik, Beebe Haji!" ("Congratulations, wife of the *Haji!"*) I exclaimed as I greeted her.

"Tashakor, Susan. *Khosh Amadi, vali tu na amad bad as Haj."* (Thank you, Suzanne, but you did not come to greet me after the *Haj.*)

"Babeksheyn, Khonum, vali ma na tanest miyayam." ("I'm sorry, ma'am, but I couldn't come.")

My perceived exclusion from the post *Haj* celebrations had been a sore point with me. Although I have been the only foreigner invited to their major family events, I was not invited to participate in any of the many gatherings held during the winter to honor the returned *Hajis*—Walid, his sister, and his wife. Walid was adamant that I wasn't being excluded from these gatherings. He said that I would have been welcomed to their home. We concluded that the issue was my inability to discern between the occasions on which I needed a special invitation and the occasions on which I could just drop in, as Afghans do to welcome returning *Hajis.*

Shortly after I was seated among the women, Sayma came in to greet me on her way to the beauty parlor. She practiced her English as she greeted me with a handshake.

"Hi Susan! How are you? Thank you for coming."

A Girl Becomes a Bride

"Hello, Sayma. I'm fine thank you. Congratulations!"

"Thank you, Suzanne. I am going to the *arushga* (beauty salon) now. I will see you later. Bye."

"Bye, Sayma. I'll see you later," I said.

As she left the room, I wondered whether she didn't feel a mixture of sadness and excitement on this occasion. While Sayma was the focus of the celebration and was about to be showered with engagement gifts by her fiancé, she was also leaving her girlhood behind on this day. After today, she would be treated as a woman who was promised to a young man who would become her husband.

During the next two hours, I joined the women of the family who sat on cushions arranged around the perimeter of the salon and greeted new arrivals. Those of us who were able to stand easily rose to embrace the new guests. The older women and the mothers holding infants remained seated. The grandmothers of the engaged couple received the greetings of guests who dropped to their knees and kissed the grandmothers' cheeks or hands, depending on their relationship and age difference. In between arrivals, we sometimes talked and other times just sat together in silence. Afghan men and women don't feel a need to talk continuously when they are together. They have developed the art of quietly enjoying each other's presence. I was grateful for the periods of silence. I am used to conversing in Dari and felt at a distinct disadvantage among this group of women, most of whom only spoke Pashtu. I understood about 50% of what they said, but I grew tired of relying on the few Dari speakers in the room to translate my every utterance to the others.

The quiet lull in Sayma's party was broken around 11:00 a.m. with the sound of music outside the house as the oldest sister of the groom arrived in a heavily decorated red *shalwar kamize* and a veil hung with brass coins. As she was greeting everyone, her four sisters arrived at the door banging *tambours* and singing Pashtun songs. They wore heavy makeup and traditional formal clothes. One sister wore a green organdy dress with a huge skirt, like the prom dresses that the girls in the United States wore in the 1950s. I concluded that she was recently married, as new brides wear fine clothes to all formal events for the first year after their marriage. The other three sisters wore *shalwar kamizes* of colored nylon in pink, turquoise, and yellow.

By now over seventy women and dozens of children filled two salons—one was dominated by the groom's sisters who were singing and playing the *tabla* while the other was occupied by women with babies and toddlers. At noon, the rooms were quickly rearranged for tea service. The cook from Walid's NGO office ordered young girls from the family to roll oilcloths down the middle of each room. Under her guidance, the girls efficiently distributed plates of cookies, dishes of sweets and nuts, and small bowls of cream. Then they poured cups of green tea. Because we were packed together on cushions surrounding the oilcloth, there was no room for the servers to walk down the sides, so they walked down the middle of the eating area in their bare feet, a custom that I have experienced at every Afghan meal served to large groups and which I try not to think about as I eat.

The singing and conversation stopped while everyone enjoyed tea. Children crumbled cookies, got sticky fingers from taking candy in and out of their mouths, and wandered across the table surface. Most of the women were so absorbed in drinking tea that they did not seem to notice the intense activity going on in the courtyard visible through the large windows of one room. As I sat opposite the window, I had a clear view of the scene. In the corner, a cook was stirring a large cauldron of *pilau*. Meanwhile, Walid was ordering around squadrons of young boys who were carrying armloads of bread and platters of cups and dishes to the gate. Obviously, the lunch for the men was being carried to the office building where two hundred were celebrating.

After a half hour, tea was done. The young girls collected the dishes and cups and rolled up the oilcloths that were now full of crumbled cookies. The grooms' sisters changed their position in the room so that the occupants of both rooms could now participate in their singing and *tabla* playing. The sister wearing the green organdy gown started dancing. I did not understand the Pashtun songs, but some were repeated over and over. Some women joined in, others listened, and at least half went on with their conversations. At 1:00 p.m., Walid tried to get the singers to stop so that the servers could make preparations for the women's lunch. He started by tapping on the window, but no one paid attention. Then he came in the room and motioned for the singers to stop. Again, he was either not noticed or ignored. Finally, he had to enter the crowded room full of women and ask the lead *tabla* player to get the group to stop playing and move out of the center of the doorway.

The lunch was the best that I have had at an Afghan engagement party. Instead of the standard, greasy *Kabuli Pilau* with a sprinkling of carrots and raisins, we had *shirin pilau*—a special occasion dish with candied orange rinds, almonds, pistachios, and saffron rice heaped over tender pieces of chicken. Side dishes included bowls of beef with boiled onions called *shesh piaz*, plates of fresh sliced cucumbers, tomatoes, radishes, green peppers and green onions, bowls of yogurt, and slabs of *naan*. Large platters of sweet green melon were offered for dessert.

After lunch, I asked to see Sayma, as it appeared that her formal entrance to the party would be delayed until after 3:00 p.m., when I had to leave for a conference call with my agency's office in the United States. Walid's wife took me upstairs to the salon in which I had shared many dinners with Walid's family. Sayma was there in her traditional green— the color of Islam—organdy gown and veil. A tiara was fitted onto her elaborately styled hair. Her young face had been covered with the traditional whitener and painted with rouge, eye shadow, and red lipstick. Long false eyelashes changed the look of her eyes from an innocent young girl to an indifferent prospective bride. Although she was eager to pose for pictures with her siblings and girlfriends, she did not smile in any of them. Afghan culture requires that the brides-to-be look solemn and show no emotion. If they look happy, the wedding participants would suspect that they are not virgins and are eager to be with their husbands. Instead, they are supposed to be focused on leaving the security of their family to go to their husband's family. As virgins, they are also expected to be unaware of the potential pleasures of marital intimacy. Some young brides-to-be don't have to be told not to look happy. I have seen some who look sad, resigned, and even terrified of the new life ahead of them. I was relieved that Sayma wore none of these expressions. She seemed content with her situation.

As I returned to the salons on the main floor, the prospective groom arrived with two large suitcases containing the clothing, jewelry and other items he had bought for Sayma. I hadn't seen him in many months, so we exchanged greetings and I congratulated him on his engagement. Meanwhile, his sisters had wheeled the suitcases into the salon in which

Sayma's female relatives were seated. Each item was removed from the suitcases and handed to the women for inspection. I watched as the gifts were approved or rejected by the females in the family before Sayma even had a chance to register her opinion. This ritual is such a contrast to bridal showers in my country where the bride-to-be is the center of attention. She is the one who opens and expresses appreciation for her gifts. Moreover, the way that the gifts are received in Afghanistan makes it seem as if the bride had been sold to the groom for these goods. The women urged me to join them in inspecting the gifts. Masking my emotions, I thanked Walid's wife for including me in the gathering and noted that I had to leave. Then I wished everyone farewell.

I saw Walid the next day in a meeting. He told me that I had missed one of the best parts of the event—the men's procession with the groom to the women's gathering, the formal joining of the families, and the presentation of the couple together. I was sorry to have missed it, though I had participated in this ritual at an engagement party for a female doctor who had been my colleague.

I also knew that it might have been difficult for me to enthusiastically respond to the arrival of the young couple while silently mourning the abrupt end to this girl's childhood.

Sayma's wedding day came a year later. Despite my misgivings about her marriage before she completed high school, I could not miss this celebration, which I attended with my friend Ruby. Walid and his male relatives welcomed us as we got out of the car and ushered us into the wedding hall. We were immediately taken to the women's side of the hall and escorted to one of the front tables by the stage so that we could easily see the bride and groom and visit with the female relatives.

Although there were over five hundred guests, this was a medium-sized wedding by Afghan standards. This afternoon wedding was more restrained in tone and in dress than the evening Tajik and Uzbek weddings that I've attended. Only the younger women, beginning with the female relatives of the bride and groom, danced to the live music that we could hear from the men's side of the hall. The rest of us visited with each other and watched the dancing. The women at this event did not evaluate each other's attire and dancing skills the way I had seen at other weddings. Instead, they spent their time minding their children and

A Girl Becomes a Bride

waiting for the highlight events—the appearance of the bride with her mother and father, the appearances of the bride and groom at the beginning and end of the event, the greeting of the bride and groom by special guests, the arrival of the wedding meal, and the cutting of the cake.

The Pashtun women at this wedding were dressed modestly. They did not follow the custom of Kabul women from other ethnic groups who wore Las Vegas-style tight, glittery dresses. Instead, some women wore traditional large, elaborately embroidered skirts with loose-fitting embroidered blouses and light veils over headdresses. Others wore *shalwar kamizes* that were brightly colored and beaded or in light summer colors. Older women wore long skirts and jackets in pastel or neutral hues. The widows in attendance wore the traditional white veils that I had seen at all Afghan weddings that I have attended. However, they sat with their female relatives rather than being segregated as I have seen at some gatherings. (I have often wondered what Afghans think of my violation of the expected dress and behavior for widows in this part of the world. I wear brightly colored clothes and join in the fun of women's gatherings along with the women who are still married.)

The ceremony of the father and mother giving away their daughter in marriage had already taken place in the family home, so it was not included in the public ceremony of Sayma's wedding. After the wedding, Sayma would go to live with her husband's family. Since her family and her husband's family were on good terms, she would be allowed to visit her family regularly. Other brides, particularly those in rural areas, might not see their own families for long periods of time. When the bride lives with her in-laws, she is under the direction of her mother-in-law. If the two women do not get along, the situation for the young newlyweds can be very unhappy.

Although parents don't literally give away their daughters during the wedding ceremonies in our country, the walk down the aisle that a bride takes with her father and the father's handing of his daughter to the groom is both emotional and symbolic. I clearly remember Michael's mixture of pride and wistfulness as he walked our older daughter Rachael up the aisle, just eight months before his death. Six year later, I saw a mixture of sorrow and love in my father's eyes when, at the age of eighty-five, he took on the role that Michael would have had and proudly walked his granddaughter Sarah up the aisle to her future husband.

In Sayma's wedding, the scene was one of family solidarity. Once the bride and groom had entered and taken the stage, they were joined by the parents of both the bride and the groom, as well as by members of the extended family that I have come to know and love. As I left the celebration, I wished the couple happiness and told Ruby that I hoped Sayma would finish her education. Happily, Sayma's father has prevailed. She finished high school before she became the mother of a baby boy who is now two years old. Her university education has been further delayed, however, with the arrival of a second child—a baby girl. Sayma is one of Afghanistan's lucky brides. Because the families are close, Sayma and her mother see each other almost every week.

Chapter 20

Unfinished Business

Instead of returning to the familiar realm of higher education in America as I intended in 2009, I joined the effort to rebuild the Afghan higher education system. On walks across campus at Kabul University (KU), I often thought of afternoon walks that Michael and I used to take along the tree-lined pathways of the campus during our Peace Corps days. In a city in which poor security no longer allows leisurely walks on public streets, Michael would have valued the peaceful walks on the campus as much as I still do.

I wondered how Michael would regard the new buildings constructed by foreign governments to replace the ruins of war. With his urban planning background, I am sure that he would have been critical of the apparent lack of an overall design plan. Regardless of the architecture, KU has come a long way since the hot summer days in 2002 when I visited the shattered buildings on the dusty campus where most trees were dying because of drought. During those visits, professors who had offices sat at battered desks next to broken windows and wept when I asked if they had any books left. When I mentioned getting computers, they laughed bitterly and asked me how they could operate computers if they had no electricity. At that time, the idea of internet connectivity on the campus seemed impossible.

Thanks to the NATO Silk Afghanistan Project, the entire campus is now networked. There are computer labs in many KU departments, the KU librarians have been trained to electronically catalog tens of thousands of donated books and have implemented an electronic check out system. Ten years after the Taliban barred women from the campus, more than a third of the students are women and the number of female university instructors is increasing at a steady rate. KU classrooms are filled to capacity during both the daytime and evening sessions.

When I leave the university buildings of the many campuses that I visit, I love being enveloped by the chatter of students as they pour out of the classrooms and gather in groups in the courtyards and breeze-ways. I note the changing fashions of the girls who experiment with ways to balance fashions they see in magazines with Islamic requirements for modesty. The current fashion among female students on Kabul campuses is colorful veils or Iranian style headscarves and knee length, belted trench coats over skinny jeans.

The outcomes of U.S. funded projects with Afghan universities will positively impact the post-secondary education of current and future generations of young Afghan adults. Since few foreigners are involved in implementing the projects, the accomplishments are, in large part, the results of the work of talented Afghan teams. Young men and women who have just received their degrees in Computer Science have provided computer skills and English instruction to hundreds of university in-structors and thousands of university students. University librarians were trained on cataloging by an intelligent Hazara woman with a Master's degree in Library Science.

Both male and female university instructors have returned from overseas Master's degree programs to revise curricula and instruction in Law, Engineering, Computer Science, and English. Through partnerships with American universities, new Master's degrees have been established in universities in Kabul. These programs have made graduate degrees available to students within the country for the first time in thirty years.

The university projects have given me the opportunity to work directly with the chancellors of the universities in Kabul, as well as the regional universities—Balkh University in Mazar, Herat University in Herat, Nangarhar University in Jalalabad, Sheik Zayed University in Khost, and Kandahar University. Some chancellors of those institutions are impressive men who received advanced degrees in Europe, North America, and Australia, and who have left their families and comfortable lives in those countries to come back to help rebuild their homeland. I never dreamed in 2002 that I would be able to participate on equal footing with these men to implement the Ministry of Higher Education strategic plan, as well as work with them individually on plans to use the e-learning centers on their campuses to help their faculty members upgrade knowledge of their disciplines and integrate technology into their instruction.

Lessons of Love in Afghanistan

I have recently returned to the classroom at Kabul Education University to help prepare university English instructors for their Master's degrees in TESOL. I have also guided university English faculties developing curricula, materials, and textbooks to help them address the needs of thousands of students who need to learn English to read their textbooks in Agriculture, Economics, Engineering, Journalism, Humanities, Medicine, Pharmacy, Public Policy, Sciences, and Education.

When people ask me why I keep returning to Afghanistan despite security concerns, I try to articulate my feeling that I have unfinished business in the country. Each time I've decided that my work is done, one of the Afghan ministries with whom I have worked comes up with new projects for which I am "uniquely qualified." Knowing that there are only a few foreign women with my professional experience in Education and who are familiar with the Afghan educational and health systems, I feel compelled to keep doing my part in promoting a woman's perspective in this process of nation building.

Despite the progress the country is making, extremists still threaten the security of Afghanistan's citizens, as well as the internationals like myself who are trying to help Afghan institutions address the many unmet needs that still exist in every sector of society.

We have grown to equate a resumption of terrorist attacks with spring and early summer, as the extremists find it easier to make their way from the provinces into Kabul when the winter snows have melted. Most attacks of this past year have targeted government institutions and government officials. Just after I returned to Seattle in June of 2012, my former housemates in Karte Se watched helicopters fly over their roof to support Afghan troops defending the Parliament building from a day-long terrorist attack. My friend Walid, who now serves in the Parliament, said the Members of Parliament (MPs) could not leave the building until that evening. He described how MPs from Kandahar and other provinces gathered the weapons that had been checked at the door on entering the Parliament building and climbed up onto the roof to support the Afghan Army by shooting back at the terrorists. Afghans around the country cheered when they heard this news. These acts of bravery confirmed for the electorate that their MPs are not going to allow terrorists to defeat their efforts to establish a secure government.

Prior to the attack on the Afghan Parliament, I had firsthand experience with the security precautions that Afghan government officials must take in order to protect themselves against the daily threats of kidnapping and assassination. Walid and I needed to travel to the Qarabagh District of Kabul Province to select sites for implementing a women's literacy project. We had conducted projects in villages in Qarabagh for over a decade and had previously traveled there without any security personnel. This trip, however, was different.

Walid's personal driver, Fahim, picked me up at the guesthouse in the morning. When I asked where Walid was, the driver told me that we would meet him on the road. As we neared the edge of town, a pickup truck with men sitting in the cargo area pulled out in front of us. They wore black masks, stocking caps, army fatigues, and were holding AK-47s. I was instantly on guard.

"Keep your distance, Fahim. These guys are not to be messed with," I said in Dari.

"Don't worry, Dr. Suzanne, I know them," Fahim responded. "Walid is in that car."

"Oh!" I said in surprise. "I thought we would be riding in the same car."

"In a little while," he said.

As the driver completed his response, one of the masked men waved to him and we speeded up. At an intersection, we pulled alongside the truck and I saw many men inside, but I couldn't see Walid. We moved at high speed until we were outside the city limits of Kabul. Suddenly, one of the armed men in the back of the pickup truck gave a hand signal, and both vehicles pulled to the side of the road.

"Dr. Suzanne, you need to get out here and get into that truck," the driver said.

The back door to the pickup opened and three armed men got out. One of them opened my door and motioned for me to go to the pickup. The transfer took about a minute. I had barely settled into the back seat of the truck when both vehicles pulled back onto the road. I was surprised to see Walid in the driver's seat. He and his driver were both wearing traditional Afghan dress—*shalwar kamizes* and the traditional felt *pakhol* hats.

"I am glad *(actually relieved, I thought)* to see you," I said. "Why are you driving?"

"Sometimes I drive and sometimes my official driver drives," Walid responded. "Just relax for the rest of the journey."

Easy for you to say, I thought as a looked at the backs of the armed men in the cargo area behind me. I never expected that I would be traveling with this level of security in the provinces of Afghanistan.

As we drove toward Charikar, I thought about many trips I had taken on this same road in the past years without any thought of threats. I had made frequent visits to the district hospital and health clinics to check the progress of midwifery training and patient care between 2003 and 2006. For three years after that, I traveled monthly through this district on the way to teacher training assignments in Mazar and Shiberghan with an escort car but without any security personnel. Decades ago, Michael and I had traveled alone through this area. I am sad that the security situation in the Afghan provinces has become so dangerous that responsible Afghan government officials like Walid who are traveling with foreigners engaged in activities to rebuild Afghanistan now require the protection of heavily armed men.

Two days before my departure for my 2013 summer "R and R" to the United States, two of my colleagues and I shared a farewell brunch on a warm, peaceful Friday afternoon in the gardens of *Le Jardin,* a French restaurant in the Kal-i-Fatullah district in Kabul. Scores of rosebushes in the garden were in full bloom and the calls of a resident peacock interrupted the conversations of at least 100 internationals gathered at tables of sun umbrellas under a bright blue sky. Two hours after we returned to our guesthouse on the other side of the city, we heard a series of loud booms that echoed as they bounced off the mountains around Kabul. We started getting frantic text messages from friends who live in Shar-i-Nau that explosions had occurred near where they lived and that black smoke was rising from the explosion site. Through later texts, we learned that gunfire followed the explosions. The gunfire which started in the late afternoon continued as darkness fell.

Through e-mailed security reports, we learned that an INGO guesthouse located just a mile from where we had shared brunch had been attacked by the Taliban who claimed that the building housed "military spies." The attack and the subsequent firefight between the Afghan army and police and the extremists left ten dead (including the six attackers and a policeman who responded to the attack) and thirty wounded. Events like this are a constant reminder that we could be next. They prompt discussions about topics that are familiar to those of us in a conflict zone but seem extraordinary to our families and friends at home. We are concerned, for example, that our landlord still hasn't installed the blast film that we ordered for our guesthouse. We have friends who were injured by flying glass in attacks over the last few years because their windows weren't covered with blast film.

My friends and former colleagues in the United States are starting to retire, but Afghanistan keeps calling me back. During each assignment, I think about what Michael would have to say about what is happening there. In Kabul, he would be concerned about the apparent lack of urban planning. He would regret that this lack of planning has resulted in a smoggy city with multi-storied glass-fronted office buildings and shopping malls and a population that is nearly ten times the 750,000 people who lived there more than four decades years ago. As he travelled the dirty, traffic-choked streets and passed government buildings and hotels surrounded by concrete barriers and guarded by soldiers with machine guns, he would remember the pristine blue skies of an earlier time, as well as the lovely tree-lined boulevards where there were once as many sheep and camels as cars. Michael would be saddened by the terrorist attacks and the necessity of barriers and armed guards around public buildings and by the environmental damage that smog and overcrowding have done to this city. However, he would also be happy to see that Kabul has risen from the rubble that was here in 2002, and he would remark on the energy of life that has returned to the city.

In Mazar, Michael would have been surprised to see the growth and development of the city, complete with wide paved streets and roundabouts. In Jalalabad, he would have been pleased to see that agriculture is still thriving and amazed at the growth of Nangarhar University.

Michael would have mourned the loss of historical buildings and shrines in Herat, but he would have marveled at the rebirth and expansion of Herat University with large pastel-colored buildings populating the vast campus at the foot of the hills at the edge of the city. He would have visited the beautiful mosque with me and probably would have recited lines from Iranian poets when he visited the beautiful, restored gardens in that city.

When I was working in Herat, I thought of Michael whenever I put on my Iranian style *chador* to go to the campus. I heard his voice inside my head describing how effortlessly Iranian women managed this process and how some younger women developed a flirtatious manner for gathering the *chadors* around their faces. I wondered how the Iranian women managed such grace, as I found it a constant struggle to hold onto my possessions while maintaining a firm grip on the cloth that the Herat winds threatened to rip off my head as I made my way across the campus. Each afternoon as I unpinned the *chador* from under my chin and removed it in the privacy of my room, I offered a rebuttal to Michael:

"It's not easy, Michael. It's a struggle to hold everything together and maintain the appearance that is expected of a woman wearing this garment."

My struggle with the *chador* is symbolic of my life without Michael. Each time I celebrate a joyful event—a holiday, a birthday, a milestone for one of our grandchildren, an accomplishment of our daughters, a marriage, birth, or anniversary in the lives of our families and friends—or when I take pride in my successful completion of projects in Afghanistan—I wish that he was here to celebrate with me. I miss him terribly and will do so for the rest of my life. At the same time, I thank him for the life he gave me. With Michael, I came to know and love the country of Afghanistan. Somehow, I think he is aware of what I am doing there.

I came full circle emotionally, as well as professionally during my recent assignments in Kabul.

I resided near the neighborhood in Karte Char district where Michael and I spent our honeymoon years. As I passed the location of our little house, I had sweet memories instead of tears. On my visit to Spozmai Restaurant overlooking Qargha Dam on a snowy day last February, the retro décor of the dining room and the disco ball lying on the table in the entry hall brought back memories of the special occasion nights when Michael and I dined and danced with our friends there. (Spozmai was nearly destroyed in 2013 when the Taliban attacked it because young Afghan men were drinking alcohol and engaging in other illicit activities there.)

Unfinished Business

My shorter, intense assignments with Afghan universities have permitted me more time in Seattle and have allowed me to rebalance my life. When I am home, I revel in the roles of grandmother, mother, daughter, sister, and friend. I virtually drink in the lakes, bays, rivers, clean air and (yes!) rain that makes the Pacific Northwest a welcome relief from the dryness of Afghanistan. My family—especially my five grandchildren—and friends fill me with laughter and love and refuel me emotionally and culturally so that I can return to my work in Afghanistan with new energy. Every time my plane enters Afghan airspace, I gaze at what appear from the sky to be endless waves of mountains before we swoop down to the Kabul plains to land, and I realize that I now have two homes and two very full lives—one in the United States and one in Afghanistan.

Michael also has a place in both countries. There is a park bench dedicated to him on the east side of Queen Anne Hill in Seattle. His family, friends, former co-workers, neighbors and strangers can sit on the bench and look across Lake Union to the beautiful Cascade Mountains on a clear day.

In Wardak Province of Afghanistan, there is a small marble plaque with his name (and mine) inserted into the wall of an Afghan village school built in his memory. The school serves nearly 400 students (girls in grades 1-6 and boys in grades 1-3) each year. His school, which was built under the supervision of Walid's NGO and funded by members of Emerald City Rotary Club and other clubs in the Seattle area and by donations from family, friends, and community members in the United States and Afghanistan, is a testimony to what can happen when committed people from two countries combine their efforts to give the next generation a future.

Life has taught me that I can plan all I want, but I cannot know what my future will be like. Afghans have shown me that the best way to live is to make the most of each day and to be ready to deal with whatever the future brings. I am ready for whatever that is. I'm not sure when my work in Afghanistan will be finished, but part of my heart will never leave that country.

About the Author

Suzanne M. Griffin grew up in Oregon. She attended college in Indiana where she met her late husband Michael, who had completed a Peace Corps tour in Iran. In 1968, the newlyweds arrived in Afghanistan to serve as a Peace Corps field team. While living in San Francisco in the 1970s, Suzanne balanced her roles as mother and wife with professional responsibilities. She achieved tenure as a university English instructor, co-authored textbooks, and co-produced an ESL video series for the BBC.

In 1978, the couple and their two young daughters relocated to Iran where they anticipated a three year stay. Suzanne was a university English instructor in Isfahan and Michael led the housing department of a U.S. contractor. Six months later, the family was evacuated at the start of the Iranian Revolution.

Seattle has been home base for Suzanne's family since 1981. Suzanne held leadership positions in Washington State education agencies and institutions while earning her Ph.D. in Education from the University of Washington. In 2002, she received a sabbatical from Seattle Community Colleges to research ways of improving literacy skills of Afghan women. When she arrived in Kabul, however, she was assigned a larger role in rebuilding the country's educational system. Suzanne has spent over eleven years there leading projects in health, education and higher education.

Please visit www.suzannemgriffin.com.

Reader's Guide

Questions and Topics for Discussion:

1. What role do you think her marriage and widowhood plays in the author's commitment to developmental aid in Afghanistan? How do her memories of the time spent with her husband in Afghanistan influence her work upon her return following his death?

2. In many of Suzanne's stories about the lives of Afghan colleagues and friends, there are themes of honor, respect and commitment to family values. With Western world media so focused on our differences, are you surprised by our similarities? Are there specific people or instances you can relate to or especially admire?

3. Even with the cultural and religious restrictions on women's rights and education, Suzanne's work, along with the work of many others, has accomplished an amazing increase in both basic and secondary educational opportunities for young girls and women with the support of their husbands and fathers.

   • What particular aspects of Suzanne's identity and character contribute to her success in working with these conservative men to allow women access to education?
   • How is it that she gains the trust and respect of these men?

4. In the current age of terrorism, Suzanne shows remarkable courage as well as an acceptance of the risks involved in travelling in Central Asia. She holds a non-judgmental perspective and position on religious and political issues.

   • Which situations did you find the most dangerous or frightening?
   • What do you think protected her?
   • In similar situations, how might you have reacted?

5. Even with the remarkable advances in female education, women and girls in Afghanistan still suffer from extreme restrictions most western women cannot imagine accepting. However, some women, particularly of the older generations, appreciate the protection and privacy of their isolation.

- What pressures are evidently placed on the men who are responsible for their family's safety and keeping?
- What would be your greatest objections about living within the confines of a conservative culture? What aspects of that culture would you appreciate having in your life?

6. Women make up 17% of the current U.S. Congress, 22% of the United Kingdom's Parliament, 20% of the French Parliament, and 15% of the Japanese Parliament. However, women account for over 27% of the current Afghan Parliament because that country's Constitution requires that women make up 25% of each house of Parliament.

- Do these 2012 figures about women in politics surprise you?
- What impact do you expect Afghan women in Parliament to have on their government and the position of women in their society?
- Do you think that other countries should amend their constitutions to ensure that women have a higher level of representation in their parliaments?

7. In 1968, approximately 60% of Afghan men and 85% of Afghan women were illiterate in their native language. Today, Afghanistan's Ministry of Education reports an overall adult literacy rate of 36% (with a target of 59% by 2020.)

- Does this rate surprise you, or alter the way you think about Afghan's traditional attitude toward education for women?
- How do you think the shift from agrarian to urban and internet-connected lifestyles will impact these rates?
- Do you think education should be mandatory in Afghanistan for both genders?

8. In terms of women's rights, what do you find the most objectionable of the issues Afghan women face?

- How do you see these being addressed by work such as Suzanne's and other developmental and humanitarian efforts?
- What more is needed to support these efforts?
- Are you moved to help? In what ways might that be possible?

Recommended Reading and Websites

Books:

Afghanistan by Louis Dupree. New Jersey: Princeton University Press, 1973.

Afghanistan: A Modern History by Angelo Rasanayagam. London: I.B. Tauras, 2003.

Afghanistan: Crosslines Field Guide, Second Edition by Edward Girardet and Jonathan Walter. Geneva, Switzerland: Media Action International, 2004.

Afghanistan Over a Cup of Tea by Nancy Dupree. Stockholm, Sweden: Swedish Committee of Afghanistan, 2008.

Descent into Chaos by Ahmed Rashid. New York: Penguin Books, 2009.

The Dressmaker of Khair Khana by Gayle Tzemach Lemmon. New York: Harper Perennial, 2011.

In My Father's Country by Saima Wahab. New York: Crown Publishers, 2012.

Opium Nation by Fariba Nawa. New York: Harper Perennial, 2011.

Paradise Beneath Her Feet: How Women are Transforming the Middle East by Isobel Coleman. Council on Foreign Relations. New York: Random House, 2013.

Samira and Samir by Siba Shakib. London: Century, 2004.

The Sewing Circles of Herat by Christina Lamb. New York: Harper Collins, 2004.

The Turkoman Carpet by George O'Bannon. London: Duckworth, 1974.

International Humanitarian Organizations Working in Afghanistan:

The Asia Foundation, www.asiafoundation.org

Ayni Education International, www.aynieducation.org

International Medical Corps, www. internationalmedicalcorps.org

International Rescue Committee, www.rescue.org

The Lamia Afghan Foundation, www.lamia-afghanfoundation.org

Marshall Plan Charities, www. marshallplancharities.org

Mercy Corps, www.mercorps.org

PARSA, www. afghanistan-parsa.org

Rotary International, www.rotary.org

Save the Children International, www.savethechildren.org

Acknowledgments

By introducing me to Afghanistan and Iran and sharing with me unforgettable life experiences and lessons of love, my late husband, Michael Fitzpatrick Griffin, prepared me to write this book. Afghans who have educated me in Afghan history and culture and shared their stories contributed immeasurably to the pages in this text. They also advised me on how to work successfully in a country with a diverse population, a continually evolving political situation, and an uncertain security environment. Most importantly, Afghans taught me how to move on after personal tragedy. My deepest gratitude goes to those (not named for their own security) who have opened their homes to me and shared the risks of making positive social changes in a resistant environment. I will always love the Afghan friends who have worked side-by-side with me in their country and who (despite real or potential risks to themselves and their families) have continued their friendship and support for many years.

Most of my writing projects are collaborative efforts and this memoir follows that pattern.

I began writing to document my adventures with Michael in Afghanistan for our daughters and grandchildren. After hearing some of my stories, Dr. Larry Mulkerin (Michael's sister's husband) and his son Mark convinced me to expand my book to include current experiences and reach a larger audience. I joined them at the Maui Writer's Conference where I received valuable guidance in the memoir writers' workshop. My friend Donn Callaway and my sisters Mary Lou, Deborah and Beth read and gave valuable feedback on early chapters. Peter Bussian, who has documented Afghans' resilience in his beautiful photographs (some of which are included in this book), has kept me focused on the theme of this memoir from the early drafts to publication.

Celeste Bennett agreed to publish this memoir because she believed that my story needed to be shared. She introduced me to editor Adam Findley who, through his comments, helped me find my voice and show readers the Afghanistan I know. Celeste's questions, significant suggestions, and edits greatly improved the manuscript. Her design skills are evident in the book format and cover.

I am grateful to my deceased parents Tony and Betty Seidl, both of whom were teachers, for their sacrifices and support that allowed me to follow the road less traveled at the end of my college years. I thank my daughters Rachael and Sarah for patiently playing next to my desk while I drafted textbooks during their childhood, and for actively contributing to my professional projects when they were teenagers. They are accomplished women who make time to help manage my domestic affairs while I'm in Afghanistan and juggle their family schedules so that I have quality time with my five grandchildren when I am home. Finally, thank you to fellow Rotarians, colleagues, friends, and family members who have raised funds for an Afghan girls' school built in Michael's memory and supported my work in Afghanistan in numerous ways for over eleven years. Their love has made my life rich.

Suzanne Griffin
Seattle
2014